Flying Alaska Gold

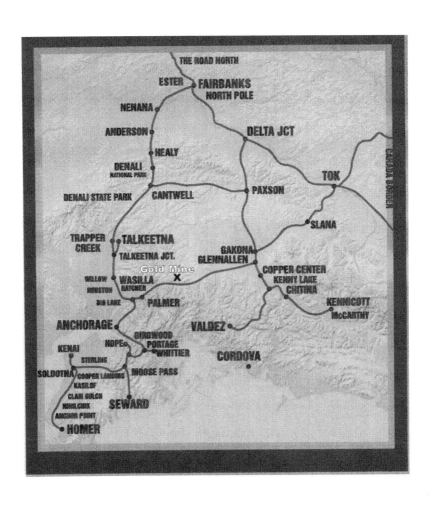

To order additional copies, please contact us.
BookSurge, LLC
www.booksurge.com
1-866-308-6235
orders@booksurge.com

Flying Alaska Gold
Grizzlies, Gold, Gangsters

David Hoerner

2005

Flying Alaska Gold

ACKNOWLEDGEMENTS:

Special thanks to Linda and Sarah for editing, to Shanon for his computer expertise, and to Susan for getting this project to the publisher.

DISCLAIMER:
This book was written from the author's memories, so other people may remember the same events differently. Except for those belonging to the author's immediate family, names have been changed to protect the identity of people described in the book.

CONTENTS

Prologue
THE LAST DANCE

July 1, 1981

I'd pushed my luck all summer, but this time I had gone beyond the point of no return. Time and again the airplane had managed to get me out of life-threatening situations. Ice-laden wings, sticky mud, or the turbulent mountain winds of Alaska hadn't stopped my progress. I had survived many close calls.

I had everyone believing that my exceptional flying skills had saved the day. My ego wouldn't let me admit the truth hidden deep in my soul. Lady Luck had been on my side.

While in Anchorage I loaded this brute of an airplane with a half-ton replacement piece of equipment. The gold mine operation was shut down momentarily, and my family was counting on this delivery to get the operation back up and running. I knew the weight and size of this load could be too much for a safe landing on our short mining airstrip, but the whole year's success was dependent on this delivery.

Veteran pilots stood back with wide-eyed stares at the overloaded plane. Even their shaking heads didn't bring me to my senses. I was never known for being timid, and for sure wasn't going to be now. Not much would stop me once I set my mind on a job. My attitude had always been, "Come hell or high water, full steam ahead!" I'd get our mining camp operational if it was the last thing I did!

As I glanced at the sheer granite walls closing in, I realized that it very well might be my last dance. Was it stupidity that brought me to this moment, or stubbornness?

I never thought this would happen, but now the nearness of the craggy cliffs was making me a believer. Adrenalin was gushing through my veins like water through a pipe. My senses heightened, my mind kept screaming, "Fly the plane!" My only chance of survival depended on maintaining control. Sweat burned my eyes as I blinked hard to clear my vision.

The stall horn in the plane was screaming like a locomotive whistle. No plane was engineered for these conditions. As the airspeed got slower, the noise got louder, creating even more doubt in my mind about surviving.

I was headed upstream in a very steep and narrow brush-covered canyon. Hitting turbulence, my heavy load shifted back, moving the center of gravity aft. This small movement was now making it impossible to gain airspeed or lower the nose of the airplane. The engine was producing a boisterous rumble, using all its horses to keep the plane airborne. As the seconds flew by I knew I was getting closer to my first failure.

I should have known better than to let this demanding flight even start. The warning signs were there, but I pushed on. While flying toward the mine, I had to put my knee against the control yoke and push forward. Any backward movement of the yoke would cause the plane to nose up uncontrollably. The plane required constant inputs to keep it under control. My elevated breathing and heart rate should have been adequate warning to bring me to my senses. The equipment was just too heavy and too far back in the fuselage.

Like race horses pounding around a track, thoughts darted through my mind. How in the hell did I think I was going to land this plane? Turn around and head for the safety of a long and paved runway? No, not me, that would be too easy. Push on, my family at the mine needed the equipment and I wasn't about to let them down.

The moss-covered cliffs of the canyons grabbed at the wings. A metal-twisting crash was inevitable with certain death in the boulder-filled ravine below. I knew that the heavy cargo directly behind me would be coming my way on impact, destroying everything in its path.

Time and space seemed to close in, my peripheral vision made the green canyon walls blur as one continuous paint stroke. The closeness of the sheer cliffs invaded my space, creating a suffocating feeling in my chest. The brush striking the wing tips sounded like rain hitting a metal roof.

I knew I was a dead man. It felt like a dream. Movement, space and time switched into slow motion. My time had come but fear was absent. A calm sensation swept over me. My stubbornness had brought me to this dilemma. Now was the time to pay up....

DEDICATION

This Alaskan adventure started in the winter of 1980 and is an account of the next summer's gold mining operation in the Talkeetna Mountains. My job was to fly supplies and miners in and out of their gold mines. This book is dedicated to my Uncle Tony, a very special friend.

Going to Alaska and mining gold had been his lifelong dream, and he was able to fulfill this wish. Even though he is gone now, I have a lot of memories of him sitting in the right seat of the plane and sharing the adventures. He was the most sincere and honest-hearted person I will ever know. Thanks, Uncle Tony, for the adventure of a lifetime.

'Uncle Tony'

I

IN THE BEGINNING

September 10, 1980

My Alaskan adventure started with a phone call from my cousin and best friend, Alan. He wanted to know if I was interested in mining gold and flying an airplane for him in Alaska. He didn't need to say much to sway me, considering both subjects had been on my mind for a couple of years.

His father and mother, my Uncle Tony and Aunt Delores, and his brother, Leo, were considering mining gold in Alaska. The price of gold had hit an all-time high, and finding the illusive yellow rock had been Tony's lifelong dream.

Alan's call gave me a lot to think about. Quitting a secure job for a pipedream could be a big mistake. Hard as I tried, it was impossible to sleep. Thoughts of rocky airstrips, grizzly bears, shiny gold and snow-capped Alaska Mountains raced through my mind continuously.

Born and raised in northwest Montana, I had been a logger for ten years. The job paid well, but carrying a chainsaw up and down the steep terrain took a constant toll on my body.

I fantasized about flying in Alaska while sawing down trees. I'd watch eagles fly over and resented the freedom they enjoyed. As a child I had pretended my hand out the window of my dad's car was an airplane. Later, I promised myself that someday I'd be flying for a living instead of dreaming about it.

At the time Alan called with the news I had managed to build a grand total of 250 hours of flight time and believed my pilot skills were a little above average. But the future would prove my knowledge was lacking in a couple of areas.

I remembered one of my instructors telling me certain people just couldn't fly, implying that I was one of them. I was determined to prove him wrong. He was a helicopter instructor and what right did he have to tell me I couldn't fly an airplane? (In my first seven hours of flight training I used three different airplanes and five instructors.) His comments were warranted, but not called for.

The doubt still nagged me, maybe he was right. Did I have what it took to fly in the wilds of Alaska? I had dreamed and wished for the opportunity to find out, and now I had the chance.

Becoming a so-called Alaskan "bush" pilot would be a dream come true. Most pilots living in the lower forty-eight believed that Alaskan bush pilots were the better pilots. With nerves of steel and the ability to handle every difficult situation that comes along, these pilots could land on short and unimproved airstrips in any kind of weather. Could I do it?

I could think of little else. Alan needed a pilot to fly supplies from Anchorage to the mine and a plane would be the most cost-effective transportation. I was overwhelmed, yet apprehensive about this offer to go North. My pilot skills would be tested with the very first flight.

I also had a family to think about. For six months my wife, Noreen, and son, Ryan, would be in Montana, not knowing if I was dead or alive. My gut feeling told me even though this could really stress a marriage, a chance like this might only come once in a lifetime. I spent many grueling hours debating whether or not to go. It was exactly what I wanted to do, but I had more to think about than my dreams. This decision would impact my family.

I would be living my dream, flying airplanes. I called Alan and told him I would take the job. Once I finally made the call it was impossible to hold back my excitement. To my surprise he increased that anticipation by saying, "Pack your bags, we're heading to Anchorage to acquire the mining claims needed for the summer."

All I could say was "You're kidding," not believing that this was possible so soon. It was no joke. Alan, Leo, Tony and I would be on an Alaskan airliner in two short weeks.

Thoughts of the adventure to come played over and over in my mind like a broken record, bringing many sleepless nights. I really needed to relax, but it was impossible to think of anything else. With so little rest, I feared I would injure myself working in the woods before the trip.

I managed to stay in one piece, and the reality of it hit home when the jetliner lifted off the ground in Kalispell. I was going to Alaska!

Conversations about mining and flying went on incessantly

until we passed over Prince William Sound. Then the sights out the aircraft windows grabbed everyone's attention.

Rivers of giant glaciers, dark blue in color, changed to aqua as they traveled out of the vertical granite mountains. They seemed to flow as rivers, twisting down long narrow valleys. Along their journey they gnawed away at solid rock walls, leaving dark-stained lines on the ice that moved with the glaciers. As the million-year-old ice neared the end of its journey, mile-long bottomless crevasses cracked open, leaving a ravaged landscape. The ice then calved into the sea with a new name, iceberg. In time, the warm water would slowly melt the giant forms into nothingness. Incredible!

The jet was going too fast to take in all the sights. I wanted to go up to the pilot and ask him to slow down. Looking at all the mountains made my heart race. Seeing the vast size of the country and crystal-white ice fields made me shudder.

Had I bitten off more than I could chew? Would I be able to fly through these giants, and how in the hell would I ever survive? Cold shivers ran up and down my spine at the sight of the granite jaws. The beautiful and threatening spectacles out the airplane window finally brought actuality and added doubt to my nagging dream.

Anchorage soon came into view, stretching over the flat land that extended from the base of the high, snow-covered mountains and right out to the ocean. The Alaskan soil called out to me. It was hard to stay seated while taxiing to the terminal.

After departing the plane, we rented a car and drove to the International Airport Inn, near Lake Hood, where the largest floatplane base in the world is located. The lake was frozen, but every space was occupied with a plane, patiently waiting for its owner. Some had skis on, while others still had floats installed. Every make and model I'd ever heard of was there. A Cessna 180, which was tied down near the motel, had its tail feathers frozen into the ice. To a pilot, treating an airplane like that is like committing a mortal sin.

An appointment was made with Shorty, the owner of the mining claims we were planning to lease. We spent the next two hours driving across Anchorage and enjoying the sights. I sat speechless as we passed Merrill Field with at least 500 planes filling the ramp. I looked at Alan and said, "I think there are more planes at that airport than I've ever seen."

Shorty met us at the door. We were somewhat surprised to see a frail man with dark beady eyes looking up at us. I guessed his age to be in the sixties, and my first thought was he looked like an older Danny DeVito.

To our surprise he escorted us in, or rather, pushed us in, without any greetings at all. As he peeked out the darkened shade-covered windows we looked at each other, wondering what the problem was. Then he turned around to introduce himself.

He wouldn't look anyone in the eyes and babbled a hundred miles an hour. His face was lined with deep wrinkles, and when he looked up through dark bushy eyebrows, the horizontal lines deepened as he glanced to see if we understood.

We listened intently, not wanting to miss a word about all the gold at his claims, and how easy it was to get out of the ground. In a flash he left the room and returned with four bottles of sparkling yellow gold. Our eyes glowed with anticipation.

Opening a bottle of dime-sized nuggets, he dumped them on the table and said, "This is what makes the world go round, boys, thirty ounces of gold. You want gold? I have plenty of gold in my claims. Sometimes you can walk around and pick it right off the ground. I don't let just anyone on my claims, but I like you Montana boys and I'll make you a deal. You can work my claims for 50 percent of the take. This is a great deal for ya. Everyone else pays 70 percent."

The nuggets were solid gold. No quartz rock mixed in. Our eyes lit up as he said, "The gold in my claims is 100 percent pure. *Everyone* wants my gold."

Each of us rolled the marble-sized nuggets in our hands. This is what we were after. He was right. We wanted his gold.

Alan stood up and said, "Fifty percent is way too much!"

Shorty yelled back, "That may sound high, but once you start mining my claim you'll see how easy it is to find. This is the best offer you will ever get. Besides, I have a lot of people who want to mine my claims. There's a lot of gold, easy to find, easy to get out of the ground. If you boys are serious about mining gold you won't pass up this deal."

For the first time Shorty stopped talking and stared at each one of us. Then he grabbed a Bible from the table and said, "I'm an elder of the church, and I wouldn't lie. You guys mine my claims and you'll make a lot of money."

His words rang in our ears. Those words were repeated many times that summer! We believed that a man's word is the truth, and Shorty's church status added to his story's credibility.

We all agreed that the little guy was indeed odd, but our desire to find gold outweighed any suspicion of deceit. It would prove to be an enormous mistake. We would soon learn that his 30 ounces of gold was really about 10 ounces. No contract was signed, just a big Montana handshake.

All four of us were walking in a blissful haze when we left Shorty's place. Soon we would be mining gold! The day had been strenuous, dinner and a good-night's sleep would hit the spot, instead Leo, always the partygoer, insisted on stopping at the Red Hot Cherry, a striptease joint not known for fancy clothes.

With a little arm bending, very little, we all agreed except Uncle Tony. We insisted he go along anyway. Tony was known for his practical jokes and would never pass up a chance to scare someone. All of us were sure he would get us thrown out of the motel if we left him alone. He soon realized that his arguing wouldn't get him anywhere, so he agreed under one condition, that he could take his Bible along for protection.

We entered the strip joint and sat down, using the elevated dance floor as the bar. The girls promenaded right in front of us; their knees level with our eyes. They didn't leave much to the imagination.

Tony knew that as long as he had Bible in hand, nothing could harm him. Just for good measure he put his hands over his eyes while the girls danced in front of him. I noticed, however, that Tony's fingers were spread apart slightly. Good old Uncle Tony!

Leo waved five-dollar bills around so we had most of the action right in front of us. After a couple of beers, Tony started to get a little giddy. One of the girls took his cowboy hat and used it in her dance routine. He thought that was pretty cool. Normally Tony was bashful and shy but as the beers flowed he got to the point where he was definitely Bible-in-hand flirting.

The best part was after the dance routines when the girls came over and served us drinks, topless, of course. It was amazing to see my uncle visiting with the barely-clad girls like everything was normal. This was his opportunity to tell them that they should go out with his boys, because they were so big.

During all the excitement he accidentally dropped his Bible, and in a flash was off the barstool hunting for it. For a 71-year-old, he moved pretty quickly. The girls loved him and laughed with us at Uncle Tony's antics until our stomachs ached. It was great seeing him have so much fun. Alan and I strained as we packed him out to the car like a sack of potatoes. Tony looked at us and slurring his words said, "I think those girls liked you guys." We laughed as we headed to the Inn for some much-needed sleep.

Being in Anchorage for two days was an amazing adventure. The fast growth found the city with log cabins surrounded by sled dogs next to shopping malls. It didn't matter where you were or what time of the day it was, an airplane was always in sight. Alaskans use their airplanes just like Montanans use their pickup trucks. The sight of the planes, the awe-inspiring mountains around Anchorage and the giant ice fields put a permanent smile on my face.

We accomplished our goal; with gold claims in hand it was time to head back to Montana to prepare for and acquire the necessary equipment for our gold mine.

While flying high above the clouds and heading south to Seattle, I had time to contemplate the upcoming summer. Although my excitement bred different thoughts that came and went like cars at a stop sign, my concern was for my family. Up until now it was all a dream, but being there made it all too real. Joy and sadness consumed me—was it fair to leave my family? That question would only be answered with time.

Leo, Tony and Dave
If only we knew what the future would bring.
Buying the 206 in Seattle.

II
CESSNA 206

The rest of the winter was spent preparing to go to Alaska. As the time to leave grew close, it was harder and harder to go to work. The same anxiety I had earlier of getting injured while sawing trees still plagued me.

Alan had asked me to find an airplane, so I spent my evenings and weekends searching for a Cessna 206, which I was sure, would be the best plane for the job. I soon realized that finding one in the short time we had left would be a big project.

A D8 CAT had been purchased in Seattle. It needed to be loaded on a barge bound for Anchorage, so my search for an airplane was centered on that area. Luck was on our side. Renton Aviation in Seattle had a plane for sale. Alan, Leo, Tony and I flew out to Seattle to take care of the Caterpillar and look at the plane.

The plane was being used to haul mail. I took one look and knew it was just what we needed to get the job done. The big tires along with the bright orange and white paint made the plane look awesome. It was manufactured for hard work and hauling heavy loads. It didn't have the best paint job or interior, but the engine and prop were new.

The biggest fear I had were the short airstrips in Alaska. Most of them were built for Super Cubs, small two-passenger planes with high lift wings. The Cub's skin is made from fabric, which makes the plane real light. Balloon tires and the thick wings make it possible to land and take off in real short distances. But because of the size of the small plane's cabin, hauling heavy loads is out of the question. So a Super Cub wouldn't work for us.

After a lot of talking, I managed to persuade Alan into purchasing a Robertson STOL (Short Take Off & Landing) Kit, which would modify the wings to handle the short runways. I would need all the help possible to land and take off on the short muddy and rocky airstrips. Just maybe the modification would give me the edge needed.

Over the preceding two years I had spent a lot of time flying in the Bob Marshall Wilderness, which is located on the continental divide in Montana. The airstrips in that area don't compare to the Alaskan strips, but it is a very mountainous terrain and the elevation is a lot higher, with windy conditions most all the time.

A couple of local pilots had Robertson STOL Kits installed in their planes. They had told me the kits made a big difference in takeoffs and landings. If I'd only known how the kit would save my life in the upcoming summer! This purchase would prove to be the smartest decision Alan made.

Because of the time needed to install the STOL Kit, we left the plane at Renton. Apprehension and questions filled my mind. Could I do it? Did I have the ability? Would I die trying? Days seemed to blend into weeks. So much to do, so little time to get it done.

Timing was crucial. All of the mining equipment needed to be transferred back to the mine location before the ice melted out of the tundra, and we were still in Montana. If this move were not completed in time, the whole summer would be lost, not to mention the family farm, which was borrowed against to finance the first year of mining.

Finally the day came when Alan and I left Montana for Alaska. It was hard to say good-bye to our families not knowing what the future would bring. We talked continuously as we crossed the Continental Divide in Montana and hit the flat lands of Alberta. Our first goal was to get to Fort Saint John and the beginning of the Alaskan highway.

The famous road was mostly gravel and rocks that slammed our pickup as big semi-trucks passed. It twisted and turned its way through swamps, prairies and then over the north end of the Canadian Rockies. We only stopped for fuel and one slept while the other drove. The pickup was crammed full of mining gear.

Alaska was like a magnet pulling us. Two long and grueling days put us in Whitehorse, capital of the Northwest Territories. I had expected to see a lot of great scenery while driving the Alcan Highway, but up to this point all we had seen was a tree-lined gravel road, no animals or mountains to speak of, just endless twisting roads.

Whitehorse is a very interesting place; a gold rush town from times past. Many a gold miner traveled over the dangerous Chilkoot

Pass, ending up in Whitehorse. A lot of fortunes were made and a lot of lives lost.

A McDonald Douglas DC3 caught my eye as we drove through town. It was mounted on a pole, 20 feet in the air, at the entrance to the airport. What a feeling to be standing under this airplane and looking up at its awesome size. This type of airplane had been a venerable war hero during World War II, carrying troops and pulling gliders all over Europe. The trustworthy giant was now mounted on a pole, strutting its stuff for all to see.

Anxious for a shower and a good meal, we pulled into an older hotel with a sign indicating that a shower cost two dollars. The woman behind the counter took the money and said that it was down the stairs, first door on the left.

In short order I was enjoying the soothing warm water, deep in thought about the next leg of our journey. I heard someone come into the room, but didn't pay any attention. Behind the shower was a toilet with a short wall beside it. I turned around to let the warm water hit my back, and noticed a pair of shoes under the wall. Women's shoes! Instantly I turned around. The shower was out in the open, no privacy at all. Did that lady at the counter say, "Take a left"?

Needless to say, I hurried up the remainder of my shower, got dressed, and scurried out of there, avoiding eye contact with my bathroom comrade. As I left the bathroom, I noticed a sign on the door, "WOMEN". Alan and I laughed all the way to Alaska.

One more day of driving put us at the Alaskan border. High, steep mountains with snow-capped peaks surround the road from Whitehorse to Alaska. As we drove we continually stared up each canyon to see pure white mountains hundreds of miles away. This was the prettiest part of the trip so far.

Our enthusiasm was hard to keep in check, but the excitement was short-lived when we started hitting all the famous Alaskan frost heaves in the highway. Our heads bounced off the roof of the pickup. Despite our zeal, we slowed to a crawl. At this pace we still had a full day's drive to get to Brandt's Texaco, our immediate destination. From there we would journey cross-country 30 miles to the mine.

Brandt's is named after the owners of the establishment, Eldon and Mary. Their facility is located on the Glenn Highway, at Tahneta Pass, the highest spot along the highway.

Our excitement was hard to contain as we left Tok, heading south to Glennallen. My eyes strained to take in all the sights; tundra with black, stunted pine trees filled the landscape. It was hard to judge distance with the immense view. I strained to focus watery eyes as I looked at snow-capped mountains that seemed to reach to heaven. For the remainder of the trip we gazed at the hypnotic vistas of the Wrangell Mountains.

This was the Alaska I had dreamed about, big and wild, with never-ending mountains, rivers and valleys fingering out in every direction. As we rounded a corner just north of our destination, a small herd of caribou crossed the highway in front of us. I slid to a stop; their white manes and rumps reflected the midday sun. They took a second to eye the intruders and then trotted out of sight.

Confusion set in when we rolled into Brandt's. There was still three feet of snow on the ground. We had been worried that we were late getting to the mine, but with three feet left to melt, we seemed to be early. Off the highway and on Brandt's parking lot was about six inches of gooey, sticky mud, which clung to tires and shoes like glue.

Brandt's consisted of one big building that held a Post Office, café, bar and curio shop. It was pretty well kept, except for the mud that was being dragged in by customers. Outside there was a two-stall garage with an old-time gas pump. The parking lot consisted of fuel barrels, trailers, Caterpillars, swamp buggies, all sorts of mining equipment—basically a junkyard.

All the gold miners in the area were there, getting ready to head out to their mines. Excitement flowed through our veins as we stood on the deck and took in all the surrounding mountains and activity around Brandt's. A small black string, which we could see was a road or trail, snaked its way over the top of the treeless tundra mountain north of Brandt's.

"I'll bet you a hamburger that trail leads to our mine," I told Alan.

Sure enough, Eldon confirmed my guess. As we ate our burgers Eldon explained that all the miners in the area used his place for final preparations. He said, "Don't let the snow fool you. When the winter ends and the thaw begins, the snow is gone in short order. At the bottom of that mountain," he pointed to the trail we could see going over the mountain, "there is a swamp that has to be crossed before the ice melts. I saw a Caterpillar get stuck in the swamp and sink out of sight."

We both laughed, thinking he was teasing. He told us that the ice in the tundra would melt down about three feet during the summer, leaving solid mud before freezing again in the fall. This conversation made us anxious to get going.

Before we left for Anchorage, Eldon wanted to show us his airstrip, which was located between the café and a lake in back. The small lake was used for a floatplane base during the summer. His airstrip was unusable right now because of the mud. "An Alaskan bush pilot could use it right now, but you better wait a week or two," said Eldon.

He continued, "I heard that you were bringing in a Cessna 206 to fly for the mine? You'll kill yourself with that plane in these mountains."

I had no reply, wondering what he knew that I didn't.

Before heading out to the mine, we would need to spend a few days in Anchorage purchasing additional supplies and equipment. Leo and Tim Wheat showed up a day later.

Leo and Alan had grown up on the family farm, taking care of horses, sheep, cattle and pigs daily. Leo seemed to flourish working around the animals. Years of lifting buckets of feed had bulged his arms and shoulders. He was strong as an ox, but was better known for his carefree 'don't give a shit' attitude. He was generous to a fault, and wore a permanent smile.

Tim had worked for Alan's construction company for the past few years. When the business was sold to go to Alaska, he stayed on to mine gold. He had long stringy hair and beard and one tooth missing in front, but knew the inner working of heavy equipment and could operate it with precision. Basically a jack-of-all-trades, Tim proved to be an asset. Alan's parents, Uncle Tony and Aunt Delores, were coming in later.

Shorty owned an old, run-down lodge located two miles north of Brandt's. We used it while preparing for the big trip to the mine. Naive, we thought we could make the preparations and journey to the mine in a couple of weeks. The few weeks became more like a month. The D8 CAT broke a final gear when it was unloaded from the barge.

Shorty had promised us a sluice box to use. Now it wasn't

available, so we needed to design and weld one together. Alan was fit to be tied—it was going to take a lot of money and work to get everything ready.

We had talked to Shorty while in Anchorage, and he suggested that we hire a miner named Melvin to help design a new sluice box and help us mine. Shorty said Melvin knew his claims and what he knew would more than pay his way. He wanted $300 a day and 5 percent of the gold we found. These were developments that weren't anticipated and cost a lot of money. Having no choice, Melvin was hired on his terms.

Before we could make the trip to the mine, the repairs on the D8 CAT had to be completed. Tok Equipment in Anchorage would make the repairs. This would give the rest of us time to rent a truck and haul all the metal for the sluice box to the old lodge. Alan purchased a welder for putting the box together.

Tim and I had the task of welding the two tons of metal together, piece by piece. It took thirteen 20-hour days to get the job done. Both of us got sick from breathing the fumes. I was glad not to be a welder by trade after that experience.

Alan and Leo stayed in Anchorage gathering equipment and helping repair the D8. They were staying with a guy named Andy who worked with Tok Equipment. He was from Missoula, Montana, and immediately became a good friend.

When Alan got back he told of his adventure. "Andy invited me to go to a Chinese restaurant. Every Friday a group of downtown businessmen would gather there for lunch. What Andy didn't tell me was that a numbers game was played to buy lunch. A number was picked, between one and a thousand. Each person, in order, had to pick a number. If you were the closest to the number then you would have to buy lunch for everyone." Alan continued, "You guessed it, my heart sank when I picked the number. The bill was over $800. I think they set me up. The laughter just about brought the house down. Then Andy paid the bill."

All the equipment was eventually gathered at the old lodge. A D3 CAT had been purchased. Its primary function was to feed the sluice box with the dirt and gravel the bigger CAT pushed to it. A high-lifted 4 x 4 Dodge pickup, which was overloaded with gear, would be going. It might need to be dragged in, but one way or the other, it was going. We also rented four war surplus 500-gallon tires that were hooked together by axles. The tires stood six feet tall when filled with diesel fuel. A tongue ran back from the first set to the second set of tires, making it possible to roll these four tires full of fuel to the mine.

Bringing up the end of the caravan would be an old gray Dodge swamp buggy. It had four-foot tall tires and a crew cab. It moved along at a snail's pace, but could climb a cliff. We learned early on to keep our thumbs out of the middle of the steering wheel. If one of the big front tires hit a rock or hole the steering wheel would make two unstoppable turns, and if the driver's thumbs were in the way, it could break them.

Everything was ready for the trip to the mine except the D8 CAT, and delivery was expected in three days. Fuel needed to be hauled or rolled to the mine, so I offered to take a load while we waited for the CAT. Melvin's words were, "Two days tops to take a load of fuel to the mine and return." He drew me a rough map and wished me luck. I wondered what he meant by that.

I hooked up the four tires and headed to Brandt's. It took three hours to pump fuel into the tires, a total of 2000 gallons. Finally, I was on the mud trail to the mine and it seemed like everyone watched me go as if they wouldn't see me again. The weight of the fuel in the tires put a good strain on the little D3 CAT; any incline at all brought the machine to a crawl. The tires had good flotation, so I rolled across the swamp without a problem.

Then came the uphill terrain, the part of the road we could see from Brandt's. The rain had recently turned to snow, so the trail now had a layer of snow on the mud. At the first steep incline the little CAT pulled hard but just spun to a stop. Backing up the connected tires was impossible, what could I do? I feared the tires would pull the machine and me right over the steep bank. With caution, I jack-knifed the tires into the bank and unhooked them, knowing that if they rolled over the hill they would be irretrievable, with 2000 gallons of fuel and our means of hauling it gone.

The next ten hours were spent plowing the mud and snow off the trail all the way to the top of the mountain, and then I drove back down the steep trail and rehooked the tires. The little CAT strained in low gear. I held my breath as the churning tracks slipped toward the edge of the 400-foot vertical drop. Looking down past the tracks, I could see the bottom of the mountain a quarter mile away.

It was so steep I couldn't see any of the hillside below me. I gently unhooked the seatbelt and slid to the uphill side of the seat. That way if it rolled over the edge I could dive off at the last second.

Alan and I thought we were late for the mining season.
Three feet of snow at Brandt's changed our minds.

With determination and full power, I crawled toward the top of the mountain, which slowly grew in size. Once I reached the top I thought I had survived the worst part, but the clouds were so thick I couldn't see 50 feet, a complete whiteout. The top of the mountain was as flat as a pancake. Melvin's map showed that I had about two miles of this cloud-shrouded mountain to cover before starting down a long, narrow ravine toward the mine.

I'd been in whiteout conditions many times, especially while training for my flight instrument rating. An airplane has instruments that keep the plane flying right side up, but on the top of this mountain I couldn't tell up from down.

Melvin's words played over and over in my mind. *You won't have any problems following the trail to the mine.*

For the next two miles I walked out ahead of the CAT and made a trail in the snow, then went back to the idling machine, moved it forward over my tracks and started the process all over again. It took four hours to go two miles. I was exhausted and probably lost.

I walked forward slowly, making sure I could hear the CAT idling behind me. Discouraged, I decided I'd gone far enough. There hadn't been any evidence of a trail for an hour. As I turned, a dark object appeared in the murk. Closer examination revealed a stick protruding out of the ground, the stick that Melvin had drawn on the map. It marked the turn to the left where the trail started down the canyon. *Thank God I'm not lost* was all I could think.

Moving down the draw took me out of the clouds. With great relief I could now see one big canyon with small ravines flowing into it like fingers to a hand. The landscape was void of trees, and short tan-colored grass covered the tundra. The bottom of the clouds was so flat it looked like a ceiling. Somewhere down the canyon miles ahead our home for the next five months awaited our arrival.

I was on a steep side hill going down a narrow valley. The weight of the fuel, about six tons, was doing its best to shove the D3 CAT and me over the steep bank at every turn. With great effort I eased my little caravan off the side hill and into the creek bottom. What a relief!

I was pretty sure that I was on the right trail, but no matter what, this machine didn't have the power to go back the way I had just come, at least not with the fuel in the tires. The canyon I was following got narrower until both sides were cliffs going straight up, forcing me to stay in the water-filled gorge. Rocks falling off the cliffs above showered the top of the canopy and splintered into smaller pieces. It felt like I was under attack as the smaller rocks ricocheting off the machine peppered me.

Being the first traveler of the year made it more dangerous for me because normally a bigger machine would first clear the trail. This I found out later. Boulders as big as pickup trucks were strung along the creek, forcing me to crawl around or go over them. At times my little caravan acted like a dam with water building up behind the giant tires, forcing the CAT along at out-of-control speeds, which under these conditions was almost suicidal.

Fear gripped me as I saw water rolling over the six-foot high tires. This flood of water was ready to swallow me like Jonah and the whale.

Just when I felt like I couldn't handle much more of the beating, the creek flattened. Without the seatbelt, I would have been thrown off the machine. Weak from exhaustion, I was shocked to realize I had been on the trail 20 hours. The map showed I was close to an old trapper's cabin, with the fuel barrels three miles beyond it. I rounded the next corner, and there it was, the cabin. Relieved, the next three miles went quickly. It was a little disheartening to realize I was the only human within 30 miles.

The barrels were right where they were supposed to be. I had strapped an air compressor on the top of the cab of the D3 to unload the fuel, and now air needed to be pumped into the tires to force the fuel out. This was a slow process, but three hours later my load was in the fuel tanks and I was headed back to Brandt's.

I had been gone about 30 hours, most of it in clouds or in the dark. As I approached the trapper's cabin on the way out it started snowing, cutting my visibility to a quarter mile. Disoriented from the lack of sleep and the snow, I decided to take a quick nap at the old cabin. The door on the cabin was frozen open, but there was a bed in the corner and a stove in the middle of the room. Melvin had warned about bears so I was a little concerned about sleeping with the door open. I parked the CAT as close as possible to the door, providing a big noisy protection from curious intruders. Keeping warm was no problem with my rain gear on and I was so tired I don't even remember lying down.

Something startled me awake. It was light out; I sat up and looked out the open door. I could see fresh tracks just outside the door, big grizzly tracks. The whole area was covered with them—the bear had been standing outside the door and looking at the strange object on the bed. I couldn't get on the machine fast enough. The bear had been there for a long time and I was sure he was close by. The hair on my arms stood on end, he was watching me, but I couldn't see him. At least he wasn't hungry!

The trip out to Brandt's was easy compared to the trip in, with the tires only full of air. I sailed up the canyon; going upstream against the flow of water was a little scary. I had to angle the blade on the CAT, forcing the raging water to flow along the side of the machine, instead of over it. There were a couple of times that the water splashed on my lap, but with slow, deliberate effort I made it over the top of the mountain and down the other side to my destination.

By now I had been gone about 40 grueling hours. Everyone had been worried about me, and thought something for sure had gone wrong. With great relief I sat down to the best-tasting hamburger I've ever had and told of my narrow escape down the rocky ravine. It was hard to put into words my feelings and the worries I had just gone through, and I was glad it was over.

The D8 CAT had shown up and would be pulling the newly built grizzly end of the sluice box. The grizzly is the part of the sluice box where the gravel would be dumped. It was twenty-feet long, four-feet high and four-feet wide. Six-inch casings were welded across the top of the box, thereby keeping the big rocks out of the sluice and also making it possible to drive the little CAT across the grizzly end.

The D3 pulled a forty-foot trailer, with the rest of the sluice box stacked on top. We put everything we could into the sluice box. I thought to myself as we lined up to start the trip, "It will be a miracle if everything makes it to the mine." The whole procession reminded me of the Beverly Hillbillies.

The first obstacle, and the one that concerned us most, was crossing the swamp. Two days earlier I had floated across it with no problems. But there was a big difference between the D3 and the monstrous D8. Now the 20-ton machine would be crossing it, pulling a heavy load.

We knew that we were a couple of weeks late. As we walked out across the swamp to find the best route, we sank up to our ankles in the gooey mud. We all came to the same conclusion. There wasn't a best route. Everywhere we walked was slimy mud. If we didn't clear the swamp, the season would be over before it even got started.

It was like the start of a drag race. Leo gunned the big diesel engine. The old machine blew gray smoke and lurched forward at its top speed. When it hit the edge of the swamp it sank momentarily, then climbed back to the top of the bog.

The tracks threw mud in all directions. At about the halfway point the behemoth slowed, and the tracks sank deeper. The gray smoke turned black as the big engine fought for more power, twenty more feet. I clenched my eyes and yelled, "Go, go!"

As the machine slowed to a stop, the front part of the tracks caught hard ground. With agonizing effort the CAT pulled itself free of the mud. Cheers and yells went up, but I knew better than to be excited. The steep gorge was next.

Our big caravan crawled over the mountain. At the gorge, Leo unhooked the grizzly and eased the big machine into the narrow ravine. The channel was so narrow that the CAT acted like a plug. As Leo worked feverishly to clear the narrow route of boulders, the water depth behind him grew deeper and deeper.

A big boulder that was completely submerged in the middle of the creek wouldn't budge. Back and forth Leo went, trying to get the big dozer blade under the giant rock. I held my breath as the water level climbed to the top of the fuel tank. Leo jumped like he was shocked with a cattle prod as the ice water poured onto his back. I could see the fear on his face as he sat back down and fought the stubborn boulder.

If the engine started sucking water it would quit, and the big machine would be lost. Finally with the help of thousands of gallons of water pushing, the boulder moved. Leo kept the pressure against the rock. When he finally exited the lower end of the ravine he had ten rocks the size of the D3 rolling in front of him The water splashed over the back of the machine and drenched Leo. Alan looked at me and said, "I thought he was a goner for sure."

After watching him go through the ordeal I couldn't believe that I had survived going through the same spot a few days earlier. It had to have been a miracle. I shouldn't have made it. It took us two days to cover the 30 miles of bad trail to the mine, which was located on Alfred Creek.

Alan and I spent hours plowing the mountain trail.

Sluicebox on trailer   Tony and his companion "Bow"

The first time I saw our mine, which was three miles downstream from the fuel barrels, I knew we were in the wilderness for sure. Fortunately, there was already an airstrip in place at the mine. Well, at least it resembled an airstrip. It was more like a long stretch of dirt and gravel, suitable for a cross-country bike race! It was about 800 feet long, and about 10 feet wide, as wide as the wheels of the Cessna 206. Scattered on the runway were rocks the size of baseballs, with a couple of two-foot humps in the middle.

Using the D8 and D3 CATS, we were able to lengthen the strip to about 900 feet. We used the bottom of the sluice box, which was made from railroad ties and was flat on the bottom, to level the runway.

I felt a little sick as I walked the full length of the airstrip. It still looked short. I had been using airstrips in Montana that were three times the length.

The improved airstrip was located at the bottom of a canyon surrounded by steep, rugged terrain, and paralleled the creek. Standing at the north end of the strip and looking downstream didn't give me much comfort. My immediate thoughts went to the 400-foot hill that I would have to climb over, or drop down over, during every takeoff and landing. The airstrip was pretty much one way in, one way out. The north end terminated right at the base of a cliff and a creek crossed the airstrip at the south end.

It made me uneasy to think about how exact my flying would need to be in order to use this airstrip safely. No second chances, I had to do it right on the very first landing. If, for any reason, I wouldn't be able to climb over the hill, it was possible to make a turn to the right after takeoff, following the canyon downstream. But I knew I wouldn't want to be in that canyon for very long. Down lower it turned into a sharp, narrow ravine, where our camp was located. The cliff at the north end went straight up for several hundred feet, making a go-around nearly impossible while landing.

I spent a lot of time thinking about the landings and takeoffs, trying to anticipate all the different problems that could happen. If I came in too fast, the plane's speed would cause it to float and then I would need more runway to stop. I would need to set the tires on the ground at minimum airspeed, get the weight off the wings, bring the flaps up and brake as hard as safety permitted. All this would hopefully be accomplished before the runway was used up.

The condition of the strip was also a big concern. It was mostly gravel, but when it rained, which was most of the time, the airstrip turned to four inches of slimy mud, making braking action real poor.

I began to ask myself, "What in the world was I thinking of when I decided to embark on this adventure?"

Fear of potential harm or death can cause one to think things through like nothing else. As a result of my fear-induced stupor, I walked the airstrip many times and repeated landings and takeoffs in my mind. Needless to say, I had my doubts and a lot of questions.

I planned to get to a bookstore as soon as I was back in Anchorage to buy all of the Alaskan flying books that I could find. I needed to study Alaskan mountain flying techniques, as well as have a very thorough knowledge of the capabilities of the Robertson-equipped Cessna 206.

While waiting for the plane's arrival, we worked the gold mining operation diligently. Melvin barked orders at us constantly, creating contempt in the ranks, but gold was showing up in the sluice box. Now we could see the possibility of all of our efforts paying off.

My thoughts were on the plane continuously. We knew it would be in Anchorage any day and supplies were getting low. The mine operation came to a sudden halt when the biggest hydraulic hose in the D8 CAT developed a leak. The machine was worthless with that line broken.

We were averaging two ounces of gold per hour. A lengthy breakdown would cost a lot of money, which could in turn break the operation. It took a couple of hours to remove the hose, and the only fix was in Anchorage. That meant Alan and I would have to take the smaller D3 CAT, our only reliable means of transportation, out to Brandt's Texaco.

We started the painfully slow trip to Brandt's. The D3's top speed was about three miles per hour. The small machine was only equipped with one seat so one of us had to stand or sit on the hood. Of course the Caterpillar doesn't have any shocks so we felt every bump in our backsides. The littlest rock felt like crossing a boulder for the hood rider. This trip meant going up steep draws full of water, over rocky ledges, up over a big high mountain pass, down the other side through the swamp, and then it was two miles of "clear sailing" to Brandt's Texaco. We knew this trip was not going to be any fun.

But it was bringing me closer to the Cessna 206, and taking turns riding on the seat provided some relief from the torturous ride.

The pickup seat felt as good as a LazyBoy recliner; our bruised bottoms were in heaven! As I drove to town I thought about the upcoming summer and what was expected of me. Even though this was my dream come true, I was still apprehensive. One thing was certain; I was going to have an exciting summer and a once-in-a-lifetime experience.

When we arrived in Anchorage, the first order of business was to get the hose repaired or replaced. Anchorage is a big town by Montana standards, making it difficult to find anything. But after identifying a few major streets, it got a lot easier. We got the hose fixed but another problem still faced us—how would we get the hose back to the mine as soon as possible? The plane had still not arrived and we didn't want to sit around and wait, as the guys at the mine needed that hose for the D8. Driving back in the pickup and D3 would take too long.

We decided to rent a plane. I talked with the people at Wilbur's Flight Service, which is a small FBO (Flight Base Operation) on Merrill Field. They said they would rent me a Cessna 172RG (retractable landing gear), which is smaller than a 206 but big enough to get the job done. The first and last thing the owner at Wilbur's told me was, "Don't land this plane anywhere but on an approved, paved airstrip. No dirt field landings!"

We both knew rough gravel or grass field airstrips could be real tough on a retractable landing gear system, for that matter on any landing system. It can end up being a costly maneuver if things don't go well.

I knew that the rental plane couldn't handle the dirt airstrip at the mine; it was too rough and too short. Brandt's was too far away to do another road trip with the D3. The plan was this: we would roll the repaired hose into a loop, fly over the camp area and toss it out the window.

This plan had been discussed with the crew before leaving the mine. When the rental plane came into view everyone would spread out on the hillside to keep track of the hose. We hoped the tundra would cushion the fall. The last thing we wanted was to damage the ends of the hose.

Alan and I departed Merrill Field and headed toward the mine. This was the first time I'd flown across the inlet from Anchorage. We flew over the town of Palmer to the north of Anchorage and started heading into the mountains. Off to the right was the Chugach Mountain Range. These mountains were steep and high, reminding me of the Tetons in Wyoming. Glaciers start high up in the mountain range and make their way right down into the valleys and are many different shades of blue and white. The aqua-colored spectacle was unbelievable! The lower ends of these glaciers had bottomless crevasses, which extended to where the melting ice turned to a torrent of brown silty water. This was a sight I knew I would never forget.

Caribou Creek came into view, with the canyon that held Alfred Creek, our mine location being 20 miles upstream. We followed it directly to the mining camp. This was my first view of the mine's airstrip from the air and what I saw didn't give me much comfort or encouragement. The airstrip looked like a small Band-Aid! After a couple of low-level, high-speed passes we came around for our "bombing run". I slowed the plane down from 150 to 90 MPH, pushed the door open with my foot and waited for Alan to throw out the hose.

Alan had a tendency to get airsick, so being smooth with the controls was important while flying with him. He was already getting sick before we even reached our destination. I signaled and with a major effort he pushed the looped hose out the door and still managed to stay in the plane. We came around for a look and saw Leo with the hose in his hands! Later that week Leo told me that it came untied immediately after it left the plane. The hose came flying at him like a boomerang, only missing him by a couple of feet.

We left the canyon and flew over to Brandt's. All the way there Alan was yelling, "I'm gonna throw up! I'm gonna throw up!"

I had to do some fast-talking to create a distraction. I assured him that we would be on the ground in just a few minutes. I chose to try a dirt landing on the existing airstrip, which was right next to the highway. It looked like it had dried out, so I thought I wouldn't have any problems.

I made a slow, low approach. The touchdown felt smooth but the rollout wasn't good. A rain shower had just recently gone through the area and when it rains in Alaska, the dirt turns to gumbo, as I should have remembered. The plane came to a sudden stop. Mud splattered the plane, and with it sticking to the tires, the plane grew in stature. I had been lucky not to wreck the plane.

I felt like a fool, especially when I had to go into Brandt's to ask for help. It took eight guys to push the plane off the airstrip and over to the highway. I received rude comments about landing on the airstrip when it's muddy.

People at Brandt's had told me that I wouldn't survive the summer flying the Cessna 206 around that area. A mistake in judgment like this one made me think they just might be right. From then on, if I had any doubts about landing conditions on a dirt airstrip versus using a nearby highway, I would use the highway. It seemed weird to look at the highway as a runway, but I soon learned that even the State Troopers would block traffic to assist a bush pilot's landings and takeoffs. I had definitely learned a valuable lesson on my first flight.

After conducting our business at Brandt's, Alan and I departed and headed back to Anchorage. I landed at the far end of Merrill Field, as far away from Wilbur's place as possible. I borrowed a hose and washed off the plane. When we returned the plane, the folks at Wilbur's weren't any the wiser. They were glad to have our business and encouraged us to rent again from them if necessary. When I stopped at Wilbur's later in the summer, the owner said he had seen me washing the plane. I apologized.

Our own airplane, the Cessna 206, was due in a couple more days, so Alan and I said our goodbyes. He headed for Brandt's and then had the torturous ride back to the mine on the D3. I went to the Mush Inn to await the arrival of the plane.

The short airstrip down in the bottom of the canyon consumed my thoughts. Was it possible to get the big Cessna down and stopped on the mine airstrip? I would have the answer in short order.

III
SHORT FIELD LANDING

May 26, 1981

I rented a room at the Mush Inn, which is directly across the street from Merrill Field. I was anxious to have a look at all the planes, so I dashed across the highway and entered wonderland. What a sight to see all the different types of airplanes! A few of them I had only read about. I saw every make and model, from a Grumman Goose and a McDonald Douglas DC3 to DeHavilland Otters. Some on wheels, others with skis and even a few with amphibian floats, enabling them to land on ground as well as water. Some had good paint jobs, while others had patches of bare aluminum and camouflage paint. The propellers on some of the planes were nicked and scraped, resembling saw blades, making it obvious which planes had been using the gravel bars and river banks.

What a great place to spend some free time. But the nagging thought of the arrival of the Cessna 206 made it hard to relax. Nonetheless, walking around and examining the planes was a great way to spend an afternoon. Each and every plane looked good in its own way.

I sat at Peggy's Café and gawked at the airplanes taking off and landing. My thoughts were on the upcoming summer. The scary thing was I wasn't convinced I could even land at our mine strip yet. My limited flying experience and skills would be tested to the max.

With zero patience, I called the Robertson STOL Company in Seattle to check on the progress of the plane. It had departed for Anchorage a couple of days earlier. My day of reckoning was close at hand! The plant manager assured me the plane would be in Anchorage the following day. His pilot had stopped in Whitehorse for the night.

What started out to be just a call for the location of the plane turned into a barrage of questions about the STOL modification. Somewhat impatiently, he assured me again that the STOL Kit would make it possible to fly at slower speeds and turn in a shorter radius. I had heard it all before but needed to hear it one more time. I hoped that maybe a repeat of the flight characteristics of the new kit would help calm me down.

With his patience wearing thin he said, "Our pilot will get you familiar with the modifications. He'll answer all your questions."

As I sat in Wilbur's flight office gazing toward the Talkeetna Mountains, I thought of our little mine airstrip. My family would be listening for the sound of the plane. Supplies were low when Alan and I left to get the hose fixed, and by now they were probably out of food.

As I watched the clouds roll over the peaks of the Talkeetna the same question nagged me: could I land on the gravel strip? The strip was short and narrow. Being anything but dead center while landing wasn't an option. After buzzing it while dropping the hose and seeing the poor conditions from the air, my courage had wavered slightly.

I couldn't relax, so I drove to a bookstore and thumbed through a couple of dozen books on Alaskan bush flying. It didn't take long to realize I was wasting my time. I just didn't have the patience to read about other pilot's stories. Everyone seemed to have his or her own way of flying; I was no different. I would do it my way.

Besides, it was hard to concentrate with the flight path of Merrill Field right over my head and a plane landing every couple of minutes. Finally I decided if I didn't know how to land the plane on a short airstrip by now, it was too late. I hoped I'd be able to get the job done when the time came.

The people at Flight Service Station started calling me by my first name. I had been bugging them every few hours over the last two days because they would receive a flight plan on the plane and the time it would be landing.

As I looked north, my thoughts went back to Alfred Creek. Alan had taken a big risk to hire me to fly the airplane. I knew there were other people more qualified, but he knew no one would give a better effort to help him succeed. Besides being cousins, we were close friends all our lives.

The weather conditions at the mine were usually rainy and foggy, creating the worst conditions possible for mountain flying. Until now the poor conditions had just been a nuisance. Now, with the reality of the plane showing up, I would be at war with the weather daily. It would be a constant enemy, one that could devour a plane and pilot without remorse. The high mountain winds and fog would remove any enjoyment and replace it with constant worry.

I promised myself that I would be careful and diligent, learning and watching as I flew.

As planes entered the traffic pattern, I stared at each one. Finally, I recognized the plane as it soared overhead. The rumble of the big engine gave the plane its own distinct sound. My heart hammered high in my chest. A deep breath calmed my nerves. The orange and white plane looked immense and over-powering as it finally rolled into the tie-down area.

Waiting for the plane had increased my desire to get my part of the mining operation going. The anticipation of things to come had been a long and hard mental strain. I had vocalized my flying abilities, and now had to come through for Alan as well as for myself. There was no more talking. All the pressure was on me now.

In the past, I had received one hour of instruction in another Cessna 206. I had flown a lot of hours around the mountains of the Bob Marshall Wilderness, but there aren't any mountain airstrips in the whole state of Montana in such poor condition as our gold mine airstrip.

Almost all my flying time had been in a Cessna 182, hauling heavy loads. Still, I wasn't 100 percent sure I could start the 206's big engine. It had a fuel-injected engine, which could be a bear to start.

The pilot that flew the plane north said he didn't have time to check me out in the plane. He knew that all the modifications to the wings made the plane fly a little different, but he wanted to go home, and all the talking in the world wouldn't change his mind. He said his flight back to Seattle was leaving in one hour and he wasn't going to miss it. So I acquired a verbal checkout while I was driving him to the Anchorage Airport.

He made it sound so simple. "Just fly the plane about ten knots slower than usual." I wondered what was usual.

By the time we arrived at the front of the terminal, I had learned everything this pilot was going to teach me. I just wanted to get rid of him. I had things to do and was tired of talking about it.

Actually, it was a relief to not have to fly with the delivery pilot. He didn't need to know how much I didn't understand about the plane. I just wanted to go fly.

I drove back to Wilbur's Flight Service and read the manual about the STOL Kit one more time. All the takeoff and landing speeds were about ten to fifteen knots slower than what the Cessna manuals listed as correct for a stock Cessna 206. Normally the stock aircraft flew like a tank when flying at such low airspeeds. I knew flying the newly modified airplane at the recommended slow speeds was going to take a little practice.

I called the factory and talked with the manager for additional information, one last time. He was upset with his pilot leaving me in the lurch. So we talked about the different speeds and techniques, which helped to bolster my courage, if only a little.

I knew I could fly the plane. But I needed to be able to do more than just fly it. The mine strip was short and down in the bottom of a canyon. The question that stressed my every thought, could I get this big plane down to the airstrip? There were so many variables: wind direction, location of the airstrip, shortness of the strip, braking effectiveness, mechanical failures, and lack of experience.

Like a continuous record it played. Could I do what I had guaranteed I could? Alan had taken my, "Piece of cake" answer to his many flying questions as the gospel.

As I sat in the plane and stared at all the gauges, my mind played these unanswered questions over and over. I had always been a person that had direction. I always did what was necessary, and then some. But now I was apprehensive.

I was tired of wondering and talking about being a pilot in Alaska. Years of dreaming and hours of learning to fly brought me to this spot. I shook my head in disbelief. Here I sat, in a plane, in Anchorage, ready to depart to an Alaskan gold mine. For an instant I thought about pinching myself to see if I was dreaming.

Knowing that I was needed at the mine hurried me up. My hands shook slightly as they touched every gauge and instrument, making sure I recalled their location. Exhilaration and nervousness clouded my thoughts as I started the plane. My eyes scanned the instruments, making sure all was well. The oil pressure was in the green, cylinder head temperature had moved. Number One radio set to the ground control, Number Two to the control tower. It was time to go, and with a little hesitation in my voice I called the ground controller. "Merrill Ground, Cessna 61101 ready to taxi for departure to the north, my present position is at Wilbur's."

I was glad to have the call completed. Then the controller asked me if I had information Romeo.

Immediately I was mad at myself for not listening to the airport information before calling the ground controller. This information is recorded on a continuous looped tape. It plays over and over until the wind or weather changes and then records the new conditions. The controller read all the information and then cleared me to taxi to Runway 16. My hands and knees shook slightly as I taxied to a stop next to the runway. I was off to the races!

I gave the airplane the most complete and thorough run up I had ever performed, making sure I used the checklist. Gas on, cowl flaps open, prop full in, flaps to 20 degrees, mixture full rich, seatbelt on, doors locked, trim tab for takeoff, all the instruments in the green. I was ready. "Merrill Tower Cessna 101 is ready for takeoff."

The controller replied, "61101 cleared for takeoff, winds from the south at 20 knots, gusting to 30."

As I taxied onto the runway I looked back down the taxiway. Eight planes were lined up behind me, ready for takeoff. I guess I'd taken a little more time with the run up than I should have.

I couldn't procrastinate any longer. Slowly I added power. The brawn from the 300 horses pushed me back in the seat. I blasted into the air, barely rolling 100 feet before becoming airborne. The added lift from the STOL Kit, combined with sea level elevation, headwind and just one person on board, made the airplane levitate upward at an alarming rate. "Holy shit," I whispered, as the ground disappeared beneath me. I told myself to calm down as a shudder ran through my body.

It took a few seconds to get all the engine settings and controls in the right places, but eventually I managed to get the airspeed, manifold pressure and propeller RPM's under control.

The radio squawked, "Cessna 61101 is cleared for a Chester Creek departure, call Anchorage Departure on 129.35."

I pushed the mike button and replied in a shaky voice, "Merrill Tower, 101 is cleared for a Chester Creek departure, I will contact departure control on 129.35."

A mile off the end of Runway 16 is Chester Creek. It flows out of the mountains to the east of Anchorage and then passes through town, eventually draining into Cook Inlet.

Voices on the radio spoke continuously. I turned right at Chester

Creek and headed for open water. This departure route was to be flown at 700 feet, an altitude that would keep me below any traffic that was landing or taking off from the International Airport. It was a strange feeling to look into offices of high-rise buildings, actually seeing people sitting at their desks.

As I flew away from land and over open water, an eerie feeling engulfed me. MacKenzie Point was seven miles away and my aiming point to reach dry land.

I gazed at the land in the distance so I didn't have to look at the cold water below. The sound from the engine seemed to be different. I thought I could detect a slight miss increasingly getting worse. I told myself, "Just keep going straight." After what seemed to be a half hour, but was really a few minutes, I reached the safety of land. The rough-running engine seemed to be running fine now. I would soon learn that the "rough-running" engine phenomenon would happen every time I was flying over open water, better known as automatic rough.

I flew along Knik Arm and headed for Palmer and thought about all the airplane traffic around Anchorage. Seeing any planes while flying in Montana was unusual. But around Merrill Field they were like mosquitoes, everywhere you looked.

I was glad I'd gone up in the Merrill Tower and talked to the controllers. They gave me a small book that explained all the area approaches and departures. With this much air traffic, everyone needed to know the same procedure for getting in and out of the area.

I passed Wasilla and then headed to Palmer. Palmer's airport is situated at the north end of the Matanuska Valley. It doesn't have a control tower facility because air traffic is light. Sheer cleft mountains with ice cream-colored tops surround the little airport. The mountains and area around Palmer reminded me of Jackson Hole, Wyoming, making it one of the prettiest spots I'd ever seen.

Approaching the airport, I was a little more familiar with the plane. I needed to make a few landings on a long runway. Trying to land on the short mining airstrip without getting familiar with the plane first could be a big mistake.

I entered the pattern with a 60-knot airspeed. On short final I lowered the speed to 55, which felt slow, but was what the book recommended. The usual sloppy feeling was gone. The plane felt as solid as a rock. As I flared for a landing the plane floated and floated. It wouldn't come down. I needed to know how slow the plane would fly. With half the runway used up, I added power and made a go-around. The plane didn't want to land.

I remembered that the speed quoted in the book was for full gross weight. With just me in the plane I was 1200 pounds light. No wonder it floated.

As I turned final I lowered full flaps and raised the nose of the plane slightly. With small adjustments of the throttle I was able to lower the airspeed to 50 and still descend toward the end of the runway. As the ground came closer I added more power, but only enough to slow the rate of closure.

I whispered, "Nose up, more power, keep it straight, more power." The wheels kissed the ground gently. I held the nose up until it settled to the ground on its own, then turned off the runway to taxi back. I had used about a thousand feet of the runway. The mine airstrip was only about 900-feet long, with real poor approaches. I would have to make a perfect short-field landing to survive the gold mine airstrip.

The power for takeoff was incredible, and the plane bound into the air using only a couple hundred feet. At least I didn't have to worry too much when departing the mine strip. It didn't take long to realize how wrong that thinking was!

I felt slightly more at ease after doing the takeoff and landings at Palmer. It was time to head for the gold mine. I mustered the courage to turn north from Palmer and headed up the Matanuska River. The high mountains along this route are steep with trees ringing the bottom half and snow covering the top. Talkeetna Mountains off to my left were still covered with snow near the tops. The brush covering the hillsides gave way to rocky steep spires that seemed to go on forever. I could see ridges and endless mountaintops fading off in the distance.

Off to the right the Chugach Mountains stood as monuments. Dark green spruce trees lined the lower slopes. Endless fluorescent ice fields connected the upper reaches of the mountain range, a sight seen only in Alaska.

Not far from the highway below was endless wilderness. A crash-landing anywhere but on the highway would probably end in tragedy. I made a pledge to myself, *whenever possible, fly close to the highway*.

I tried to enjoy the scenery in every direction. But the constant thought of landing at the mine dampened any enjoyment.

Due to the previous week's hose drop, I knew the mine's airstrip could be easily identified from the air. I turned left at Caribou Creek and followed it until it converged with Alfred Creek. Anticipation grew, as I got closer.

The strip finally came into view. It looked altogether different from what I'd remembered. Looking at the Jeep trail/airstrip for a high-speed fly-by was different than analyzing it for an actual full-stop landing. I could feel the tension building as I circled over the strip. I started breathing faster.

Suddenly, it felt very warm inside the plane. I could see everyone on the ground and of course they were ready to see me land, not so much from the excitement of seeing the 206 or being impressed by my flying skills, though. Their supplies had run out. The airplane was the only way that they were going to acquire more groceries.

As I circled overhead, I scrutinized the airstrip and surrounding area. "Now is the time to think it through," I told myself. "Don't get in a hurry, check out everything and don't make this approach until 100 percent ready."

My thoughts continued, "The airstrip is down in the bottom of a canyon with big hills at both ends, so a go-around is next to impossible." Water from the creek flowed over the approach end of this so-called runway. Where the water passed the airstrip was a three-foot bank.

"Make sure not to touch down before the bank."

I would have to fly over the top of a hill that was about 400-feet tall, then descend to the runway, not letting the airspeed increase while floating down to the touchdown spot. Touching down with too much speed would mean sliding into the cliff at the upper end. With these thoughts in mind, I circled a few times, and then turned on a two-mile final.

I skimmed along the flat on top of the hill. It looked perfect for a landing airstrip, but was actually muskeg and mud three-feet thick. Scraping off the vegetation would turn the flat hilltop into a big mud bog. I couldn't see down to the runway as I approached the edge of the hill. I just couldn't get the airspeed down to 50 knots. Being only 30 feet above the ground and trying to stay lined up with a runway I couldn't see was making it difficult to get everything exactly the way I wanted it.

As I floated over the lip of the hill the small airstrip came into view, with the nose of the plane covering all except the last hundred feet of the runway. I lowered the nose of the plane to see the touchdown end of the runway, and then lowered all the flaps. In a matter of seconds the airspeed shot up to 60 knots, then to 70.

That wasn't going to work; everything accelerated. The far end of the runway looked way too close, especially at the speed I was going. Reacting to a dangerous situation, I immediately added full power and the plane surged forward. Carefully, I raised the flaps to 20 degrees. The manual had said that the plane wouldn't climb with full flaps extended. I was glad I had remembered that bit of information as I cleared the cliff at the north end of the runway by mere feet. I wouldn't have made it over the cliff with all the flaps extended.

A million things ran through my mind at once. Why was I here? Should I head back to town? How can I control the airspeed? How can I control my shaking knees?

"Calm down, Dave," I mumbled. To get down to the runway would take full flaps and less speed. At the top of the hill I needed to be just above stall speed, then shove the nose over enough to see the end of the runway. While doing that I would slip the plane enough to get the rate of descent needed to touch down close to the end.

In theory it sounded pretty good. Pushing a lot of right rudder and cross controlling the wings to keep the plane headed in the right direction would cause the aircraft to settle toward the ground a lot more than usual. I would use this technique to get down. I had practiced this maneuver before, but it seemed to be almost a lost art and usually only used in a plane without flaps. I remembered that the Robertson manual said not to slip with full flaps, but at this point it was the only answer I could come up with.

I made a couple more circles to calm my nerves and clear my mind, then set up on another final approach. This time as I flew over the hill the stall horn screamed. This automatic warning device is put on the plane to warn the pilot that the plane can't be flown much slower. I dove down toward the end of the airstrip. Full right rudder placed the nose of the plane pointing 30 degrees to the right of the runway. The plane settled toward the airstrip at an alarming angle. At about 100 feet from the end I went to full power and relaxed the right rudder pressure. The nose of the plane swung back toward the runway.

This maneuver stopped the rate of descent. I raised the nose of the plane and pulled the power off. The stall horn blared. The plane staggered the last hundred feet. Constant adjustments of the ailerons kept me centered. "Hold it off, hold it off, power, power," I said aloud as the plane settled onto the runway with a slight bounce. I immediately lowered the nose to see down the runway, which wasn't much wider than the tires of the plane. Steady pressure on the brakes kept me on the runway and slowed the plane to a walk.

The landing had kind of been a controlled crash. I hadn't hit anything, but it wasn't pretty. Oh well, I was down on the ground and had only used about 700 feet of the runway.

Boy, were my knees shaking! I rolled out to the end of the runway, turned around and taxied back toward all the people at the lower end.

Everyone was happy to have the plane on the ground and told me what a good job I'd done. I just tried to smile and not show how shaken I really was.

I was looking forward to having a little time off to regain my composure, but Alan had a different idea. He wanted me to fly back to Anchorage and get groceries. A 10-minute break gave me time to build up a little courage, and then I jumped back into the 206 and taxied to the uphill end of the runway and turned around.

I thought a takeoff in this plane would be a piece of cake. But looking down the short runway and at the hill I would have to climb over gave me cause for concern.

It was time to think about my options. I would keep the plane on the ground or in ground-effect until 50 knots, then climb over the hill while maintaining 50. If the ground out-climbed the plane, I would turn down the narrow canyon to the right and climb out. I didn't want to be in the deep ravine, but as a last option it might give me more time to climb out of the narrow canyon. The last thing I would do was lower the airspeed to the point of stalling the plane.

So with my plan intact, I added full power. The plane accelerated forward. At the halfway point I peeked at the airspeed. Fifty-five knots already, then I pulled back on the yoke. The plane lifted off the ground and climbed for the top of the hill like a homesick angel. When the top of the hill passed under the nose of the plane indicating that I would clear the ground with ease, I took a big breath and leveled the plane. I had cleared the top of the hill by 200 feet.

A feeling of accomplishment forced a big smile. The takeoff had been a piece of cake compared to the landing. The Cessna 206 had performed flawlessly.

I now knew that I could at least land the plane at the mine. This knowledge took a little stress from me, although thoughts and concerns turned the flight back to Anchorage into a daze. I had used every bit of knowledge and experience to land at the mine. What if I had a big tail wind or big load? I'd pushed myself to the brink of my ability. Had I just lucked out?

As I approached the mine on my return I could feel nerves taking over. The plane was loaded to the ceiling with groceries and supplies. The first landing had been completed with a real light load. How would the plane respond to the heavier load?

As I flew over the edge of the hill the stall horn blared. The plane settled toward the runway. With the heavy weight in the plane I didn't need to slip the plane. Adding power right before touchdown softened the landing and rollout. The load seemed to make the plane fly smoother and the landing easier. I had been told that the Cessna 206 liked a heavy load, now I knew what they meant.

I had plenty of help unloading the plane. Everyone was craving the fresh fruit and other supplies I brought back. They tore into it like a pack of wolves.

I stood back and smiled to myself as I scanned the surrounding mountains. I felt so good about the day's events; I could walk on water.

Some of the guys had been working steadily at the mine for a couple of weeks. Alan thought it would be a good idea to fly them to Brandt's Texaco for a home-cooked meal and a shower. So with a little reluctance I loaded the plane with five guys and taxied to the takeoff-end of the runway. Everything got real quiet as I started down the runway. The plane was loaded to gross weight. This takeoff would test my skills.

I thought about unloading a couple of the guys and telling them that the plane couldn't climb up and over the hill with the weight. But I knew it could be done. Now was not the time to be weak. If anything didn't seem right I could turn down the narrow draw as a last option.

The plane increased speed unwillingly. With 200 feet of runway left I raised the nose. A small hump launched the plane into the air.

The stall horn blared for a second. The plane settled toward the hill and then started climbing. We paralleled the climb angle of the hill and floated over the top with 50 feet to spare. A few feet closer to the hillside and I would have turned down the creek.

Everyone slapped me on the back as I turned the plane toward Brandt's. My heart raced from the adrenalin rush of the takeoff. At least I knew the plane could get out of the gold mine airstrip, just barely.

I had landed at Brandt's earlier with Wilbur's airplane, so I had a real good idea as to the condition of their airstrip. It was 1100-feet long and had a big hump in the middle. The hump made it impossible to see down the runway when taking off. It also was only wide enough for the wheels of the airplane.

Those weren't the only obstacles. At one end of the airstrip was a lake, which meant once power was applied for the takeoff, the pilot was committed to takeoff. If he tried to stop he would end up in the lake. There was no room for a change of heart! The airstrip was downhill, making the possibility of stopping in any kind of an emergency almost impossible.

After the guys had their showers and meals, we were ready to depart.

The mud flew off the tires and slammed the bottom of the wings as I taxied up the hill toward the end of the runway. The farther I went, the deeper the mud got. The narrow ruts I was following were full of water and gooey mud, which eventually ended up on the side of the plane as the tires and prop blast dislodged the gumbo. It was now or never, if I went any farther on the airstrip we would get stuck.

Being stuck with a 2000-pound airplane would be a disaster. I applied full left rudder and brakes to get the plane turned around. The lack of traction enlarged the circumference of the turn, forcing the plane off the edge of the runway and out into the puckerbrush. With a lot of slipping and sliding I finally got the 206 lined up on the runway.

The amount of runway between the plane and the water at the end of the runway looked very short. I knew the four inches of muddy slop would extend the takeoff run.

I had a couple of options. Taxi back down the runway, or give it hell. It wasn't much of a decision for a logger who had been doing everything his way for years. The plane pitched forward with application of full power. The airspeed passed 40, then 50. Mud thrown off the wheels peppered the wings. The end of the runway was close.

Without looking down I pushed the flap lever to 30 degrees. As the flaps lowered, the plane took on a distinct feel. Even with six passengers and a 3000-foot elevation, the plane wanted to fly.

With 50 feet of runway left I eased back on the control yoke. Like a mallard duck the plane elevated into the air. I eased the nose over slightly, making sure I didn't settle toward the water. But I needed more airspeed before climbing out of ground effect. The airspeed went past 60 as I cautiously raised the flaps, and then smiled as we made a slow turn toward the mine.

"This is one hell of an airplane," I thought to myself.

The plane was training me well.

Everyone laughed and joked about not getting wet on the takeoff from Brandt's. I smiled and laughed along with them, even if a little shaken. I had used the entire runway for the takeoff. For a couple of seconds I wasn't sure we were going to get into the air before we plowed into the lake.

For the next few minutes I enjoyed the scenery and pleasurable feeling of completing a job. As we flew around the end of Syncline Mountain, a Dall sheep came into view. I turned the plane and passed by him at 100 feet. His magnificent full-curl horns and bleached white hair gave him the appearance of royalty. The great animal stood in defiance as we flew by. He ruled this world high on the mountainside.

The happy feeling was gone as we turned the last corner and headed for the mine airstrip. This was going to be a maximum gross-weight landing. It was a lot heavier than the supply load. Besides, this time I had the welfare of five men to think about.

I circled over the airstrip checking the wind and making sure there wasn't a caribou in the way. The cabin grew silent as I turned a two-mile final. We floated along the top of the flat plateau. At the edge of the hill, I had the plane slowed to 50 knots. The heavy load made the controls feel real mushy. The plane flew nose high and demanded a lot of power to maintain the airspeed.

(Airstrip located in creek bottom upper center.)
I flew high over the mine airstrip looking for caribou.

With hesitation I sat on the   Departing the mine airstrip.
north end of the airstrip
waiting to depart.

The small airstrip was directly in front of the plane and 400 feet down. I lowered the nose of the plane and reduced power, creating an alarming sink rate. Large adjustments of power and controls produced an angle of descent that looked perfect for an on-the-end touchdown.

At about 200 feet out from the end of the runway I added power, slowing the rate of descent. Without looking down I added full flaps. The plane's airspeed crawled lower. At the last possible second I added a bunch of power. With a thud the mains hit the dirt. Without the power I would have hit real hard.

Without taking my eyes off the runway I retracted the flaps. Full backpressure on the yoke and heavy braking brought the plane to a stop with 200 feet to spare.

A loud cheer went up in the plane. The landing was a little hard but I was down and taxiing back without any problem. I couldn't erase the big smile from my face.

My first day of flying was complete; I felt as weary as if I had just sawed timber for a week.

Alan and I sat up and talked for a while about the flying demands and how to schedule use of the plane. I tried to tell him that the weather would be a big deciding factor, but his mind was preoccupied with the whole operation. Getting supplies to the mine had been nearly impossible, so the operation had gone without. The plane would change that problem.

I was just hoping that the weather would turn nice for the next few days, giving me time to get familiar with the plane and flight routes to the mine. What was scaring me more than anything was flying to and from the gold mine when the weather was bad. When scud flying down near the bottom of the canyon, I knew the country would take on a new appearance. What would be easy flying when the weather was good could be nearly impossible when the clouds and rain pushed the plane down near the bottom of the canyons.

Alan explained that he needed my help running the machinery during the night shift. The pressure of flying the plane was all I wanted, but I agreed to do whatever it took to help. At least now I knew I might be able to get my part of the job done.

Sleep was slow in coming that night. Even though I was exhausted I couldn't help but lie there and think about the summer adventures to come.

I wondered if the landings and takeoffs I had made today were just an accident. I knew that I'd been real lucky. One bad decision could bring disastrous results.

Thoughts kept running through my head; I tried to close my eyes, but my mind wouldn't rest. "What if there's a 20-knot tailwind? I kept telling myself that once I passed over the edge of the hill, I was committed to land. What if, what if...."

"Would I live to return to Montana?" The small shake in my usually steady hands brought concern. The pressure I felt was overwhelming. Somewhere around 2:00 a.m. my confused mind gave up and let me fall asleep.

As the plane floated down over the hill I could tell I was going too fast to get stopped. Adrenalin and fear froze my body. I slammed hard onto the runway. Dirt and gravel flew off the tires as I slid toward the vertical wall. I wasn't going to get stopped in time! This was the end. The sheer cliff rock wall would kill everyone. I held my arms up as the plane.

I sat up yelling. Sweat poured down my face. As my eyes focused, I could hear Leo say, "What's wrong?"

Taking a deep breath I said, "I just had a bad dream."

He replied, "I hope it wasn't a dream about wrecking the plane."

I gave my best imitation of a laugh and rolled over. It was going to be a long summer.

IV
TRIAL AND ERROR

CREATIVE PROBLEM-SOLVING FLYING

Over the next couple of weeks, the mine operation and camp started to take shape. Alan had to keep the machinery working around the clock; finding gold was imperative. It was in the ground, but not the quantity that Shorty made us believe. By now, we realized that Shorty had lied to us about a lot of things.

Leo had a feeling about Melvin, too. He said to me, "That guy is stealing gold."

Alan had enough worries, so we kept our thoughts to ourselves, but we were going to keep a real close eye on him.

To compound the problems, breakdowns on the equipment were happening daily, which meant hurried flights to Anchorage for parts.

If the weather turned bad on the Matanuska River route, I would have to find another way to get through. This would force me to slow fly the plane toward the small opening between the clouds and the top of the ridges, trying to see if the next valley's weather was flyable. At the last second I'd either dive into that valley or turn away and find another route.

Once I made a commitment, the fear of the weather closing in behind me created a lot of anxiety. I'd make a sharp turn every few minutes to look back and check the weather I'd just flown through. But, somehow I patiently eased the plane through the rugged mountains most of the time. I knew that this type of flying could get me killed, just one mistake in judgment could end it all.

The old D8 we purchased in Seattle *looked* good, but as we now discovered, was worn out.

Everyone was working double shifts. Leo and Tim worked their normal shift running equipment, and then performed maintenance or camp chores for eight hours. Days blended together, no time for meals or hygiene. Just sleep and work. Leo would dig overburden and then push the gravel to me to ease into the big sluice. Night after night the same procedure played over.

Almost every day I would make a flight, and some day's two flights, to Anchorage for supplies.

Two pots of coffee, a ragged shave and a good pre-flight would put me in the air and headed to town. Staying awake on these flights was a continuing problem. My head would weave and bob, as involuntary dosing would be interrupted by a semiconscious state, while the winds bucked the plane.

Leo would go along on some of the flights, which helped me stay awake. The prop control knob had a tendency to vibrate in as we flew, which made the RPM's on the engine speed up. Leo had seen me screw the knob back to the normal range many times. A prankster, like his father, he took it upon himself to screw the knob out when I wasn't looking. When I caught him adjusting the knob I yelled, "Don't touch the controls! Just let me take care of the airplane." But telling him not to do something was like telling a dog not to chase cars.

As we flew toward Anchorage I caught Leo reaching for the prop control knob again, but he had grabbed the mixture control by mistake and was turning it out. This turning usually made the RPM needle move back into the normal range. But turn as he did, nothing happened to the RPM's. Well, almost nothing. Each turn leaned the mixture of the engine.

One last turn and the engine went silent.

The shock of the engine quitting and my abrupt pushing over the nose of the plane scared the hell out of him. He grabbed at the ceiling of the plane and yelled, "What's wrong?"

I replied, "You just killed the engine! I told you to keep your hands off the controls."

Evidently he learned his lesson and never touched the controls of the airplane again.

Alan hadn't left camp yet; no one could be trusted with gold around. He went without sleep or showers and I started to receive complaints about his lack of bathing. Somehow I had to get Alan in the plane and out to Brandt's or we'd have mutiny. So I had to come up with a plan to get him in the plane. Whenever possible Tim and Leo would catch a ride to Brandt's, enjoying showers and real food.

We had moved into the old trapper's cabin, which was three

miles above the mine operation. Packrats the size of cats would run around the cabin. We soon learned to pay no attention to the rats running across us during the nights. The cabin only had one room so everyone slept and ate together. The outhouse was connected to a long ago rotted-out cabin. It was just a hole in the ground with a wood structure on one side.

The present living conditions and location just wouldn't work. Something had to be done. One of us could end up with a serious disease. These conditions were just a step above the caveman's.

Cook Shack-better known as "Mel's Diner".

"Bunkhouse"   "Honeymoon Suite"

Alan made the much-needed decision to build a couple of cabins down at the mining operation. With a list of building materials needed, I flew to Anchorage. It took four trips to town to get all the supplies needed. I cut 4 x 8 sheets of plywood in half, and then loaded them into the plane all the way to the ceiling. The next planeload was 2 x 4 studs. Leo had cut trees and had one side flattened for the floor purlins. While everyone else worked the mine, Leo and I managed to get a 15 x 20-foot cabin fabricated. This building would be the sleeping quarters. The roof was flat so we stretched black plastic over the top. We christened it the Alfred Creek Hilton.

Then we framed together a 10 x 20-foot cookshack, and dubbed it Mel's Diner. This building was covered all around with clear plastic. One wall separated the dining area from the kitchen.

Next we dug a 10-foot deep hole in the ground on a small mound above the cabins. Three sheets of plywood and a roof created the outhouse. One side was wide open, giving new meaning to the saying, wide-open spaces. A bench with a 10-inch hole provided the seating arrangements. It was rustic, but would do the trick.

I just knew that one-day a grizzly would walk around the corner while the outhouse was being used. At least it was close to the mining operation and had no rats!

I flew in a refrigerator, tables, cookstove and beds, which had to be cut in half in order to get them into the plane. Then I welded them back together after delivering them to the mine.

Everything had to be flown to the mine, since the over-the-mountain road was just too muddy for anything to travel on.

Flying the miners into Brandt's to eat and take showers had turned into a common event. Everyone begged for a break from the conditions at the mine, and Alan knew a flight to Brandt's would help keep morale up. The problem was that when one shift would get off it was usually getting dark and the next crew would work the night shift. This usually meant departing in low-light conditions and landing in the dark, which created a lot of tension.

I strained to keep my eyes focused on the shadowy outlines of the crest of the ridges and mountaintops. Just finding the airstrips in the dark canyon bottoms was next to impossible. If it was a cloudy, moonless night the flight was canceled.

This didn't set well with a bunch of cold, dirty, hungry miners. We finally came up with a solution to the blackouts on the airstrip.

We would park the swamp buggy just off the end of the airstrip, with its lights illuminating the first hundred feet. I'd load the plane, taxi down to the other end and fly out passing over the top of the lights. The light was blinding until I gained enough altitude to be above the illumination. A few moments of apprehension and a couple of blinks would restore limited vision.

I climbed the plane at the slowest possible speed, which created maximum altitude gain in the shortest distance. My eyes darted from the instruments to outside and back again, trying to keep the plane in a wings-level climb and not hit a mountainside.

To say I had a few minutes of terror would be an understatement! Eventually my eyes adjusted and the outside ghostlike mountains would reappear.

There weren't any lights at Brandt's airstrip either, but the lights of the café and the reflection off the small lake would help me line up on the runway. The airplane's light would usually give me time to make an abrupt adjustment for a landing.

Flying back to the mine at night required complete silence in the plane. I instructed everyone, "Keep your eyes plastered outside and watch for the mountains."

We all squinted into the darkness, looking for any danger. Eventually the shadows of the looming mountains would come into view and pass by the windows like spirits in the dark. I stayed high until the lights of the swamp buggy came into view far below, then spiraled the plane down directly over the illuminated runway. The last turn was shallowed out just enough to line up with the lights. I strained my eyes to be close to the top of the hill and then descended with the panicked miners to the small airstrip. The swamp buggy would only be a few feet away as we passed over it and floated to the ground.

In seconds I rolled out of the lighted area and into darkness. Continuous pressure changing on the rudder pedals kept the plane on the narrow runway. The worst part of this approach was judging my altitude above the hill and swamp buggy. I had to continually change my gaze from the front to the side window to judge my elevation.

All the lights had to be off in the plane to make it easier to see the surrounding landscape. As I went over the hill on the short final I was obligated to conclude the approach. It would be absolute suicide to try a go-around in the mountains in the dark.

Caribou were always a concern. During the day I could see them; at night it was impossible. During one of these night landings I had just touched down, and as I fought to keep the plane in the middle of the runway a dark object appeared.

I smashed on the brakes as a silvertip grizzly darted across in front of the plane. He dissolved into the darkness like a ghost. Everyone was a little hesitant to leave the plane. We had seen tracks of the big bears, but this was our first sighting. We would soon learn it wouldn't be our last.

Using bush pilots on a regular basis was a necessary part of mining life at all the gold mining camps, so I wasn't the only one pulling flight duty. Most miners couldn't afford to hire a full-time pilot, so they would hire a pilot as needed to get their gear in and out of their camps. As a result, going in and out of Brandt's airfield or using other miner's airstrips was common for all bush pilots.

There was an understanding or an acceptance if another pilot had to use your airstrip, as hardships were as common as emergencies.

During one of my stops at Brandt's I received a message that Tony and Delores had left Montana for Alaska and would be here in a couple of days. I was waiting for them when they pulled into the parking lot. Tony was so excited, hugging me and pivoting around looking at the Alaska he'd spent a lifetime dreaming about.

They both asked question after question about the happenings at the mine and were glad to hear that we had moved out of the primitive cabin and built a new camp down by the sluice. I introduced them to Eldon and Mary and then loaded all their gear into the plane. Neither of them had been in a small plane before and were a little nervous about flying.

I calmed them down best I could and departed for the mine. It was great to have both of them with us. So far we had been doing our own cooking and everyone was anxious to have Delores take over that job. She had always been the boss at home and now we needed that discipline. Tony couldn't stop smiling as he surveyed the surrounding mountains at the mine. His life-long dream had now come true.

They moved right into one end of the cookshack like it was home, sweet home. Conditions were crude, especially in the cookshack and bathroom facilities, but for us it was a great improvement from the first camp. Delores immediately kicked everyone out of the kitchen and started cleaning while Tony prepared supper.

Waiting for the next load.

Leo, Alan, Tony and Delores

We all stood around outside like a pack of hungry wolves, waiting for a home-cooked meal. The arrival of Tony and Delores was a blessing, and their appearance in the camp brought a calming effect to the operation. Alan had been under a lot of pressure to get the operation up and running. Up to this point there had been a lot of setbacks, but I was sure the arrival of his parents was going to make life better for him.

Every once in awhile someone would land on our airstrip and park his plane there. It wasn't a big deal, except for a guy by the name of Liverpool who had a cabin somewhere upstream. Until we fixed the airstrip we had no idea that there was anyone else in the area.

A few days later Liverpool showed up on our strip and left his plane about 200 feet from the end of the runway. The runway was only about 900-feet long, and I needed every inch to get it stopped. It was just too dangerous to fly over someone else's plane. The short runway was scary enough when everything went right.

The first time I flew over and saw his plane sitting on our runway, I didn't know whom it belonged to. I buzzed around the airstrip and finally saw this guy at his cabin, which was just out of sight from the airstrip. He just stood there and watched me circling. I buzzed over him and rocked the wings abruptly. He stubbornly glared at me.

With time and gas getting low I staggered my plane over the top of his plane, stalled onto the ground and slid to a stop with only a few feet of runway left, then taxied back to his plane and shut the plane down. I stood by the plane waiting for the man to show. The longer I waited, the madder I got.

Finally he showed up, and as he approached I said, "I would sure appreciate it if you wouldn't park on the runway. There's enough room in my tie-down spot for both planes." I went on to explain the reason. His mocking smile told me he already knew why.

Explaining was futile as he angrily said, "You're them guys from Montana. What the hell would you know about flying airplanes?"

His reply caught me off-guard and I didn't have time to answer. He climbed into his plane, started the engine and then taxied off the runway and around my plane. The aircraft bounced like a ball as it moved through the grapefruit-sized rocks. Eventually he taxied back onto the runway and rolled to the end, turned around and took off. His underpowered plane staggered into the air and missed the 206 by a few feet.

A couple of weeks later I had a heavy load of groceries in the 206, and as usual I circled the airstrip, looking for any caribou that might be in the way. Instead I saw Liverpool's plane. The same thing; he was parked 200 feet from the end again, right on the runway. As I came over his cabin I could see him standing in the doorway, and as before, not making any sign of moving toward the airstrip. I buzzed him a few more times hoping he would move, but he just stood there like a statue.

Just like before, I eased the near-stalled plane over his and landed. I fought for control all the way to a stop and slid right up to the very end. The nose of my plane stopped off the runway surface. I shut off the engine and walked back toward his plane.

The guy saw me coming so he walked from his cabin down the strip toward me. We met close to where he had parked his airplane. This time I was more than a little upset; I had almost wrecked the plane for the second time and it was time to get his attention.

The guy moved pretty fast. I chased him around his plane two or three times but couldn't catch him. On the fourth lap he headed back to his cabin, calling me unprintable names as he went.

The only thing I could think of doing was to grab the tail of his plane and pull it off the strip and into the creek. He could see what I was doing and stood on the hill and watched, then came running toward me.

As I walked back to the 206, Liverpool yelled and shook his fist in the air, then tugged and strained until he had the plane out of the water. I stood by my plane with my pistol in sight, not knowing what the idiot would do next. He started the plane, bounced back on the runway and took off.

As he passed over he gave me his one-finger wave goodbye, or maybe he was just showing me his IQ! I never saw him again.

The next time I stopped at Brandt's I heard that he was going to have me arrested for damaging his plane. So for the time being, I'd just keep my eyes and ears open.

Melvin somehow had talked Alan into hiring his entire family, adding three more people to the camp. His wife would help Delores with the cooking, a son named Bernie would help run the machinery and a daughter, Devlyn, would help around camp. There was something strange about the whole family. I couldn't put my finger on it, but something was going on. Eventually we would find out.

Another cabin needed to be built. We would name the new cabin the Honeymoon Suite. I went to Anchorage and purchased all the plywood and 2x4 studs that would be needed for the project. The problem was that I couldn't haul everything in one load, so I came up with a plan. I strapped a 12-inch thick stack of plywood sheets to the bottom of the plane. But as soon as I leveled off in flight the plane started vibrating uncontrollably. I made an immediate one-eighty and landed.

I needed to make the front end of the plywood stack more aerodynamic. The flat end of the stack of plywood created too much drag. I took a piece of aluminum, nailed it to the top piece of plywood, then bent the metal to a point and nailed the other end to the bottom of the stack of wood. The angled metal created a wind deflector.

Surprisingly the 206 actually flew pretty well, and although the vibration wasn't totally gone, the plane was controllable.

The upcoming landing needed to be smooth; I didn't want to break the strap holding the wood up against the bottom of the plane. I eased the plane onto the gravel runway and carefully came to a stop. I was happy to get all the material in one load. The wind in the mountains had been strong for the last couple of weeks, making for a bumpy, uncomfortable ride.

There was always a lot of activity in our area. We weren't the only miners who were forced to move their camp location. Another miner moved in several miles below us and had been trying to get me to fly for him.

The first time I flew this miner it was an educational experience. He'd whined at Brandt's about his struggle to get his mine operational and bragged about the good condition of his runway. I finally gave in and filled up the plane with the miner and his supplies. I had already observed his runway as I passed over, and from the air it looked to be in poor condition.

His runway didn't parallel the creek like most, but sat at a weird angle to the canyon, making a straight-in approach impossible. The strip was down in the creek bottom with one end near the miner's cabin and the other end at the bottom of a 200-foot cliff.

We circled overhead, trying to figure how to make the approach. The miner instructed incessantly on how to make the approach and landing.

Unable to take any more, I looked at him and said, "Would you shut up and let me fly the plane?"

He nodded his head and sat back.

I turned the plane down the creek and glanced back to keep track of the airstrip. About two miles out I banked left to reverse my direction and looked upstream, trying to see any part of the little runway, hidden around a bend in the canyon.

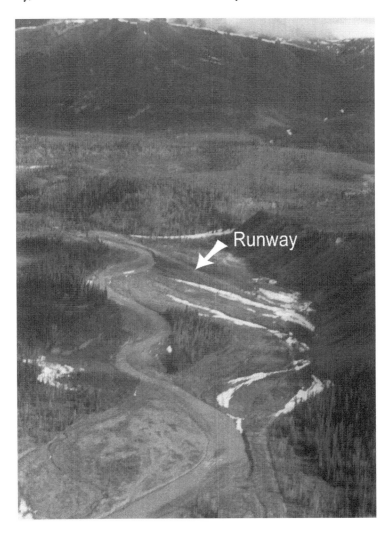

Each landing created anxiety.

As we flew closer, I lowered the elevation and skimmed the treetops. Glimpses of the runway showed through the trees and tall brush. As I glided over the taller trees and pulled the power the plane descended toward the ground, then I banked the plane to the right to get closer to the end of the runway. I would need all of it to get stopped. The cliff at the end grew disturbingly large in the window.

The closeness of the runway 50 feet down and directly in front of me seem strange. I needed to maneuver the plane now or I'd miss the runway. I banked the plane steeply left and pulled all the power. The stall horn squealed from the weird angle, which put the left wingtip dangerously close to the ground.

Power lifted the wing as the plane turned to line up with the airstrip. As the left wheel kissed the gravel, I applied full left aileron. The input kept the right wheel off the ground as the plane completed the turn. In seconds the nose lined up with the runway, forcing me to pull off all the power, planting the right wheel on the ground. Heavy braking slowed the plane to a crawl.

About halfway down the airstrip, water from the creek was eating away the edge of the flat surface, creating a 10-foot drop-off. The plane rolled past the narrow gape with a couple of feet to spare as we taxied to a stop at the miner's cabin.

I took a deep breath and said, "That's a scary approach! If the creek keeps eroding away at the edge of the runway, it won't be usable." I wasn't looking forward to landing there again.

After a long night of pushing gravel I flew to Brandt's for supplies and a shower. With a full belly, I was really looking forward to a shower. I was paying for the shower when the miner with the bad airstrip stepped into the building and headed my way. He said, "Can you fly a load of gear to the mine?"

Although we needed to make all the money possible, I was hesitant and asked, "Is the creek still eating away at the edge of the airstrip?"

He answered, "It hasn't changed since the last time you landed there. Besides, I just have a light load."

A light load would make the approach and landing easier. "I'm going to take a shower, go ahead and load the plane. I'll be ready to go in a few minutes." I'd come back and pick up my supplies later.

I walked to the plane, shocked to see it loaded all the way to the ceiling. "I thought you said it was a small load. How much weight did you put in the plane?"

He replied, "It just looks like a heavy load, everything is real light, just some groceries and light supplies."

The bottom sides of the tires were flat. I could usually figure out how heavily the plane was loaded by pushing down on the tail. If it came back up by itself, it would haul the load. If not, I'd unload gear before taking off. The tail came back up, but just barely.

I assumed the tires were low on air and taxied to the south end of Brandt's runway. Almost full power was needed to taxi up the muddy airstrip and over the hump in the middle. The load had to be heavier than I was led to believe.

I fought the controls and power as the plane wallowed and slowed through the mud. If I went any farther I'd get stuck. The plane jumped and bounced through the puddles as it sluggishly turned, throwing muck in every direction. Without reducing power we rolled back toward the hump and crested the hill. It didn't seem like the plane was accelerating normally as the runway's end and the lake loomed closer.

For a few seconds I had doubts about getting airborne in time. The end of the runway was only a hundred yards away, time was running out. Gingerly I pulled backpressure on the control yoke, making the plane stagger as the wings starting creating lift. The wheels bounced on the ground.

We lifted momentarily, then touched back down with only a few feet of runway left. Reacting, I applied more backpressure. The plane grudgingly mushed back into the air and crossed the lake with just a few feet between the wheels and the water.

I held my breath as the plane fought to gain altitude and glanced over at my passenger's smug face. He was just sitting there like nothing was wrong. The other half of my problem was still to come. The heavy load needed to be landed on the miner's so-called airstrip.

After a 20-minute flight we arrived at the miner's camp. I crossed over the top of the airstrip to check for animals and look at the water-cut section. The creek had eaten half the runway away! I looked at the miner and said, "I thought you said the runway hadn't changed?"

"You can see where I added gravel across from the eroded section. When you roll by there, move over to the new gravel. There shouldn't be a problem." he said, unconcerned.

I replied, "I can't go across your new gravel, it's not even on the runway. The gravel is in the ditch. If we go in there we'll wreck the plane." The miner just sat and stared straight ahead.

I was pretty sure I could get the plane on the ground and stopped before the cut section. We could unload the plane there and I could take off in the opposite direction.

Not being absolutely sure, I started the approach. The plane reacted to my inputs like an old stubborn mule, forcing me to over-exaggerate the controls to get it to react. With a lot of exertion and concentration we made the steep descending turn, flared the plane with full power and slammed onto the ground.

As we slowed down, lift from wings diminished, transferring the weight to the wheels, spreading them out again past normal. The runway was cut and we wouldn't get stopped. For an instant I thought about going to full power, hoping to get enough speed to lift the left wheel over the hole. But that wasn't an option. Enough speed meant going off the end of the runway in a metal-bending crash.

With 50 feet to go I applied right brake. The plane moved right and closer to the edge of the runway. The wing dipped low as the right wheel rolled into the ditch. If I went any farther we'd wreck the plane. I stared at the 10-foot hole that was full of water and held my breath as we rolled by. The left gear had to have missed the hole by inches, I thought to myself, as I moved back onto the runway and rolled to a stop at the end.

I knew I was the only one to be mad at. I shook as we stepped out of the plane and at the same time felt both anger and relief.

I couldn't even talk as we unloaded the plane and found not one, but two jeep transmissions as well as a bunch of iron. The miner wouldn't look at me, the gear was needed at his mine, and he had found a pilot crazy enough to fly it!

I looked down at the gape in the runway as I departed. The airplane's tire marks went to the edge of the hole, disappeared and then reappeared on the other side. I shook my head in disbelief as I turned back toward Brandt's. I'll never know how the tire crossed the opening, but one thing for sure, I had learned a big lesson. From that moment on nobody loaded my plane but me.

We had been finding some gold, but not even close to what Shorty had made us believe. The first two cleanouts produced only 20 ounces of gold, not very good for a couple of weeks' work.

Leo had mined on the Steese Highway, which was north of Fairbanks, making him our authority on gold mining. After the second cleanout he motioned Alan and me out of the cookshack where no one else could hear and said, "Something is wrong, there's a lot more gold in the sluice than we're ending up with. Someone is stealing gold."

The fines was all the dirt left in the sluice box when the water was stopped and was where the gold would be hiding until we ran it through a smaller sluice. Up till now Melvin had bossed everyone around like a drill sergeant and had made the decision as to when we would clean the sluice box. Everyone was starting to get tired of him. He had thinning red hair, a skinny frame, rotten teeth and chained smoked. In addition, he wouldn't do any manual labor and spent most of his time eating in the cookshack. It was hard for everyone not to grab him and shake him up with his abusive attitude.

The process of cleaning the gold out of the sluice took a lot time. The first thing to do was dam off the water running into the sluice. Then the 100-pound metal riffles in the bottom of the box had to be lifted out by hand, leaving gravel and dirt. The material that was left was where the gold was found, the fines.

Cleaning the box out was backbreaking work that shut the operation down for at least half a day. Each cleanout usually produced about 50 gallons of gold-bearing gravel, which then needed to be washed through a small four-inch sluice, one cupful at a time, leaving only gold behind. When to clean the box was always a guess. Wait too long and some of the gold could be washed out the end of the sluice box.

Melvin strongly insisted on cleaning the box every couple of days and wanted to clean the fines himself, reasoning that the summer was short and the machinery needed to be working the sluice box as much as possible. That made sense to us. So while he cleaned the gold in the little sluice, the rest of the crew would put the big sluice box back together and go back to work.

The gravel would be pushed into the top part of the sluice, called the grizzly. Then it would wash down the grizzly and drop onto a one-inch thick plastic plate, which had three-quarter inch holes drilled in it. This section would catch all the gold that was smaller than three-quarters of an inch in size.

The gravel then would wash over the plastic plate and plunge onto two-inch angle iron steel plates, where all the gold nuggets were found.

When the water was dammed up and stopped, it was possible to find gold nuggets in this section of the sluice box. We learned real fast to keep the helpers away from the sluice box during the no-water times. More than once I found nuggets in the washing machines after washing work coveralls. No one was to be trusted when it came to gold. We had a real good idea who was stealing gold, but as of yet we couldn't prove anything.

Leo refused to let Melvin clean the gold by himself again. From the very start he said that he didn't trust Melvin and now his whole family had access to the gold. I'm sure that Alan had the same feelings about the guy, but for the time being, he needed him to show us how to keep the operation working.

So on the third cleanout Alan, Leo, Tony and I cleaned the fines along with Melvin. He protested adamantly, but for the first time didn't get his way.

In the same area as the first two cleanouts and in about the same amount of time, we found 40 ounces of gold. Twice as much as when Melvin cleaned the fines by himself!

Melvin and his family were suspected of stealing in the neighborhood of 20 ounces of gold. At $800 an ounce, it was a lot of money. Alan was no fool; at the right time Melvin and his family would be gone. In the meantime we would keep a close eye on them all.

Everyone's attitude toward him changed, which created tension in the camp. The mining camp went from a place of togetherness and struggle to a place of distrust.

Shorty showed up in camp a few days later. With the lack of gold that had been promised and hint of thievery, he wasn't welcomed very well. A heated altercation between Alan and Shorty emptied the cookshack. Shorty made it perfectly clear that all he wanted was his share of the gold, any mining problems we were having were none of his concern.

That was the wrong thing to say to Alan. Alan had taken this religious leader for an honest man and was gambling a lot on this guy's word. Up till now everything that was guaranteed had proved to be a lie.

Tony and Delores standing beside the working sluice box.

D-8 pushing overburden.   Setting the sluice.

Shorty's exaggerations and fabrications were being found out and unless we found more gold, there was no way Alan could afford to keep the mine operating. So Alan made it clear that he wasn't happy with him or Melvin, but even with all the problems he was facing, he gave Shorty his share of the gold. But he made it clear that there wouldn't be any more gold for him until we found the gold that he had promised. Shorty left in a huff and Melvin stayed out of everyone's way.

I knew that money was becoming a great concern for Alan. We discussed the problems in confidence, not wanting to worry his mom and dad.

The next day was a laundry and grocery day in Anchorage. Uncle Tony was going along to help with the chores. He was like a shadow, always wanting to go with me, a great help and companion.

V
CALL ME A GOFER

I had a long list of chores to do in Anchorage, forcing Tony and me to be at the plane and ready for takeoff at first light. The clouds hung low over the ridges, making me wonder whether to go or wait for the clouds to lift. With the airstrip down in the bottom of the deep canyon, it was a constant battle to judge the weather.

I looked at Tony and said, "We'll take a look, and if the clouds are too low we'll make a one-eighty and return."

I strained to see over the hill as the plane fought for altitude. The low clouds obscured the landscape. As we flew down the valley, I was forced to change direction constantly to stay out of the fog.

When we reached Alfred Creek the clouds lifted and the sun shined through. Caribou dotted the surrounding landscape, their white manes reflecting the morning sun as they moved away from the noisy airplane. Every turn brought new and endless vistas. Deep glacier-filled canyons and high snow-capped peaks appeared in the Chugach Mountains to the south. The glaciers created a huge winter wonderland high in the mountains even in summer.

The hum of the plane and warm sunlight relaxed my mind from the ever-nagging chores of the mine, giving me time to think about my companion.

Tony had always been a friend to all the kids that showed up at his farm, and he took the time to listen and direct that day's adventure. Sneaking into his root cellar as a young boy and drinking Tony's homemade chokecherry wine was a big hit. Alan and I made a lot of new friends that way!

On one of our wine raids Tony showed up unexpectedly at the root-cellar door. To everyone's amazement, Uncle Tony sat down and pushed the wine on us. It was fun until everyone decided they'd had enough, but good old Uncle Tony had different ideas. All the wine had to be gone before anyone could leave. He said, "Wine will go bad if it isn't all drunk once the bottle is opened."

We all looked at each other in bewilderment. Getting caught

drinking alcohol would normally constitute a whipping or at the very least being grounded for while, and now we were being told, by an adult, to drink all we could and more. Something wasn't making sense.

The bottom inch of the jug was covered with the settlings of the concoction. We stared into the dark bottle trying to see what was there: pieces of cherries, twigs and things we couldn't identify. As we turned to look at Tony with blank stares he said, "Everything must be gone."

The bottle was passed from kid to kid, the remains getting thicker and harder to swallow with each sip. Tony stood by and cheered us on, making sure everyone got an equal share. With a lot of effort the contents of the bottle disappeared.

All the boys sat back with relieved looks on their faces. The feeling of bliss changed to agony as we felt the effects of the wine. One by one we each got sick. I felt like I was going to heave my guts out.

When everyone was finally finished Tony walked us up to the house and called everyone's parents. Our new friends never showed up again. To this day I can't drink wine.

As I looked at Tony he asked, "What are you smiling at?"

When I told him we both laughed out loud, remembering the chokecherry wine and Tony's way of making a point . . . .

Tony loved to point out different things as we flew, trying to see things before I did. We played that game whenever we were in the plane together. If I had a choice of any companion during all my flights I always chose Uncle Tony. I dropped him off at the grocery store and headed for the other end of town for mining parts.

We've all heard about a gofer, the guy who was always told to go for this or that and was the bottom of the totem pole as far as prestige and job importance were concerned. That was exactly how I felt most days. Go get this or go get that and hurry home. I was always late and everyone always wanted everything yesterday.

But after many trips to Anchorage I started becoming familiar with the streets and businesses, making my job a little easier. The town is spread out over 20 miles and it seemed that every time I needed a part it would be clear on the other side of town. Roads like the Seward Highway or Tutor Road became well known throughways.

I'd find a company that made hydraulic hoses, only to be told that the hose I wanted was all the way across town. It didn't take long to learn that being in Anchorage around 5 p.m. made it impossible to get anywhere. It was a total mad house.

Even with that problem, Anchorage always impressed me. There were tall, modern buildings in the downtown area. Right next to them would be old shacks with sled dogs tied up outside. The overall setting on the coastal bay was an awesome sight to a landlocked Montana logger. I could still see the old Alaska in several places, but the old was slowly being pushed out and replaced by the new.

One of the biggest problems that we had at the mine was getting everyone's laundry cleaned. We were always up to our necks in mud. There was so much laundry that I had to pack the airplane almost completely full just so that I could get it all to town in one flight. That would amount to about 20 garbage bags. It was a monumental task to get it all clean, so I'd drop it all off at the laundry, run my other errands and pick it up a couple of hours later, clean and folded. It was expensive to do it this way, but the job was always well done and it gave me time to run supplies.

After one of these return flights, Alan said that he wanted me to do the laundry myself, hoping to save money. I understood his dilemma, but didn't like that idea at all.

I already was spending all my time in Anchorage running parts. He still wanted me back as soon as possible, needing me to run the CAT at night. I was already too busy and there was a limit to what I could do.

A couple of days later was laundry and grocery day. I was dead tired, but loaded the plane full of dirty, muddy, greasy work clothes, and headed for town. I had a list of supplies to get, and I was expected to wash the clothes myself.

This money-saving idea just wasn't going to work. I came up with another idea that would help Alan see that his request was unreasonable. I washed all the clothes but somehow forgot to use soap. I don't know how I forgot such an important item, I guess I just had too many things on my mind. I didn't have time to fold them either. I stuffed the clothes in plastic garbage sacks, then raced across town to get a 25-gallon can of oil and headed for the plane.

The pressure I felt to get back to the mine caused me to fly across a section of Elmendorf Air Force Base airspace, which in turn resulted in a close buzz job by an F-14 Tomcat. The closeness of the military jet woke me right up. The pressure to work all night and fly all day was taking its toll.

I knew I put this pressure on myself; Alan never questioned where I was or how long it would take when it concerned the plane. I just wanted to help him get the job done. But flying airplanes in this state of mind was dangerous. I decided to talk to Alan about this problem.

All I could say was that I didn't have enough time to do all the laundry and run for parts. If I was to be responsible for doing all the washing, what they got was the best they were ever going to get. For some reason, that was to be the last time that I did the laundry. Thank God! Tony volunteered to go to town on all laundry days after that.

Having all my errands completed, I picked Tony up at the grocery store. He never complained when I was a couple of hours late. The weather had gone bad in the direction of the mine. Dark clouds filled the Matanuska Valley, and as I approached them it was hard not to turn around and go back to town, but the mining operation was depending on my load.

At Chickaloon Pass the weather turned real ugly, with wind and rain battering the airplane. At the Matanuska Glacier my progress came to a sudden stop; the clouds descended to the ground. The last thing I wanted to do was fly back through the pass and get beat up in the wind en route to Anchorage. So I circled, looking for a landing spot on the highway.

On the second pass I noticed a man standing in a small opening. As I passed over him I could see him motioning me to land. The airstrip looked real short, but we didn't have much choice as the weather was closing down fast. A steep turn lined us up a mile out from the runway. The stall horn was shrieking as I drug the plane onto the grass runway right on the approach end, then slid right up against the trees at the far end.

The old man walked up and greeted us. He was amazed that I was able to get the Cessna 206 stopped before hitting the trees. The airstrip was built just for his Super Cub; no other plane had ever landed there. It was 400-feet long. I was glad to be on the ground, so I didn't quiz him as to why he'd motioned me to land on the short runway.

Since his house was across from the glacier, he'd seen me fly by when the fog was low and wondered who the crazy pilot was flying in the poor conditions. Now he knew.

We ended up spending the rest of the day with the old guy and his wife and happily furnished a roast for the home-cooked meal. During supper we heard about his gold mine, which was located on Billy Creek, 20 miles upstream from our mine. He had been flying a D2 CAT to his mine for years, piece by piece.

I still remember the sparkle in his eye as he said, "Just one more year and I'll have all the pieces to the mine."

Now that's what I call fortitude. He was old and bent, but far from beaten.

Later that day the fog lifted, so we resumed our trek home. The departure on the short strip was no problem, although 400 feet looks real short. The end dropped down and away making the climb out toward our mine a piece of cake.

When we touched down Alan was waiting for us, worried because the mine had fogged in right after we'd left, and we were late. We'd enjoyed the day with the old couple, two Alaskans who loved the land and life.

Caribou standing on the runway hampered almost every landing at the mine airstrip. Tony brought up the subject of caribou meat constantly, and even though it wasn't hunting season, we decided to thin the resident airstrip population a little.

Everyone liked caribou meat and some preferred it to the fatty beef we purchased. That was right up Alan's alley, since caribou was a lot cheaper than the expensive beef. Uncle Tony would spend all day cutting it into pieces. Not even the smallest morsel was wasted.

The wrapped meat was then arranged in the order it would be eaten and put into the freezer, a 30-gallon barrel that had been buried next to an ice-cold creek. The ground and creek water was so cold that the inside walls of the barrel were covered with an inch of frost.

Tony turned into the handyman around camp. One thing for sure, as long as he was at camp we wouldn't go without meat to eat. Being the cook's helper and camp counselor was his way of helping out. Life at the mine had improved greatly with the addition of Tony and Delores. They kept the camp in working order and could turn a pan of caribou steaks into a meal fit for a king.

Tony had discovered a natural mineral lick only a couple of hundred yards above the camp. The lick drew all the local animals, giving Tony a never-ending supply of animals to try to talk me into shooting. The problem was that it was located on a cliff face. He had the eyes of an eagle and made sure that I knew there was meat right in our own backyard. Almost every day he would see Dall sheep at that lick.

Every time I wandered into the cookshack he would ask me to shoot one for camp meat. Up till now I had always had a reason not to shoot a sheep. The mineral lick sat high on the top half of a cliff and the fact that it was illegal had always been a deterrent.

The next day Tony ran into the cookshack, half out of breath, and pointed through the clear plastic yelling, "A big ram!" He hoped his excitement would persuade me to get him a sheep. At first I refused, but he kept the pressure up until I relented.

I had my hunting rifle with me, a 308 Norma Mag. It's a little high-powered for a sheep, but if the bullet were placed in the right spot, it wouldn't ruin any meat. With careful aim I looked at the ram through the scope. It was standing in a position that made it impossible to see anything other than the stomach area. Not the area to shoot. I wanted to wait, hoping the sheep would move, but Tony wasn't going to give me time to change my mind.

He agreed to clean up the mess. I squeezed the trigger gently. The big magnum rifle rocked me back as the bullet made its way to the target. The sickening sound of "whoop" told me that the bullet had hit exactly where it had been intended, in the stomach. The animal stiffened up like a board. It did exactly what I'd hoped it wouldn't. It didn't fall, hanging precariously onto the narrow ledge. The last thing we wanted was for the sheep to die on the high cliff perch and out in the open right above our camp.

I took careful aim and shot once more at the same spot as the first shot, with the same results. It was one thing shooting the sheep, but now we might not be able to retrieve it if it didn't fall. I had no choice but to shoot again. The dead sheep stayed as stiff as a board. I looked at Tony in amazement, "How could that sheep stay on the vertical cliff?"

He shrugged his shoulders and looked away with a smile, knowing he finally had a sheep to eat.

I scrounged around camp and found the best rope that was there, then waded across the creek, and angled uphill through thick brush until I found a small ravine that led to the top of the hill next to the cliff. I talked out loud the whole time, hoping any grizzlies would move out of the way. Based on the tracks, I knew where all of our four-footed furry friends spent their daylight hours.

I eased my way up to the top of the vertical drop off and swore to myself as I peered down at the white sheep, wishing that it had fallen to the creek below.

Since I had been little, I'd been afraid of high places. The only time I wasn't scared was in an airplane because I couldn't fall out of it. But the shear cliff made me cower back as I looked for an anchor for my rope. I slithered over the edge until the puny rope held up my weight. A quick glance down made me nauseous.

Trembling with fear I inched myself down to the sheep. The animal was dead for sure. I could smell him long before I arrived. The stomach shots had made a terrible mess, although I hadn't ruined much meat. I was glued to the rock as I kicked at the sheep. It slowly rolled over and disappeared. I listened for the splash in the creek 200 feet below.

I lifted my arm, looked under it and glanced down. I was flabbergasted to see the sheep right below me. It had managed to land on the only flat spot between the bottom and me! My first thought was to forget the whole thing. No sheep was worth falling off a mountain for. But then I thought about the sight of the white sheep showing up like a bright light to every plane that flew by.

With only 20 feet of rope left I eased myself down to the sheep. My arms felt like mush. A small push launched the sheep out of sight. I waited anxiously for the splash.

Tony and Leo waved reassuringly, jumped in the swamp buggy and bounced across the creek toward the sheep. I took a big breath as I looked up a hundred feet of near-vertical cliff. Inch by inch I pulled myself back to the top.

As I lay on my back taking in deep breaths, I promised myself I wouldn't do anything that stupid again. I thought to myself, "People actually do that for fun." I stumbled back to camp.

The ram was pretty smelly and in terrible shape, but that didn't bother Uncle Tony, who was ready to go to work. We hung it up, and he had the animal skinned and cleaned in short order. All the while I gazed up and down the creek, fearful the game wardens might show up. But that was impossible, considering the remoteness of our camp.

As Tony cleaned, the foul odor around camp seemed to get stronger. The memory of that smell was so strong that every time sheep meat was served, I couldn't eat it. Everyone else in camp liked the taste of it, though.

Alan decided that he had to stay at the camp, and henceforth I would be selling the gold. So far we had sold gold at the stores that sold mining equipment. They would only give the day's market price, which Melvin said wasn't enough money for Alfred Creek gold. Most of the gold that was found was nugget size and worth more money than the daily price.

Since the day Shorty had been run out of camp Melvin had been pretty quiet. He knew that we were suspicious of him.

Most of the gold that we found had to be sold immediately. The cost of running the mining camp, buying food, fuel, wages and working supplies demanded a big supply of cash.

The next trip to Anchorage was filled with all the usual chores and one more, finding a new buyer for our gold. My first idea was to go to a jeweler. The fourth jewelry shop owner said exactly what the first three said, that he would buy it at the day's price. But he knew a buyer who would pay a lot more than spot price, especially for the nuggets. He whispered, "The only way to sell gold is through the black market."

"What's the black market?" I naively asked.

By that evening I had an appointment to show the gold. The broker gave good directions. The meeting spot was in a pawnshop on Fourth Street, the bad part of town. As I walked along I stared at all sorts of low-life's who glared right back. Every race and color seemed to materialize in front of me as I hurried through the drunken crowds.

I started to receive a few rude remarks about my cowboy hat and boots; in this part of Alaska I was completely out of my element.

My destination was only a block away. Maybe I was just imagining that someone was following me, but the feeling grew stronger and stronger. The 60 ounces of gold in my pockets was making me jumpy. Halfway across the next intersection the feeling of imminent danger overwhelmed me. The hair on my arms stood erect and a shudder ran through my body.

I swung around in a flash, with my coat pulled back showing my pistol to the aggressive crowd. The crowd stopped and stared. I looked each one in the eye until their stares turned away. After a few seconds the crowd went back to its own business. I turned and hurried to the pawnshop, relieved to be off the streets and in the store.

The broker I had talked to earlier was waiting for me. He said he owned the pawnshop and could make all the arrangements for selling my gold, as well as any future shipments. Of course he expected a small percentage of each transaction.

He said, "My name as well as the buyer's name is of no importance to you. The price these people offer for your gold will be the highest price possible. They don't want to know you. They just want the gold. No questions asked. They will examine the gold and give a price. You and I will discuss the offer and accept it or reject it. Any gold bought will be paid for in cash. Do you understand how it works?" I nodded my head in agreement.

As he talked I learned that the value of a gold nugget goes up in price, as the size of the nugget got bigger. Jeweler's gold is the size that is used to make watchbands, rings or pendants. It will not bring the price of nuggets, but is worth more than fine gold. If we found any big nuggets, about the size of a thumb, they required a special arrangement and were worth a lot of money if the right buyers were contacted.

This was going to be the biggest gold sale yet. Up till now we had only sold a few ounces at a time. But now Alan had some big bills to pay and had told me, "Get the best price you can. Try to get a hold of some of the people Melvin mentioned."

He let me know how much money he needed, so I had gone to the safe-deposit box and filled my pockets with gold. There were some big nuggets that he had been saving, but now had to sell. These nuggets were special, about the size of a quarter with very odd shapes. If I did my work right, they would bring a lot of money.

I was more than a little nervous about handling the job. I knew there was a lot of money to be made or lost. Alan was counting on me.

The pawnbroker continued, "Normally the buyers won't show up for a small amount of gold. But, because of the big volume of gold you have, they will be here to examine it."

We slowly arranged the 20 small jars of gold in order according to their size and weighed each item, making sure all the weights were exact. The gold looked impressive lined up in order all over the table.

The gold represented all the effort and stress that everyone had gone through to this point. It was the sum total of what our mining operation represented. Although the pawnbroker tried to make me believe he was running the show, I knew I would have the final word on any transaction.

The pawnbroker said, "The buyers will only want the bigger pieces of gold. They can buy fine gold anywhere. But Alfred Creek nuggets are valued because of the purity and unique shapes."

I replied, "They will buy all the gold or none. That is my final word on the subject. I'm not leaving here with fine gold. The nuggets make the fine gold valuable. If they want the bigger gold, then they will buy the fine gold to get it."

The pawnbroker didn't like what I said, but understood what I wanted. As we talked a black stretch limo pulled up in front of the store. Two men in black suits walked in looking straight ahead, never once glancing in my direction. They were the classic Mafia people I'd seen in movies. They looked Italian, were clean-shaven and had coal-black eyes. One of the guys had a black briefcase, which he set on the table. As they examined the gold, they didn't say a word or look up. Each bottle of gold and each nugget were scrutinized.

After what seemed like eternity, one of the guys looked at the pawnbroker and said, "We'll take all the gold except the fines."

Immediately I said, "It's all or none."

Both guys looked at the pawnbroker like he had just committed a crime. The broker grabbed my arm and said, "Let me do the talking."

As far as I was concerned not wanting me to talk was bullshit, but I bit my tongue for the time being.

"Gentlemen, Alfred Creek nuggets are valuable. You will have to buy all the gold on this table." The tension built as both men straightened up and whispered to each other. One of the guys wrote a number down on a piece of paper and put it on the table. The number read $60,000. It was a good price, a lot of money.

My mind was going a hundred miles an hour trying to figure how much they were really giving for the fines and nuggets. It was hard to think with everyone staring at me. A quick computation told me they were trying to get the fines without paying for them. Besides, you never take the first offer. They thought I wouldn't dare turn down the sixty.

I took a deep breath, looked at the pawnbroker and said, "No deal, 72 or nothing."

Without saying a word they stood up, grabbed the briefcase and walked out of the building. The pawnbroker was flabbergasted. He couldn't believe that I would turn down their offer and caused him to lose $1800 in commission.

I felt a little sick myself. I had just turned down $60,000. A feeling of numbness overwhelmed me as I left the pawnshop with the gold. It was too late to take the gold back to the bank, so I drove to the motel with my mind reeling, scolding myself, "You idiot, you won't get an offer like that again."

The telephone woke me from a fitful sleep at 2:00 a.m. The pawnbroker had been negotiating all night. He yelled, "They want all the gold at your price." He was so excited that he could hardly talk. As I hung up the phone I sighed with relief.

I was at the pawnshop right on time the next day waiting for the buyers. They walked into the room, put the briefcase onto the table and counted out a total of $72,000 in 100-dollar bills, then placed the gold in the briefcase and walked out. Never once did they look at me or say anything.

The pawnshop owner and I spent the next hour putting the bills in stacks and then in a shoebox. It was filled to the top. I felt even more nervous walking down Fourth Street with the money under my arm!

The parking lots around Merrill Field were full of cars as I neared our plane. An air show was going on and the airport was closed. I needed to get back to the mine with the supplies and was anxious to let Alan know how good he did with selling the gold.

I called the tower to see how long I would have to wait to get out of town. They said that from 12:00 to 12:30 the airport would be open for locals to land and depart. So I sat back to watch the show.

Four Ultralite home-built airplanes were in the air. Each one was performing steep and dangerous maneuvers. The small machines were so flimsy; the wings shuddered and shook as the pilots put each machine through its paces. I grimaced as the wings distorted under the constant pressure. The mufflerless chainsaw engines on the makeshift airplanes whined at the high RPMs. As one of the machines pulled out of a dive, the left wing snapped upward. The aircraft and pilot spiraled to the ground like a maple leaf falling out of a tree. The pilot was helpless.

I closed my eyes as the injured machine slammed into the pavement. The crowd let out a sickening moan.

I opened my eyes to what I expected. The pilot lay on the ground, still in the harness, motionless. I turned my head as they loaded the injured man into an ambulance and disappeared for the hospital. The image of the small aircraft plummeting to earth hit too close to home.

Departing for the mine, my thoughts wouldn't leave the small plane. The wind rocked the big Cessna continuously as I left the highway. Even though the windblown mountains created continuous turbulence, I was glad to be headed back to my mining home. The gusty tailwind made me sit up straight as I fought the controls of the plane all the way down to our gravely airstrip.

My love affair with Alaska was strong, but the turn of each corner created a new situation that had to be approached cautiously. Selling gold or not, ending up like the Ultralite pilot was not part of the job. But I had made my boss an extra $12,000!

I was on cloud nine, and when Alan heard the story his face gleamed with surprise. He was more than appreciative, giving me a $500 bonus for my efforts. This was a special gift he truly couldn't afford.

As we visited, his odor reminded me that he hadn't been out of the mine for a long time. Maybe tomorrow I could talk him into going to Brandt's for a well-deserved cleanup.

VI
PARTY AT GUNSIGHT

A few days later I was on one of my many flights back and forth to Brandt's. As I looked to the north I noticed smoke billowing skyward from a small deep canyon. The mountains in that direction were steep, treeless and full of grizzly bears. I had flown over the area many times, but never noticed any sign of human life. To get in that canyon a person would have to come by our camp, and as far as I knew, no one had come by. I turned north for a look.

In the bottom of a deep ravine was a small tent, with two guys waving as I flew over. I banked the wings of the plane in return, the equivalent of a wave, and headed for the mine. What in the heck were they doing out in the middle of nowhere, 40 miles from any roads?

We wondered how the newcomers had traveled by our camp without one of us seeing them. Strange noises and footprints had been seen around camp for weeks—maybe these were the people scaring us at night.

Every day I received complaints about the lack of a shower, so I decided to do something about it. I had made a point of not looking too clean whenever I would get back from town, but what was a guy to do? Hot water for two bucks and good food was available in town, so I used it.

After all the heckling about my showers and complaints about who smelled, a plan was made to build a shower. Leo, who could build anything, and I took two 50-gallon barrels, fixed one on top of the other and placed them beside the corner of the bunk house. A small creek flowed right next to camp. A water line was run from the creek to the upper barrel, and the bottom barrel was fitted with a door and chimney flue. With water in the top and fire in the bottom it wasn't long before we had steaming water. Pressure from the hose forced the water out the barrel and up to a showerhead.

The crew was so excited when we proudly showed them their new luxury. But still they demanded that I be the first to try it. No problem, not wanting to tell them I had a shower just the day before. A hole was cut in the floor for the drain and black plastic was hung around the showerhead.

I jumped into the steaming hot water, in my birthday suit, mind you, and let the warm water soothe my aching body. Without warning my state of bliss turned to breath-taking panic. The hot had turned to ice water and in the confusion I had retreated in the wrong direction!

So here I was, naked as a jaybird, cold water making my manhood look like it belonged on a newborn and a bunch of cold-hearted miners laughing their behinds off. With great courage I dashed back through the spray of numbing water, only to be met with an onslaught of rude remarks. Oh well, it was all in good fun. But I'd get even with each and every one of them.

Timing was essential when preparing for a shower. The learning process speeded up after a scalding or a freeze. At least everyone in camp could get cleaned up and maybe now the complaints about smelly miners would stop.

I had been hearing rumors of an upcoming party at Gunsight Mountain Lodge for a couple of weeks. Tim and Leo had been working a lot of hours, so Alan surprised them with a flight to the Lodge. Everyone was surprised to hear that Alan was going along. With his mom and dad at the mine, he felt he could finally leave.

I had never landed at the Lodge, but I'd flown over it many times. From the air, the runway looked real short, with one end of the airstrip ending right up against the Lodge itself. It was rumored to be only 800-feet long and its intended use was for Super Cubs only.

A couple of the local pilots made it clear I was to stay off of this runway with the big Cessna. They never told me personally; neither of them had enough guts to tell me face-to-face, so they passed the message through other people.

This was the first time Alan, Leo and Tim were in the plane together. I owed all three of them for a lot of pranks they had played on me in the past, and it was time to get even.

I started talking about the stall characteristics of the plane. They listened intently as I climbed for altitude. I said, "I'll show you one stall, and you won't believe how gently the plane recovers."

All three guys were apprehensive, but I talked fast to affirm that they would like the demonstration. The plane actually had a real gentle stall, but I'd make sure they remembered this one for a lifetime.

As the plane slowed down I raised the nose to an almost vertical attitude and added some power. Alan grabbed for a handhold as the plane shuddered. Our airspeed was almost zero, and as the stall horn screamed, the wings finally gave up the fight. Normally any forward movement of the control yoke would recover the plane from a stall.

I kept the plane in the stall. The wings dipped up and down, not liking the abuse. In an instant the plane rolled, inverted to the left. Now the ground was in the top part of the windscreen. To make matters worse the plane started to rotate, the beginning of a spin. Although this plane could spin, it wasn't certified for such a strenuous maneuver.

My heart went up into my throat. I wasn't expecting this either. Everyone screamed in unison and fought for a handhold as I jammed on right rudder and shoved the nose over further. The normal reaction would be to pull back on the yoke. That would only make the plane rotate faster. My training took over: first recover from the stall, then stop the rotation, then recover from the straight-down attitude. I pulled back on the yoke, and the pressure of the recovery made us all feel twice as heavy as normal. I relaxed slightly as the plane came back to level flight.

As I looked at everyone, they stared back with frightened expressions. Alan said, "What the hell was that? Don't do that shit again!"

I replied, "I told you guys I'd get even." I smiled in triumph. They never noticed the shake in my hands. Little did they know I'd scared the shit out of myself as well as my passengers.

We flew over the Gunsight Mountain Lodge. The rumor of a party must have been true. People were dancing right on the airstrip, beside the back of the Lodge.

I made a slow drag-it-in approach, touching down close to the end and then taxied right up to the party. People grudgingly moved out of the way, not wanting the Cessna 206 close to their Super Cubs.

The same two local pilots that had been rude ever since day one stood at the front of crowd. Whenever I got close to these guys they would tell me I was going to kill myself in these mountains.

To this point I had ignore them, not sure they weren't right. I had refused to drink with them, so I guess they took it personally.

When we got out of the plane they led the chants, "Get your god damn plane off of our airstrip."

Alcohol was doing the talking, they were real tough with all the people around, but I'd had enough. With a finger jabbed in their faces, I let them both know that one day they were going to have to back up their big mouths. That seemed to quiet them for the time being, so we pushed through the crowd and went in the Lodge.

The guys took off for their showers while I ordered hamburgers. The bar was horseshoe-shaped, which made it possible to look directly at the people sitting across from me. Everyone was having a great time, a knee-slapping party, Alaska style. Everyone except the other pilots, both sitting in the corner, glaring a hole in me.

Across the bar from me were three ladies. Well, a lady is probably not the right word. Dirty, unkempt hair and 30 pounds overweight would describe them better. As they talked I noticed dark holes in their mouths where teeth used to be. With voices loud enough for my benefit, they started telling Montana sheep jokes.

I thought I had heard just about every Montana sheep joke, but these girls were coming up with new ones that made even me blush.

Finally everyone finished their showers and sat down to have a hamburger. The jokes got louder and nastier.

One of these lovely dames yelled across the bar, "I hear you Montana cowboys have short cattle prods."

Well, enough was enough. I yelled back at her, "You know what Montana guys do for you gold-mining women?"

She said, "No, what do you do for us?"

"We take you out of this wilderness where you don't know the difference between scratching and screwing; three months in Montana will turn you into respectable ladies."

There was one more sentence to my line but the beer bottles that were being launched in our direction kept me from finishing. It probably wasn't the right thing to say, and we made a hasty retreat to the plane, with a big crowd in tow. Rude and sarcastic remarks came from every direction. It was time to leave; with all aboard I lit the fire in the big engine and taxied to the end of the airstrip.

On takeoff I could have climbed over the angry crowd but decided to keep the plane close to the ground instead. It wasn't hard to pick out the people with brains and the ones without. The dumb ones stood their ground. The smart ones moved out of the way of the big fan up front. But grudgingly all finally moved, deciding not to play chicken. As we flew by the crowd, everyone gave us their favorite one-finger wave.

It should have been enough, but we decided to have the last word. In a slow turn I headed back for the Lodge in no hurry, wanting our party-going assailants to forget about us. The end of the airstrip closest to the Lodge ended at a ravine that went down and away from the party. With a lot of speed we flew up this ravine and turned onto the airstrip.

By now, everyone was outside on the airstrip dancing and having a good time again. That all stopped when they heard the rumble of the planes engine.

Everyone moved in unison to get out of the way, everyone but, you guessed it. Dan and Blacky, brave men that they were, stood their ground.

Not one to be intimidated, and having a bigger gun than them, I bore down on the weaker duo like an arrow to a target. At the last second, bravery turned to survival. We shot by a couple of feet over their heads and glanced down to see the pilots sprawled out like a couple of spiders.

We got a big chuckle out of the buzz job and the sight of the two guys diving for the ground kept the laughter going. I flew straight away from the Lodge, not wanting to give anyone an excuse to take a shot at us.

I was sure that if the tables were turned, I'd be one mad Montanan. An airplane passing within a couple of feet of you and going 150 miles an hour would be real scary. But for the time being we enjoyed the moment.

One of the bush pilots, Blacky, would get more than even in the near future.

Total darkness was left behind as the days of summer counted on. Even though it was 11:00 p.m., I could see the runway from a mile out. The possibility of caribou on the darkened runway demanded total concentration as we touched down on the hard gravel. On short final Alan noticed smoke coming out of the old trapper's cabin. This was the cabin we had stayed in before building the new shacks farther downstream. The smoke meant someone was waiting for me to return and needed a flight to town.

While we tied the plane down a couple of boys walked up to us with their hands extended. They looked to be about seventeen and twenty years of age, both in good shape and had the eager faces of youth.

They explained that Shorty had talked them into coming to Alaska from Idaho and mining gold on his claims. So far all they had managed to do was starve. He had driven them in and dropped them off without many supplies and now they wanted to know if one of them could beg a flight to Anchorage for groceries. A bear stole their remaining supplies and chased them out of their camp.

We were immediately pissed—how dare that shyster drop off these two boys in the middle of a bear-infested wilderness!

This was an area where a person could die without much effort. Shorty had used his religious influence to get these young boys to come to Alaska. What a creep!

"I'll bet he only wanted 50 percent of the gold," I asked the boys.

They looked shocked, and said that was absolutely right. We took the young guys with us to our camp. Delores and Tony had hot food for them in minutes, and they wolfed it down like ravenous dogs.

Alan told them about the promises and lies Shorty had made to us. He also explained to them that the ground Shorty said was his actually belonged to the Indians, and any gold they found was theirs.

I had a flight to town the next day, so they spent the night. Tony, the older boy and I went to town and bought supplies. Tony washed clothes and I bought a planeload of supplies and then we flew back to the mine.

Tim was going to drive the young Idaho boys back to their little canyon in the swamp buggy and help them reorganize the camp. I told them I would fly by every once in awhile to check on them. As they drove out of sight, I couldn't help but admire their bravery. Grizzlies had torn up their camp a couple of times, but the boys were determined to find gold. The wall of a tent wasn't much protection.

Both boys were more than upset with Shorty. I think he was in for a big surprise when he showed up for his share of the gold.

There were a total of six mining operations on the creek, each one from the outside or from the lower 48. There weren't any local miners in the area, but we were all mining claims owned by local people. We never questioned why no locals were mining; that answer would be realized eventually. Each miner was trying to take advantage of the high price of gold. I would fly supplies for all of them before the summer was over.

The lowest mining camp on Caribou Creek was owned and operated by a construction worker from California. He was hoping for the same thing we were, to strike it rich. He used a different route to his camp than we did, so the only time I would see the owner of the mine was when I was at Brandt's Texaco. He traveled a trail down Squaw Creek, which was a torturous 20-mile bog.

This mining operation was having a hard time getting going. They had new equipment, which we found out later was mandatory for finding gold, but had no clue as to how to find it.

They had heard the same old story from Shorty. "Lots of gold, easy to find, and easy to get out of the ground." The miner was mad as hell when I told him that we had heard the same story. My heart went out to him; at least we were finding some gold. He hadn't found any.

I flew them to town from Brandt's a couple of times, then they fought the 20 miles of impossible trail back to their camp. I tried to talk the owner into building a little airstrip, but he decided to buy a small helicopter and hire a pilot to fly in their supplies.

A few days later I heard that the helicopter pilot had landed with one skid teetering. When the engine shut down and the blades slowed, the rear end of the helicopter tipped backwards, hit a rock and bent the tail-rotor blades.

The owner of the helicopter was so upset that he made the pilot walk out to the highway to hitch a ride to Anchorage to get a replacement rotor. The blade wasn't that big, only about four feet long, but the pilot had a 20-mile walk through wilderness just to get to the highway. They never did get the helicopter up and running again. Instead, they made just enough repairs to move the helicopter to town, and as a result a small runway was built for supply trips to and from Anchorage.

The tough times didn't stop there. They had purchased a new 955 front-end loader. One day it stalled right out in the middle of the creek. It had lost hydraulic pressure and wouldn't move without repairs. That night a big rainstorm hit the area, and with the water rising the mechanic had to retreat to higher ground. All night the water washed around the machine, at times only leaving the top third showing.

The next day they discovered the cap to the reservoir hadn't been put back on. It was now full of water and sand. The big machine moved only a few feet and stopped after the repairs were completed. Sand and mud had contaminated the whole hydraulic system. The front-end loader never moved for the rest of the summer. I flew over the mine a year later; it was still sitting in the same spot.

I flew over this camp on every trip to town. The request for my services had dwindled to a stop. Rumor had it the miners were completely broke and didn't have much in the way of food supplies. I thought about their dilemma often. We were struggling, but not like they were. So on my next trip to town I stopped at a deli and requested a turkey with all the trimmings.

Their wide eyes and big smiles were my reward. They couldn't thank me enough for the Thanksgiving dinner. The miner had decided to call it quits and had given everything he had to make his mine work. I gave them enough food to last them one more week. Shorty had claimed a victim.

I never heard from this guy or his crew again. I'm sure he lost his entire life's savings. Unfortunately, I was hearing about this happening to a lot of people. Everyone came to the gold fields thinking they could strike it rich quick. Truth was it was hard work and took a lot of money just to run an operation correctly. If money and equipment were not a problem, just the mining environment could break the toughest miner's spirit.

I had a flight the next day with a miner located downstream from our camp. He had a load of supplies as usual. The condition of the airstrip at his camp made it hard to sleep.

As I lay on my bunk, the thought of the short and narrow strip sent chills up my back. Each landing on his runway was pure survival. If I had any brains at all, I'd refuse to land there.

VII
JAPANESE TOURISTS

Somewhere around midnight Alan and Tim wandered into the cookshack, cold and hungry. Both looked like they hadn't slept for a week. The arctic environment had turned their faces a bluish-red color. As they soaked up the heat of the stove and sipped hot coffee, the shaky chills departed.

Now it was Leo's and my turn to work the gold sluice. The cold air cut like a knife as we walked the short distance to the CATS. Both of us felt a little uneasy as we separated and stepped up on the tracks of the machines.

Over the last couple of weeks I was getting a real strange feeling that someone or something was spying on us during the night shift. The uneasy feeling would start with my mind telling me someone or something was glaring directly at me. Then shivers would run down the length of my body, immediately followed by the hair on my arms and back standing erect.

A suffocating pressure in my chest would be the sign that I'd had enough. At this point I had to stop the machine, step to the ground, stand behind the Caterpillar and peer into the darkness.

Somewhere out there in the high brush on the hillside was a set of eyes, looking directly at me. After awhile the strange feeling would slowly leave. But this time as I climbed back onto the seat the feeling struck me harder than ever.

I usually wouldn't strap on my pistol while running the machines, but lately I felt more comfortable with the sidearm close-by. I slowly backed the D3 up and turned to get behind the pile of dirt Alan had left for me. The lights of the CAT brightened the surrounding area. The feeling was stronger than ever, and my eyes strained through the bright lights. As I turned the machine a movement caught my eye, and for a second I thought something just out of the range of the lights moved. I hurried the machine off the ramp and rolled at full speed toward the image.

As hard as I looked, I couldn't see anything. I drove back up on the ramp next to the sluice and Leo turned the big CAT so the bright lights shined in my eyes. I shrugged my shoulders. He knew why I had left my post. Both of us had been on edge for quite awhile and understood the other's reactions without even talking about them.

While I was gone Leo had pushed a pile of dirt the size of a house to the ramp. Now I'd be behind for hours. The feeling of danger subsided and then was totally forgotten as I pushed overburden into the sluice box like a madman.

The cold wind blew through the canyon continuously, which meant we had to wear gloves, earplugs and rain gear. Back up, push forward, repeated hour after hour. The drone of the big engines induced a semiconscious state of mind. Eight hours slipped by with no remembrance of time. It was an awful job, but one everyone did without complaint.

It had been a rainy, cold night, but Leo figured we'd pushed somewhere around 2000 yards of dirt and gravel through the box. Both of us were in need of a gallon of Tony's coffee, then Delores's ham and eggs would set everything right again. The thought of that breakfast kept us going for the last two hours of our shift.

When we entered the cookshack Tony handed me a message, the miner that needed equipment hauled to his camp wasn't going to make it. Another miner would take his place instead. The message gave me some relief because the new passenger's airstrip had a good approach and a nice level surface, making my job a lot less stressful. The thought of landing at the other miner's bad airstrip had plagued me all night.

As I drove the old swamp buggy up to our airstrip the lack of sleep hit me like a rock. Maybe if I hurried I could get some shuteye before my passengers showed up.

As I taxied to a stop at Brandt's, Eldon walked up to the plane and said, "Your passengers are going to be a couple of hours late."

It felt great to have a hot shower, especially one that could be adjusted for comfort. Having a couple of hours to spare, I needed to find a peaceful place to get some sleep. I drove Alan's pickup up to Shorty's old lodge; the same one we had used to build the sluice box in. The area in front of the lodge was cleared of any trees or brush. I stopped the pickup in the middle of this open area. The warm sunshine filtered through the clouds, prompting me to lie down in the back of the pickup. With the heat of the sun and warm rain gear I was asleep in seconds, comatose to the world.

A loud sound startled me awake. For a second I couldn't get my bearings or comprehend what made the noise. Whatever was making it was real close and getting louder. I jumped to my feet, still half asleep, and turned toward the sound.

The shiny reflection off the propeller of the plane coming straight at me gave me my answer. It grew bigger as the pilot bore down on his victim.

At first I stood my ground stubbornly, but survival took over as I dove out of the pickup and hit the ground with a thud. I gasped for air and rolled over to see Blacky's laughing face gawking out the side window.

For a few seconds I was madder than hell, but then I thought about the buzz job I'd given him a day earlier. As I drove back to Brandt's I had to laugh, he sure got even. I was still smiling when I lay down in the open doors of the plane. Just maybe I could still get a little shuteye.

The sound of voices brought me out of my stupor. When I opened my eyes I found myself encompassed by Japanese people.

The second I stepped out of the plane I had thoughts of Gulliver's Travels and the Land of the Lilliputians. I felt like a giant. The tour guide said they were with a bus-tour group and had stopped at Brandt's Texaco for a backcountry lunch. They couldn't pass up the opportunity of seeing a real live Alaskan bush pilot and his plane, even one with a Montana cowboy hat.

I smiled as the tourists stared at me with my cowboy hat, boots and two-week old beard. I'm sure I was giving them a new image of a bush pilot. Each tourist had two cameras hung around his neck, with the shutters clicking away like crazy.

Their tour guide interpreted all the questions they had for me. Then came picture taking, each one wanting to get his own picture. The process went on for about a half hour, and was kind of fun for a while, but with my lack of sleep it was hard to remain friendly. They reminded me of little hummingbirds, never standing still or stopping talking. I kind of enjoyed all the attention but was glad to see my passengers show up, which meant I could be on my way.

They all wanted a picture of the plane as it was taking off, so I motioned them back, telling their tour guide to make sure they didn't come on the airstrip. "There would be no way I could avoid hitting one of them once I came over the hill, so please keep them all back."

My passengers got in; I started the engine and taxied away from the crowd. All cameras were up and aimed at the plane.

For a moment I felt like Lindbergh taking off for his fateful oceanic flight.

We slowly taxied up the hill and then eased over the hump in the middle of the airstrip. From this point on I wouldn't be able to see the crowd of tourists until I rolled back over the hill on takeoff. My instructions were clear about where they could stand and not stand, so I wasn't worried about them.

The north end of the strip was always muddy. As we taxied the wheels started throwing mud against the bottom of the wings. Not wanting to get the 206 stuck, I jammed on left rudder and brake, forcing the plane to turn around, and immediately added full power for takeoff. The plane wallowed in the quagmire as speed slowly built. I was now committed to follow through with my takeoff; aborting it would mean sliding off the end of the runway and into the lake.

As I plowed through the mud and over the hill I couldn't believe my eyes! Standing right on the side of the strip was a little Japanese guy, camera up and taking pictures. The remaining airstrip was short and not much wider than the wheels of the airplane. Normally I would use this entire runway to gain enough air speed for lifting off the ground, but with the man standing on the airstrip, I wouldn't be able to do that. If he didn't move I would have to plow right over him and still lift off at the water's edge.

My little picture-taking menace was standing at least a hundred feet from the lake. My immediate thought was, tourist or not, I had to complete the takeoff or wreck the plane.

I was getting closer and closer to this guy and he wasn't showing any sign of moving. I'm sure that looking through the lens of his camera gave the appearance of a lot of distance between him and the plane.

Glancing at my airspeed confirmed what I already knew, too slow to fly.

The muddy condition and heavy load was forcing me to take the rotation and liftoff all the way to the water. Still no sign of the guy moving and we were boring down on him like a freight train. The plane was starting to bounce slightly, indicating that the wings were starting to produce lift. At 50 feet from the victim, I applied full flaps and rolled in full right aileron. The plane reacted sluggishly to the mistreatment.

The added lift from fully deflected ailerons forced the left wing to rise, with the right wheel still firmly on the ground. The stall horn bellowed immediately, warning me of my dangerous situation.

I would only have one chance of not hitting him, but the plane wasn't built to take the abuse I was forcing on it. If we missed the guy, the chance of getting into the air before plowing into the water was poor.

Brandt's Texaco airstrip, the highway looks better.

Ready for takeoff at Brandt's.

At the last possible second the Japanese man lowered his camera, realizing he was face to face with my left wing strut and only a few feet from the spinning propeller. The last thing I saw was the look of terror on his face, with eyes wide as silver dollars. Out of the corner of my eye I saw him get slammed to the ground by the force of the impact.

I was at the lakeshore in an instant. Reacting, instead of thinking, I lowered the left wing and applied full backpressure on the control yoke. "Fly, you son of a bitch, fly!"

The last thing that was needed was full flaps with a heavy load for takeoff. The plane's fully deflected flaps were only designed for landings, not takeoffs. Grudgingly, the plane lifted its heavy frame into the air, but not before it sprayed a little water off the tires from the lake.

The plane staggered inches above the water, and then slowly climbed a couple of feet. I leveled the climb, wanting to stay in ground effect, or in this case, water effect until I had gained enough speed to climb safely. Gingerly I retracted the flaps, not wanting to settle back into the water. Half of the small lake was crossed before I managed to get 20 feet of elevation.

I was sure I had hit the man, although I hadn't felt the impact and couldn't see any sign of damage to the plane. I knew we had to go back to see what had happened. Leveling my altitude at 100 feet, we made a slow turn to the left to come back over the accident sight. I envisioned this man's friends and family standing all around him with heads bowed in grief. With my heart pounding in my throat, I wiped the sweat off my face and stared at the scene.

From a mile out we could see the crowd standing in a small circle. As I flew overhead I had to force myself to look down. Then, to my surprise, right in the middle of the crowd was this little guy waving his hands harder than anyone else. His smile extended from ear to ear!

I couldn't believe what I was seeing, he was alive and not hurt. I must have missed him by inches. The force of the plane going by was probably enough to drive him to the ground, a lucky break for both of us. I am sure that he had stories for everyone back in Japan for years to come.

Turning the plane toward my passenger's airstrip, I imagined the Japanese man sitting on his back porch, talking to his grandchildren about his Alaskan vacation and the adventure he had with a bush pilot who almost ran over him with his airplane.

I dropped my passengers off at their camp and headed for home. Tony gave me a tall cup of coffee and listened as I relayed my story. My hands shook, spilling my coffee. I had done everything right and still just about killed someone.

As we talked, Alan walked into the cookshack and said, "Dave, I need you to fly to Glennallen and inform the troopers that someone is stealing gold and supplies from us." He continued, "When I went down to the sluice this morning, there were footprints all around it. They didn't match anyone's shoes here."

That explained a lot. Even though we suspected that someone was wandering around at night, this was the proof we needed.

VIII
GLACIER FOG

That night the clouds rolled in and the rain beat down. We'd never seen sheets of rain like this in Montana. Day after day the rain pummeled the little camp. Water levels rose, forcing an emergency pulling of the big sluice box, bringing the operation to a complete stop. With the creek bed overflowing, all we could do was sit in the cookshack and hope that the downpour would end soon.

Tempers flared as the days of inactivity brought dissension to the camp. For the first time Alan had time to analyze the first couple months' mining. Leo was adamant that Melvin was stealing gold, and now the whole family was probably in on the act. From the very beginning he hadn't trusted him, and although I tried to give Melvin the benefit of the doubt, I came to the same conclusion. Having had time to hear all the evidence, Alan finally started to think about what Leo was saying.

Gold nuggets showing up in washing machines after they were emptied of clothes, and gold missing from sealed jars was proof enough. Alan went on to say, "You're probably right, but we still need his mining experience. The season is only half over. From now on we are going to high-grade the creek and only mine the hot spots. We need Melvin to show us these spots, but don't leave any gold with him, and one of us needs to be around him all the time."

The solid cloud layer parted and let the sun shine through. In an hour's time the creek level started lowering. The floodwater had turned the familiar creek into a new landscape. The big tailing piles we had left behind had washed down the creek. The material that we had pushed through the sluice earlier would now be pushed back through the box. There was no way of knowing what had been worked or not.

The supplies were getting dangerously low. I hadn't been able to fly for a week, so it was time to depart for Glennallen and then to Anchorage. Like a water-soaked duck, the plane had sat out the storm. As I added full power, the plane slushed through the mud and water, gaining speed slowly. The suction of the wet earth finally let go and we bound into the air.

The aircraft felt like it had a mind of its own, and the engine felt stronger than ever. The big plane was finally back in its element. Even though fog and clouds hung low, forcing me to fly a zigzag route to Glennallen, it felt great to be back in the air.

The trooper said that there was nothing he could do about our intruder. We were to keep our eyes open and let him know if we caught anyone stealing gold. I was surprised that he wasn't a little more sympathetic to our problem.

As I walked into the flight service station to check on the weather conditions down in the Matanuska Valley, I noticed five airplanes sitting side by side on the ramp. The pilots stared at me as I asked the weather briefer for the information.

As I thought, a weather system had pushed in from the Pacific Ocean. The whole area around the Anchorage Basin was packed with low clouds and fog. Almost all the small planes were grounded until the weather improved.

As I filed a flight plan to Anchorage the pilots gathered around. The one nearest me spoke up and said, "You can't get to Anchorage. I tried to fly through an hour ago. There is no way you can possibly make it."

What he didn't know was that I had just spent two months flying this route through the same conditions. Through trial and error I had managed to find a route that usually let me slip under the fog and on to Anchorage.

As I walked to the plane the pilots explained that they had all flown up from the outside, meaning the lower 48, and had been stuck at Glennallen for the last four days. They couldn't wait much longer for the weather to clear. Every day these men had been trying to fly to Anchorage, only to be stopped by the clouds and fog. Then they'd fly back to the Glennallen Airport and wait out another day.

By the time I arrived they were frustrated and discouraged, yet still hoping for a miracle. I guess I was the miracle they were looking for.

"Can we follow you to town?" the pilots asked.

I replied, "Listen Guys, I know you want to get to Anchorage, but the route that I use is dangerous. I have been using it daily and know every rock and turn like the back of my hand. Believe me when I say you do not want to follow me."

All five pilots talked at once. "If we don't like it, we'll turn around."

I didn't like the idea at all, too many things could go wrong. But after a great deal of talking, I agreed to help them out.

As we studied a map I pointed out the unfamiliar terrain. "Right here is a narrow canyon. To stay out of the fog you have to be below the rim of the canyon walls. The creek and walls get narrower as you go downstream. There are six steep turns; slow your planes down to about 60 knots or you won't be able to make the corners."

One of the pilots looked at me and said, "You're kidding, right? What happens if the canyon is filled with fog?" They all stared at me waiting for an answer.

"Up till now, the fog hasn't been any lower than the rim of the canyon."

A couple of the pilots swallowed as they thought about my answer.

I continued, "The creek will get real narrow, when it does you're about to cross over the Glenn Highway. Just remember this, once you have entered the canyon, you can't turn around. In a couple of spots the walls will only be a hundred feet wide.

"After you cross the highway, lower your elevation with the terrain. Right in front of you will be a tall rock called the Lion's Head that will protrude up into the fog. Go around the rock to the left and then make a sharp turn to the right. The Matanuska Glacier will be right in front of you. Fly slowly by the glacier and head downstream until you see the mouth of Chickaloon Gorge."

I took a deep breath and looked at my new flight squadron. They all stared with wide eyes and slacked jaws. "The gorge has vertical walls and is real narrow. You must enter it at the top; don't try to fly up and out of the gorge. The top of it will be covered in fog. The narrow, deep gorge will make you feel like you're flying in a coffin. Once you fly out of the gorge it is about fifteen miles to the Palmer Airport, which sits right beside the river, so you can't miss it. Any questions?"

I answered four or five questions. As I turned to walk to my plane I remembered a couple more things that needed to be said, "Guys, the reason you fly real low in the Chickaloon Gorge is because there's a cable car that crosses from one side to the other. It's near the top, you do not want to be anywhere near the top of the walls. In bad weather I never see the cable. The other thing is, once you make a decision to drop down into the bottom of Caribou Creek you are committed to this route. Trying to turn around at any time could be fatal."

As I completed my engine check, I taxied in front of all five planes and saw the fear and hesitation on each pilot's face. I could imagine what they were thinking. *We must be fools to follow this Pied Piper down the path of no return.*

"I still could put a stop to this," I thought to myself, pushing the mike key and asking one more time, "I don't think you should follow me. This isn't a good idea."

Lower Caribou Creek.

All five of them talked back immediately. "If we're not comfortable, we'll turn back."

The Cessna was faster than all the other planes so I circled around the airport. When all were in the air I turned down the highway heading for Sheep Mountain. I turned to see the other planes flying single file, each one about a quarter mile behind the other and trying their best to keep track of the guy ahead of him. I was glad I was in front, not having the worry of keeping track or running into anyone. As we flew by the north side of Sheep Mountain I turned and started toward Caribou Creek.

The low fog and clouds came into view. As I had experienced many times, it was right where it should be. I talked fast as I headed for the narrow canyon.

"You can see where the creek flows under the fog. We need to slow down and level out about a hundred feet above the bottom of the canyon. As you can see, the fog isn't lower than the rim. You guys circle out here in the clear air and let me make sure that the canyon is open all the way to the highway."

One of the pilots replied, "You're really going to fly under that fog? It looks like it's all the way to the ground."

I answered, "From up high it looks that way. When I cross the Glenn Highway I'll give you guys a call and let you know what the conditions are."

I couldn't worry about the other people. I had flown this route quite a few times, but it still demanded total concentration. One wrong move could put the plane into a rock wall.

Leveling off at such low altitude and entering the tunnel-like conditions under the low clouds always panicked me. I could just imagine what these outsiders were thinking. They had just hooked up with a pilot who hadn't shaved for a week and dives out of sight below a fog layer.

I slowed the plane more as I made a sharp left turn to stay over the creek. "Five more corners," I said to myself as I stood the plane on its right wing to make the next turn.

"Are you all right in there?" I heard someone ask.

I didn't have time to reply. The canyon walls were slowly narrowing in. The fog touched the wingtips as I made vertical turn after turn. I took a big breath as the 100-foot wide creek straightened.

I had made it through all the steep turns and now the highway was a quarter of a mile away. At least the area on the other side of the highway flattened enough to make it possible to maneuver the plane a little bit.

I keyed the mike and said, "I'm just crossing the highway. The canyon is full of fog; whatever you do, don't try to follow me." I hated to lie to the pilots, but I had flown this route four or five times when there wasn't any fog. I knew each turn of the creek and where it was leading me. Someone could get hurt if they followed me.

The radio came to life with everyone behind me talking a mile a minute and wanting to turn around at once. I'll bet it looked like a Chinese fire drill in the sky. I was thankful to be in the lead, and wished I hadn't agreed to the plan.

The rain beat down, making it hard to see the highway as I crossed over it. The white of the glacier illuminated the steep side of the Lion's Head. I dropped lower as I turned right. The full view of the aqua blue and fluorescent light reflected off the old ice. Wind blowing down the glacier rocked the plane. This wind and cold would create fog, or as the locals called it, glacier fog. Almost every morning it would appear only to dissipate with the heat of the sun.

As I flew past, the glacier fog lowered, forcing me down closer to the ground. I strained to see the opening of the gorge as the gray clouds surrounded the plane. Usually I had Tony to help keep track of the ground. Now I leaned back and forth, looking out the corners of the front window making sure I was still over the river.

Like a shadow in the mist, the opening to the top of the gorge appeared. The river dropped sharply as I lowered the power to descend to the bottom of the steep ravine, leaving the fog high above me. I strained to see the cable that crossed from one side to the other, but with no luck. The sheer walls off the wings were a lot better sight than the gray clouds that had engulfed me moments earlier.

In seconds I flew out of the gorge and into clear air. The cloud base was a thousand feet above. I could see all the way to Anchorage.

After tying the plane down, I called the Glennallen Flight Service back. All the pilots had returned without any problem. One of the guys said, "We all agree that you are completely crazy!"

As I shopped for groceries I thought about what the guy had said. Even though he was teasing me, there probably was some truth to his statement. But I had found the dangerous poor-weather route to Anchorage during clear conditions and had flown around every sharp corner or down in the bottom of the gorge many times before the weather forced me to be there.

The Lion's Head, with the
Matanuska Glacier in the background.

The weather had gotten better so the flight back to the mine was a lot easier. I stared down at the route I'd flown earlier. Questions nagged at me as I thought about all the flying I'd done up to this point. Did I think I was better than I really was? Or was I just being cocky. Was I pushing too hard? Had I just been lucky? I finally concluded that I was only doing what I needed to do to get the job done.

I didn't know that answers to these questions would be forthcoming. The most dangerous and life-threatening flight would soon shake my world.

IX
LUCKY TO BE ALIVE

Leo and I spent another bitter cold night working on the CATS with the north wind sapping the life from our bodies. Our stiff, cold muscles ached as we stood up to restore circulation after hours of sitting. The steady vibration of the machine had numbed my lower body.

Leo or Tim usually operated the D8, both guys being masters on the big machine. It was the workhorse for the whole mine, and if it wasn't working, the mine was shut down. Moving boulders that were ten feet tall, or scraping bedrock and then moving it all to the sluice was demanding both for the machine and operator.

Since the flood, we'd been high-grading the gold, digging on the inside corner of a bend in the creek and only pushing the last foot of soil through the sluice. We scraped about six inches of the hard bedrock before pushing it to the sluice.

Leo loved to keep me buried in material; he always had the ability to outwork three people. I had to run the little CAT at full speed to keep up with him. A bump from his Caterpillar would bring me back to reality after hours of endless backing up and pushing gravel into the sluice. I'd look up to see Leo's toothy smile.

Somewhere around 2:00 a.m. Leo was upstream and in the creek. Something was wrong, for the first time in hours I was out of material to push into the sluice. There was no way Leo could sit still that long. Then I noticed the unique odor of hydraulic fluid permeating the air.

I slowly drove the D3 up to where he was sitting. The big machine was still out in the middle of the creek in three feet of water. Leo was sitting in the CAT, the glow of his cigarette giving away his presence. The CAT wouldn't move; without even talking, we both knew the problem. The maintenance crew had just finished some work on the big machine right before our shift. Whenever maintenance work was done on the CAT, the bottom rock guard, which is a piece of metal an inch thick, was taken off and had to be replaced when the work was finished. It protects the engine, torque converter and transmission from damage.

The lights of the small CAT reflected off the oil-soaked water and told us what we already knew. Leo had backed over a big boulder, which broke the housing of the torque converter. The machine wouldn't move without repair, shutting down the operation again.

We spent the rest of the night pulling the canopy off the CAT and took turns standing in the icy water. The complete top half of the CAT had to be removed and carried to dry ground. Around 12:00 the next night we finally had all the broken pieces of the torque converter removed. Tony and Delores kept us in warm blankets and hot coffee the whole time.

The converter came apart and each piece took four guys to move. It had been raining for a couple of days, causing the airstrip to have four or five inches of mud combined with deep puddles of water. Because of the condition of the runway I decided to make two flights to get all the broken parts to town.

The stars shined brightly as I lifted off at 2:00 a.m. I couldn't sleep anyway and told Alan I'd be back right after daylight.

Climbing at 50 knots and keeping the wings level was necessary to get over the hill. Ghostly forms emerged in the shadowy darkness of the deep canyon as I eased my way down Caribou Creek. My thoughts moved from the darkness behind me to the upcoming Chickaloon Pass. As I approached the pass, rain started hitting the windows, which meant the glacier fog might not be present.

I was right, no fog in the canyon. The anxiety of the lack of visibility and knowledge of the closeness of the unseen mountains eased when car lights on the Glenn Highway defined the hidden road. As I flew by the glacier the white luminous color faded into shadows.

It wasn't common to be asked to do such a flight, but getting the broken pieces to Anchorage quickly was a matter of survival for the mine. This night's flying conditions gave me the same feeling I had the first time I flew in the clouds back home, a squeezing and almost panicked feeling.

After dropping off the first piece, I went to Peggy's Café and had a big breakfast. I'd had enough night flying for a while. The steady shake in my hands told me that it was time to slow down a bit. Daylight finally broke and I headed back up to the mine for the remaining part.

The second load was going to be a lot smaller than the first. The rain battered the plane as I added power. Mud squirted out both sides as the tires rolled through water. The heavy rains turned the uneven airstrip into pockets of shallow lakes. The suction felt like an unknown force that didn't want to release its grip. I straightened in the seat as the end of the runway rushed toward me. With only a few feet left I applied backpressure on the controls. The nose lifted and then the main wheels.

The plane shot skyward like a rocket, but because I had used every inch of runway I was dangerously close to the hillside. I struggled to out-climb the hill and strained my neck looking out the side window, making sure I didn't get any closer. With a cry of relief the plane finally crossed over the lip of the hill.

It took a week to get all the parts put back together. When the unit was repaired and intact, it weighed about 1200 pounds. Measurements indicated the newly repaired piece would barely squeeze through the cargo doors of the plane. The Cessna 206 and I would be pushing past our abilities to get the 1200-pound piece back to the mine.

A loader lifted the rebuilt converter onto the back of my pickup, tilting the small vehicle backward from the weight. I couldn't possibly get the piece into the airplane by myself. A detour down Fourth Street produced six winos willing to help for $10 each.

The first thing to do was block the tail of the plane up. With all seven of us working together we inched the heavy load off the pickup and into the cabin of the plane. Each effort moved the piece a mere quarter-inch.

"All together now, heave!" Finally the piece was right up against the back of my seat.

I returned my helpers to their little heaven, each one wanting to be let off at the liquor store, then went to a hardware store and purchased two rolls of wire. In an hour I had all the wire wrapped securely around the converter and attached to the floor.

Every few minutes I would look toward the mine, wondering if I should really try to get this heavy load in the air. I knew if the equipment moved aft even a fraction of an inch the plane would probably be uncontrollable.

I gingerly removed the blocks out from under the tail of the plane. The tail sagged down a couple of inches and then slowly moved up until all three tires sat firmly on the ground, which up till now meant the plane would carry the load.

Veteran pilots stood back with wide eyes staring at the over-loaded plane. Even their shaking heads didn't bring me to my senses. Everyone had an opinion, but no one offered to help. I was on my own, with the outcome solely my responsibility. As I looked at the over-loaded plane the doubt grew stronger. I wasn't one to be timid and had always had the attitude, "Come hell or high water, full steam ahead." I'd put all my effort into getting the operation going again. But, I'd better go now or I might change my mind.

I started the engine and then promised myself if the airplane didn't handle correctly after takeoff, I would return to Merrill Field immediately.

While taxiing, the nose of the plane bounced into the air for a few seconds and then went back down to the pavement. A lot of power and brakes kept the front wheel on the ground. As the plane rolled down the runway and gained airspeed the sluggish feeling left the controls. I held my breath as gravity was overtaken by lift. Because of the weight being so far back, the nose of the plane shot skyward. I trimmed the nose full forward, which relieved the backpressure slightly. It still took both hands on the control yoke to keep the plane in some degree of level flight.

My arms tired quickly. There wasn't any way that I could keep so much forward pressure on the control yoke all the way to the mine. With a little squirming around I managed to get one knee up against the yoke to help keep it forward.

Thoughts of returning to Merrill Field haunted me, but the importance of getting my load to the mine won the battle being waged in my mind.

I tried small adjustments in power settings. If I pulled the power back at all, the nose would balloon upward. The only way to keep the plane flying was with full power and full forward pressure on the elevators. The plane resembled a roller coaster as I flew, which indicated too heavy of a load and an aft center of gravity. Sweat ran down my face as I neared the mine. I felt like I'd just run ten miles. Alfred Creek finally came into view, now all I needed to do was land.

I wasn't sure how the plane would act down in the bottom of the deep, windy canyon. So I flew over the airstrip at about 200 feet to feel the conditions. As I approached the strip I gently backed off on the power, my second big mistake. The first was taking off. Immediately the nose of the aircraft shot upward, which created more drag. The plane reacted immediately, settling toward the ground.

Instant fear and adrenalin grabbed my soul. Full power made the problem worse. Because of the climb attitude of the plane, the thrust-producing propeller wanted to pull the nose higher. For an instant I thought, "At least the power stopped the plane from descending." But in a second I realized that I wouldn't be able to get the plane flying at a normal attitude. I was in big trouble.

At the north end of our airstrip the creek ran through a steep-sided small brush-filled canyon. I had no choice, that narrow slit was my only chance. The flight path and the altitude of the plane remained level, but the ground was getting closer as I flew upstream. The stall horn screamed louder as the speed lowered, bringing the plane closer to a stall.

I glanced at the sheer granite walls closing in. Although the thought of dying always remained hidden, now I had to face the inevitable. This could be the end.

Was it stupidity that brought me to this moment, or stubbornness? Adrenalin gushed through my veins. Breathing was labored and my mind screamed, "Fly the plane!" Maintaining control was my only chance. At least then I could pick the best spot to crash. Sweat burned my eyes as I blinked to clear my vision.

The turbulence that I'd hit while flying to the mine had shifted the heavy load back, making the plane unflyable at this slow speed.

Like horses pounding around a track, thoughts darted through my mind searching for a way to survive. A metal-bending crash was inevitable with certain death in the boulder-filled ravine below. The heavy load behind me would be coming my direction on impact, destroying everything in its path.

The moss-covered cliffs of the canyon walls grabbed at the wings. Time and space seemed to close in. The walls blurred as the closeness of the abrupt cliffs invaded my space. Brush striking the wing tips reminded me of rain on a metal roof.

It felt like a dream, I was a dead man, everything around me switched into slow motion. My time had come; fear was absent. My stubbornness had brought me to this time and place. Now was the time to pay up.

The lack of noise brought me to back to reality, the brush that seconds earlier had been swatting the wingtips had stopped. Somehow, I had miraculously flown through the narrow ravine and out into a more open area. The canyon walls now spread out, creating a bowl-shaped opening in the narrow valley ahead.

Why wasn't I dead? The narrow crevasse I'd just flown through should have smashed the plane. How could it be possible I was still flying?

The calm feeling I felt moments earlier turned into a panicked survival mode. I wasn't dead, and now was the time for action.

The controls were sluggish. Any abrupt movement would induce a stall. As I gingerly adjusted the control yoke I whispered aloud, "Gentle, gentle, Dave, keep her flying. Easy, easy."

Clearing the cliffs of the narrow canyon hadn't solved all of my problems. I had just won this battle, but the war was still being waged. I was still dangerously low and headed upstream, with the ability to turn around slim. I wiped the salty taste of sweat from my face. The blurred ground rushed way too close to the plane and I grimaced as I passed two boulders the size of a house. Only inches separated the plane from the rocks, but I was still in the air.

To survive, I had to fly up and out of the steep canyon or gain enough speed and altitude to turn around. If I remained over the creek, somewhere up ahead my luck would run out. The airplane would impact the steep boulder-filled gorge. I had driven a Caterpillar through this very spot earlier. Rocks as big as cars filled the gorge, making it almost impossible to get machinery through.

There weren't any possible landing areas in the direction I was headed. With that thought in mind, I racked my brain for a solution. Now was the time for action, the canyon ahead was impassable, but I wouldn't give up without a fight. I yelled at myself, "Get this plane turned around!"

I had an empty, feeble feeling deep in my gut, too low to turn and too slow to climb. I prayed for the luck I'd had all summer, *just one more time.* Two hundred feet of flat creek bottom, I had honed my skills; with just two hundred feet of flat ground, I could do it.

With that thought I was starting to scan the steep hillsides, knowing at the last possible second I'd make a sharp turn up the steep tundra hillside. At least that would get me out of the boulder-infested creek and on grassy tundra. Even landing on the hillside would make for a slim chance of survival. Sweat ran into my eyes again, time was running out. The tight grip on the control yoke made my hands ache. I was in deep shit.

The canyons walls seemed to be getting farther away, giving me instant relief. The lack of vertical rock walls just off of the wingtips changed my thoughts from dismay to optimism. The steep mountain slope leveled out just slightly, creating a canyon that seconds earlier was 100 feet wide to a valley a quarter of a mile wide.

The nose of the plane angled up dangerously. I only had seconds to get it down before the plane stalled. But lowering the nose even slightly meant crashing into the ground.

All 300 horses under the engine cowl were performing at maximum power. The only thing I hadn't done was adjust the fuel mixture. If I could get it just right, then maybe the engine would put out a little more power. My shaky hand could barely grasp and turn the mixture control knob.

The engine noise increased slightly, I kept my eyes glued to what was happening outside the plane. The creek bottom seemed to be only a few feet away. I held my breath as I passed over another big boulder.

It was now or never, the canyon was narrowing down again and my one chance would be gone in seconds. With great care I turned the plane toward the steep hillside to my left. I needed all the room possible to get turned around. The slope climbed toward the plane.

Waiting until my nerves and mind couldn't handle the nearness of the left hillside, I started my right turn. The stall horn screamed. Relaxing the backpressure slightly on the control wheel kept the stall away. Any raising of the nose of the plane at all would force the wings to quit flying, resulting in a nose-straight-down collision.

I forced myself not to pull the nose up as I flew over another little hump in the hillside, holding my breath as I cleared it by a few feet. I was so close to the ground I clenched my teeth and face muscles, waiting for the impact. Luckily the plane never touched, it just slid on by. I had been concentrating so hard I was surprised to see the creek pass under the plane, completing half of the turn. The downhill slope of the creek made it possible to drop the nose slightly, gain a little extra airspeed, and steepen my turn.

Seconds passed like minutes; a quick glance at the vertical speed indicator confirmed what I had just felt, a slight climb. Sudden relief ran throughout my whole body, I was actually climbing and gaining speed! I relaxed for the first time since I started this fight for survival. The stall horn finally quit squawking and I started gaining altitude as I headed down the creek and back over the airstrip.

A new form of adrenalin hit me like a mule kick, making my knees shake so much I couldn't keep them on the rudder pedals. My whole body shook uncontrollably. I was actually alive and for the time being I was just going to breathe and live.

Everyone was standing by the airstrip and waiting for the equipment that was right behind me. I wondered if they knew how close to a crash and death I had come.

I jolted my mind back to the present. I still had to land the plane, and the first try almost killed me. I circled in an attempt to regain my composure.

This landing was going to be performed a lot differently. I had tried to make a 200-foot high pass on the first attempt, wanting to feel the wind conditions. When I added full power the weight and position of my load created a nose-high attitude that made it impossible for the plane to climb. I had let the plane get too slow, learning a valuable lesson the hard way.

There wouldn't be any hesitation this time, just straight in and land. I was determined to do this right. I could do this, for the last two months I had been landing on short, harrowing airstrips.

Now was the time to pull all my experience together and do it right. I turned the plane on a three-mile final approach to the runway. My target airspeed was 90 knots, way too fast for this short airstrip, but with this load I needed that speed to stay in the air.

I cleared the hill with 50 feet of elevation to spare, applied full flaps and shoved the nose over toward the end of the runway. I had to touch down close to the very end of the runway or I wouldn't make it. No room for error.

The combination of speed and full flaps was making my approach too high. Pulling the power off would only get me into the same situation I had just barely survived minutes earlier. I jammed the right rudder all the way to the floor, which created a settling effect on the plane, but also lined the nose of the plane with the creek instead of the runway.

The end of the runway came shooting at me like an arrow; my rate of descent was way too high. With 100 feet to go I jammed on full power, which accelerated the plane forward and swung the nose of the plane back toward the airstrip.

An eight-foot high bush, which was about 70 feet from the end of the strip, hit the tail as I started my flair to arrest my speed. Immediately the nose came up to an alarming angle, but this time I was prepared. The runway was right in front of me and I was taking the plane all the way to the ground.

I slammed onto the runway with full power. Reducing power and retracting the flaps put all three wheels on solid ground. Heavy braking and full backpressure on the control yoke slowed the plane. Mud slammed into the bottom of the wings and the airplane grudgingly gave up its momentum and slid to a stop. The tail of the plane slowly lowered to the ground. I had stopped about 50 feet from the end of the runway.

My heart pounded in my chest, breathing was labored. What a relief to be on the ground and alive! The shake in my hands came back with a vengeance. Grabbing the mixture control was next to impossible. I had no strength left; the last 30 minutes had drained me. With concentration I reached over and shut the engine down. Because of the weight in the back of the plane, the tail crashed to the ground. The nose pointed toward the sky, a weird angle for this type airplane.

Alan drove up and helped me out of the plane. As I tried to stand my knees buckled; I would have hit the ground if he hadn't caught me. He then helped me over to the pickup, where I steadied myself.

I had hit so hard the front cowling on the plane had a new six-inch crack.

Alan said, "We thought you crashed when you went through that narrow canyon." They had heard the brush hitting the wings and from their angle it looked like I had gone down.

I didn't have the composure to answer him. They were already headed up to the crash sight when I flew back over them on the way back down to the strip, much to their surprise.

With great effort the equipment was removed from the plane, and it was good to see the plane sitting on three wheels again. I tried to help but my legs were still too weak, so I just watched.

That evening Alan and I sat in the cookshack, nursing a bottle of whiskey. We talked about the gold mine, the past and future events. It was great to be alive. He didn't want me to work the machines anymore. He needed the plane flying and didn't need a dead cousin. It was music to my ears, although I felt I was letting the rest of the guys down. So we agreed that I would fill in if needed, but my new title was Pilot only. Alan suggested that I take a couple of days off from flying, and I couldn't have agreed more. I lay in bed thinking about the day, and all the events that brought me to this time and place.

I wondered about all the pilots who had come before me, flown these rugged mountains and had not survived a day just like today. Why had I? I couldn't answer that question. I knew more than luck had saved me.

As tired as I felt, sleep would not come, so I starting thinking about the circumstances that brought me to this little mining camp. I thought back to the day I saw the plane at Merrill Field. My heart almost pounded out of my chest. It was a remarkable machine that had brought me through one more time. I had learned a lot since then and developed a special bond with that flying machine. I'd keep that to myself; people might think I was a little crazy.

Maybe that's it, crazy. Had I had lost touch with reality? Any person in their right mind wouldn't have left with that heavy load. Did I have a death wish? Was I too proud to say no? One thing for sure, I was alive.

Nothing would be worth going back to Montana in a body bag. Flying in these rugged mountains and harsh conditions was like going to war against an enemy that was around every corner, trying to claim another victim.

It took two days to put the torque converter back into the D8 and get the mine back in operation. Everyone in camp got sick from standing in the cold water. We had lost a week of valuable time. The summer was slipping by and if more gold wasn't found, the chances of returning were slim.

A few days later I had to go to town for more groceries and do the weekly washing. Delores wanted to go and do the shopping while I ran parts. I had run the CAT half the night and was tired, but was thankful I hadn't been up all night. I was glad to have her along to help keep me awake. The sky was slightly cloudy with a broken overcast. It was going to feel good to be off the bumpy Caterpillar and in the warm airplane.

As I added power for takeoff it felt like something was wrong.

The plane just wasn't performing like usual. All the gauges looked normal, so I thought I was being paranoid. The plane slowly climbed over the hill. Delores looked at me and asked, "Did we hit that brush with the tail of the plane as we crossed over the top of the hill?"

I replied, "We were close, but not that close."

We continued down Caribou Creek. It felt great to be flying again. I could actually relax and enjoy the country.

As we passed Sheep Mountain, Delores spotted young Dall sheep running and playing with each other. They were quite a sight to see. Unlike us, they had no worries in the world.

We headed for Chickaloon Pass. The weather toward Anchorage looked bad. Dark rainy clouds filled the horizon and descended all the way to the ground. Halfway between Palmer and the Matanuska Glacier is a remote radio station called Sawmill. This station made it possible to call the Flight Service Station in Anchorage and get the current weather. The report was about what I thought, heavy rains between Anchorage and Palmer. But there were some cloud openings south of town, with blue sky. They said the Matanuska Valley was completely covered with clouds and reported the tops of the clouds at about the mountaintops.

Instead of fighting the weather around Palmer I decided to climb through an opening in the clouds and fly in clear blue sky above the clouds to Anchorage. Flying above a solid overcast is a risk; any mechanical problem meant flying down through the clouds without being able to see outside the plane, then trying to make an emergency landing. Not an adventure any pilot would like.

Delores and I were enjoying the warmth of the sun, which was a rare occasion at the mine. The sight of the top of the white fluffy clouds and Mount McKinley protruding skyward like a giant ice cream cone made both of us smile.

The sun got the best of my passenger. She was sleeping soundly. I was also feeling the effects, and opened the side vent, hoping the cool air would keep me awake. I had just passed Palmer VOR, which meant I had flown past the town of Palmer. I tuned in the Anchorage VOR to get a straight route to town. The sky was still completely overcast. The earlier weather report indicated I should find a few breaks in the cloud cover real soon.

Delores and I enjoyed the sun and the sights of the
mountain tops, until the engine of the plane
started running rough.

Then I felt the plane shudder, just for a split second. My first
thought was we had hit a little turbulence, not surprising considering
the cloud cover and winds. All of the engine instruments were
functioning normally. I forgot about it, thinking the complete cloud
cover was making me a little paranoid.

The approach controller talked without hesitation, busy keeping
the flow of traffic smooth into the International Airport. Even
though my destination was Merrill Field, I still needed permission
from the controller to enter the airspace, which encompassed all the
airports around Anchorage. I was getting close to my destination
and still hadn't seen any openings in the clouds, so I scanned the top
of the clouds looking for the opening that would get us down to the
airport.

Then I felt the shudder again. There was no mistaking a
problem this time as the shaking reappeared. Suddenly the engine
compartment exploded, with an instant loss of power. The propeller
still turned, but the manifold pressure dropped to eighteen inches.

The plane descended toward the clouds; applying full power didn't help. We were going down.

In as calm a voice as I could muster I called Approach Control and declared an emergency, talking on top of other pilots.

The answer was immediate, "Cessna 101, repeat the problem."

I took a deep breath and said, "This is Cessna 101, I'm on top of the overcast with only partial power. I'm going down, I repeat, I'm going down!"

The reply was immediate, "Squawk 3465 and ident."

"Squawking 3465 and ident," I said back.

Delores looked at me and said, "Don't you kill me!"

The controller needed to identify me from all the other planes in the area. I dialed in the numbers on the transponder which would send a signal to the controller's radar scope with the numbers I had dialed in. "Fly heading 185 for Merrill Field. Five miles distance."

I turned to the heading as I repeated his words. The engine was still producing power, though not enough. Instant claustrophobia hit as we sunk into the top of the murky clouds. The radio was silent, as was Delores. I was glued to the instruments. "Fly 185, airspeed 90 knots," kept repeating in my mind.

"One zero one, how's it going?" asked the controller. The clouds' color lightened as we dropped into clear air. Instant comfort hit home as I told the controller we were in the clear and directly over Merrill Field. I had the field made! He gave me a frequency for Merrill Tower, I replied with a big thank you. The Merrill controller had moved everyone out of the way and gave me the runway of my choice.

Not wanting to do any more damage, I shut the engine down. A small left turn lined me up on Runway 26. Then we floated down to a soft landing and turned off onto the south taxiway.

Delores gave me a big smile and said, "I knew you could do it," as emergency vehicles pulled up. Bob's Maintenance towed the plane to their hangar. After pulling the cowling off the engine compartment it was easy to see the problem. The top of the back left cylinder had blown off. A heat shield had broken on the intake manifold, wearing a hole in the tube. This hole produced more air to that cylinder, which provided too lean of a gas-to-air mixture, burning up the cylinder. The hard landing the previous day must have broken the shield.

The maintenance shop had mechanics on duty and parts available to fix the broken cylinder. The mechanics worked all night after we explained the urgent need for the plane. The next morning we filled the plane up with all of our groceries and headed back to the mine, just like it was another day at the office. We had been real lucky. If the cylinder had blown anywhere but where it had, we would have had a forced landing in the wilderness.

As we flew back toward the mine I thought about the last few days' near disasters. Every day was producing overwhelming challenges. My love for Alaska was strong, but it seemed that this great land had no love for me. Mining gold and flying a plane under these harsh conditions was turning into a concerted effort for survival.

Alan wasn't at all surprised hearing about the exciting ride that Delores and I had taken the day before. His luck had been bad for a long time, why change now? Nothing had gone right for the mining operation since we had arrived, Melvin was stealing gold, and the D8 was a piece of junk.

The air around the mine could be cut with a knife. Tension was high and good attitudes in short supply. Alan was under a lot of pressure to come up with a solution. We had been hearing a rumor that Shorty had more miners coming into the creek. They were going to mine a portion of the creek that was directly below us. It was the spot we had been planning to move to next, an area that had never been mined before. Exploring in that area had produced a lot of gold, so Alan hoped that area would save the operation. Now it might go to someone else.

Leo was upset with Alan for not getting rid of Melvin. On the next trip to Anchorage Leo went along and didn't return. He was finished with the gold mine. Both he and Alan had been at odds all summer, so it was probably best. Leo ran the big D8 like a surgeon, and would be missed.

Alan was so mad he could hardly talk. That night we had a family meeting about Shorty. All agreed that he wouldn't receive any more gold and was not welcome at the mine. It was time to put an end to all agreements with Shorty. Alan would go to Anchorage and face him to let him know how it would be. We would stay where we were for the rest of the season.

Leo had told Alan about some mining claims for lease north of Fairbanks. The gold up there was supposed to be easier to find. So Alan wanted Leo and me to fly to Central to see if we could acquire the claims for next season. Central is a one-building mining town situated on the Steese Highway, just south of the Arctic Circle.

Although no one said so, we all knew that our present mine wouldn't produce enough gold to survive another year. Early the next morning I headed for town. I told Alan that the trip would take about four days and that I would be back as soon as possible. The mine had supplies for five days, so the pressure to return quickly was present, as usual.

X
TO THE ARCTIC CIRCLE

Leo had mined gold north of Fairbanks on the Steese Highway a few years earlier, but that was all he would say about it. That seemed a little strange, as normally he was real talkative. The area was northeast of Fairbanks, not far from Fort Yukon, a small village situated on the banks of the Yukon River.

Leo knew some miners that lived near the town of Central. This potential hot spot was not too far from the Arctic Circle, land of permafrost and long winters. The mining season up there was shorter, but gold more plentiful.

I told Leo, "I've heard a different version of the same story."

He just smiled.

It had been a learning experience to land at Merrill Field daily. At first tension would build as I flew along the Chugach Mountains and closed in on Anchorage. If the pattern at the airport were stacked with planes, the controller would make me stay out of their airspace until planes had landed or left the area. I didn't have the patience to be circling and wasting time, and at first I thought the tower wouldn't give me a clearance just to slow me down.

When I did receive a clearance I usually would have to fly behind a slow plane that seemed to be crawling through the air. The big 206 wallowed in slow flight staying behind the slow traffic. In truth, they were flying at normal speed and then I had my speed, along with zero patience. The air traffic was always heavy with ten or so planes in the pattern and I realized the controllers had a high-pressure job trying to keep all the planes separated and flowing.

But something had to be done about the delays. I decided to visit the people in the tower. Up until now, all I knew of them were their demanding voices in my earphones.

To my surprise, they turned out to be nice people and told me what I needed to do to speed up my landings. They said I should plan my flight to Anchorage so that I would pass by Palmer, then fly close to the mountains east of Anchorage. After Palmer I would pass

Birchwood Airport and Elmendorf Air Force Base, then the next stop was Merrill Field. A couple of miles past the Air Force Base, I needed to make a shallow turn to the right which lined me up with Runway 26 at Merrill, although I was still about ten miles from the airport.

If I'd use this approach the Control Tower would usually give me a straight-in clearance. That meant, as I got closer to the airport I could adjust my speed to fit in-between any planes that were in the pattern. I was thankful for the advice and used the new knowledge for the rest of the summer.

I got a room at the Timbers Motel, located right next to Merrill Field. Whenever I stayed there I walked around the airport and looked over the field of airplanes. I was always amazed at the number of airplanes tied down on the airfield.

The next morning I met with Leo at the airfield and loaded his gear into the airplane. The one thing I wouldn't let Leo do was smoke in the airplane, but he was as sneaky as a cat. I'd learned this firsthand. As we loaded the plane he placed a little sack behind his seat. It was his carton of cigarettes plus a little bit of marijuana, I guessed. In those days, marijuana was legal in Alaska. When he wasn't looking I threw it back into the pickup.

The Ground Controller had me taxi to Runway 16 and gave me the Chester Creek departure. After getting airborne, I flew straight ahead until I came to Chester Creek and then followed it out to where it enters the ocean. All this was done at 500 feet or less, which meant I could look right into some of the higher office buildings as we passed by.

After getting to the bay I stayed below 800 feet until I reached McKenzie Point, which was about ten miles across the inlet from Anchorage. I never liked that departure because of all the cold water below. The problem with the engine a few days earlier added to the spookiness of this departure. Chances for rescue were slim-to-none because of the tides and fast currents in the area.

We were maybe an hour out of Anchorage when Leo started digging around the plane looking for his little sack of goodies. He knew I didn't want him to smoke in the plane but he would always try anyway. It wasn't long before he realized his sack wasn't where he'd put it. I just stared straight ahead, innocent as the new-fallen snow. Panic set in as he crawled into the backseat and dug around like a madman.

He reminded me of a badger digging a new hole; finally realizing his stash was gone. He knew that I had removed his survival kit and was so mad he just sat way in the backseat, staring out the window. The silence was a lot better than smoke! He was getting more nervous and broke the silence with a pleading question about the little brown sack. Of course I had no idea what he was talking about. He was even starting to shake a little from not having his cigarettes.

We headed north looking for the Parks Highway, and intersected the highway at the little town of Willow. Mount McKinley stuck up like an out-of-place giant off in the distance. It was amazing how huge it looked, even 80 miles away.

The town of Talkeetna passed under the right wing. This little town was famous for two things: Don Sheldon, a famous glacier pilot, ran his business out of the town airstrip. He spent his entire life flying mountain climbers up to the Ruth Glacier and back out again. The other thing was a tavern called the Bucket of Blood Bar. It was a well-known place that people from all over the country came to see.

We continued up the highway toward Windy Pass. With a name like that I always wondered when the big wind was going to hit. Mount McKinley or Denali, as the Natives call it, was on my left. Flying right next to the mountain made me feel very, very insignificant.

I turned the corner and entered the pass, which was plenty wide to turn around in, if, need be. We hit a few bumps, but all in all the winds of Windy Pass were tame compared to Caribou Creek.

As we continued on, the little town of Clear came on the horizon. My sectional chart told me to turn all the radios off because of the high power output from radar domes in the area. I promptly followed orders and flew right by all the towers with no problems, but wondered if there was any effect on the human body from so much energy output.

Twenty miles later we left the mountains and started across the flat land that is south of Fairbanks. I could see a big cloud that was hanging over the ground. It was about where Fairbanks should be, as we got closer the cloud got bigger and bigger. I called Fairbanks Approach to get some clarification on what I was looking at. They said there had been a huge tundra fire just south of town and that the smoke had been hanging over the area for a few days. Visibility was about two miles and the field was operating under IFR, Instrument Flight Rules.

I slowed the plane as we entered the smoke. The forward visibility went to zero, although I could look straight down and still see the ground. I divided my attention between the instruments and the ground. The smell of the thick smoke stung our noses as it entered through the air vents of the plane. I immediately asked for a special VFR (Visual Flight Rule) clearance, which was allowed if the pilot had one mile of visibility, and stayed clear of the clouds. I didn't have clouds, but I had smoke. The controller told me to make a 720 turn, which was two complete turns in either direction. Other traffic in the area was closer to the airport and needed to land.

He said that he would get back to me shortly. When he told me to make the turns I was already in the smoke and the visibility was poor. I was basically on instruments at 500 feet elevation and could still see some swampy ground straight below, but had zero visibility straightforward.

As we circled, the engine coughed a couple of times and then quit. I straightened in the seat, trying to figure out what had happened. My hands shot at the boost pump switch and then switched the gas lever to the other fuel tank. For a few anxious seconds the engine sputtered and then came back to life. Leo said, "You scared the hell out of me!"

I replied, "It didn't do my nerves any good either." I had been concentrating so hard on keeping the airplane flying straight and level that I forgot to switch tanks.

As we completed the last turn the controller called. He said that Fairbanks International Airport was too busy for me to land, but he could get me to Metro Field, which was a small strip three miles to the east of the big airport. I needed fuel and going to Metro suited me just fine.

It was time to land; I'd had enough of the smoky conditions.

The controller gave me a heading, said Metro was six miles away from my current position, and wanted me to let him know when I had the field in sight.

Silence broke the air as the controller said, "Cessna 101, Metro two miles and twelve o'clock."

I repeated his message and told him I didn't have the field in sight. Forward visibility was still zero, but we had to land, fuel was running low. Both of us strained to see the little grass runway.

The controller's voice, now sounding more anxious, said, "Metro one-quarter mile and straight ahead."

He wanted to know my intention if I missed Metro. Missing hadn't entered my mind. Without thought I pushed the nose of the plane over slightly, hoping to get a glimpse of the airstrip.

The controller said, "101 you just passed over Metro, what are your intentions?" The only intention I had was to land. I stared straight down, staining to see the airstrip. The smoke cleared slightly and there it was, the west end of it. Instantly I turned left and started descending. It was more than a little scary flying on the gauges and turning to a final approach without seeing the runway.

"Look for the runway!" I yelled to Leo as I concentrated on instruments and strained to keep an eye on the ground directly below.

Full view of the end of the runway finally materialized out of the gloom. The feeling of terra firma was heaven as we rolled out to the parking spot. I had just spent fifteen minutes in near-zero visibility and I needed some mental rest before going any farther.

By the time we landed Leo was so mad at me about his cigarettes that he got out of the plane and headed for town. Didn't even say good-bye. About a half-hour later he returned with a sack of marijuana and a carton of cigarettes, and I was his best buddy again. That was Leo. As long as he had his stuff to smoke, he was fine.

An hour later I was starting to get nervous about going. We still had a couple hundred miles to fly before dark and the smoke was as thick as ever. The weather station said the top of the smoke was about 2500 feet. This meant that we would be in clear air only a couple of minutes after takeoff. I knew those two minutes could be deadly if control of the plane was lost.

As the plane rotated for takeoff I changed my observation from outside to the instruments, holding the wings level as we climbed for the top of the smoke. It was a great feeling and relief to get out of the smoke into the clear blue sky again.

Turning north, I picked up the haul road that led north out of Fairbanks to Prudhoe Bay. The Steese Highway took off toward the northeast about 30 miles farther. At this point the highway became a two-lane gravel road that went all the way to the Yukon River. That was the road we wanted.

Leo had mined gold for a man by the name of Red. Their mining operation had been right next to the Steese Highway, so he wanted to stop and visit him. In a half hour we arrived at Red's mining operation and circled the so-called landing strip, which was on the road and also on an uphill grade.

To make a successful landing I would need to fly over some spruce trees and then land going up the steep hill. It looked dangerously steep from the air, but Leo said that other planes had landed at that exact spot. Not one to be outdone, I decided to make an approach. If the landing didn't look right, I would abort.

Over the trees we went. Looking at the ground rising in the windscreen demanded immediate action; full power slowed down the rate of closure on the road. The plane started to climb, but not as fast as the road. I pulled back on the yoke and jammed on full power, but I was a little late, we still hit pretty hard and taxied up the hill.

The problem was that I had to turn around on the uphill road. The road was steep enough to tip the plane over when turning around, so Leo got out and held onto the wing strut while making the turn. Then we coasted down to the bottom and into a little parking lot.

I was glad to be off of that steep hill and was looking forward to a little rest. Leo had headed over to the mining operation to visit with his old friend, and since I had a few minutes to myself I thought I would take a walk up the hill to get a better look at the slope for the departing takeoff. This was the steepest grade I had ever landed on.

The truth of the story was that only Super Cubs had ever landed on the hill, but I always figured that this 206 could land just about every place a Cub could. Well, almost every place.

As I walked back down the hill to the plane, I could hear Leo and Red arguing heatedly. I quickened my pace to find out what was going on. Leo was standing by the plane and the other guy had a rifle aimed at him. The man said, "You'll leave right now if you know what's good for you!"

He was serious and he didn't have to say it twice. I was in the plane in a flash, with Leo on my heels. The engine started and we rolled out of the parking lot. Just to get up the hill took almost full power. I thought if I turned around quickly, Leo wouldn't need to get out and hold onto the strut.

It was a bad decision; the wing tipped precariously as I swung the plane around. I looked down the hill at that steep grade and felt a rush.

At the bottom of the hill stood Red, shotgun in hand. "Let's get the hell out of here!" I yelled. In mere seconds the plane's airspeed built and we lifted off. It was the steepest slope I'd ever taken off on. The acceleration at that angle with the high horsepower of the 206 was incredible. I was amazed how fast we got into the air.

After being safely airborne and turning to head up the highway, I asked Leo what caused all the ruckus with Red. All I found out was that Leo had spent a couple of nights with this guy's wife and he also owed him money. It happened a couple of years prior to our arrival and Leo had forgotten all about it, but the other guy hadn't!

We continued on in search of the trapper with the mining leases. Leo explained that trappers in the area would stake out gold claims during the summer and then lease them to miners for development. All they had to do was find ground that hadn't been staked before, register the claim and clean all the borderlines of brush and trees. Leasing mining claims was a way for them to make some money during the summer months.

The trapper we were looking for had mined with Leo in the past. He had an old log cabin situated next to the Steese Highway. There was no airstrip, just the road to land on. The cabin was about where Leo remembered, but the brush on the side of the road was high and the road, narrow. I turned onto final approach and slowly lowered the plane to the top of the brush, which seemed to be inches from the wing tips. I needed to think this over, so added power and climbed a couple of hundred feet.

Leo said he knew planes had landed there before and it shouldn't be a problem. Of course that was years ago. I had heard this from Leo before and knew his ability to judge dangerous situations were questionable.

Not having many options I lined up on final approach. As we descended to the road the brush got closer and taller. Being dead center on the road was imperative. With great care I eased the control yoke back. The wheels touched the ground like a feather as the tall brush gently whisked the last foot of the wings.

I wasn't able to miss the chuckholes, so the gentle noise from the brush intensified as we bounced through the holes. Slowing to a crawl, I taxied to the cabin. The approach from the highway to the cabin was uphill, but looked smooth and had room for the wings, so I powered up the grade to a stop.

As the propeller stopped we had our first look at the old cabin. Moss grew on the roof and discarded garbage lay around. It definitely wasn't the Alaskan cabin of my dreams. By the looks of the place, no one had been there for a long time.

When we opened up the door of the plane, a black cloud of mosquitoes came swarming in, thousands of them. They were little, but boy did they sting! We closed the doors quickly and spent the next ten minutes killing them.

I reasoned to Leo that he should be the one to check out the cabin. He couldn't afford to have his pilot weak from lack of blood, after all. Leo made a quick run to the cabin, pounded on the door while slapping at his attackers, and then sprinted back to the plane. It was funny until the door opened and a dark silhouette of blood-hungry bugs headed for me.

Another ten minutes of war brought victory. We left no survivors, but we each received a couple dozen stings.

So here we sat, facing uphill with a gazillion mosquitoes slamming into the windows. I formulated a plan, started the engine and let the plane roll back down the grade. I hoped that we'd have enough coasting speed to get all the way back to the highway and be able to turn enough to line up for takeoff. Everything was working fine until I was almost on the main road. Our timing was off.

An old windowless truck pulled up behind the plane. We hadn't seen any vehicles for the last 50 miles and one had to show up now! I had to slam on the brakes to keep from hitting the truck.

An old long-bearded man stared out the glassless window. He had on an old leather flying helmet with goggles to match and motioned me to get out of the way. He was shouting something, shaking his clenched fist and honking his horn.

Not wanting to endure the wrath of the mosquitoes again, I applied power and slowly taxied back up the grade.

The old fart shook his fist and yelled unheard messages as he sped by.

We hadn't taxied far enough up the hill, so now both of us had to get out of the plane and push it back onto the road. After returning to the security of the plane we killed bugs again for ten minutes. Both of us had welts everywhere.

I carefully added power and lifted off the narrow road. The dust from the old truck grew as we headed straight down the road hunting for the old-timer. The dilapidated army truck was moving at its top speed of 30. It was time to get even!

I bore down on our unsuspecting victim. When directly overhead, I pushed in the propeller control, making the prop go into a flat pitch, which produced a very loud rattling noise. I must have made my point about social graces, because as we circled around we could see the old truck was sideways in the ditch. The old man was leaning out the window shaking his fist at us.

We both laughed for a few minutes. That was payment enough for all the mosquito bites that we had. I admit it was a dirty trick to play on that old man, but oh well.

It didn't take long before the town of Central came into view, a small village with half a dozen buildings. A guy wouldn't want to blink twice or he'd miss it.

The sectional map showed an FAA-approved airstrip about three miles northeast of the town. It also showed a private airstrip in the center of town. We flew to the government-approved strip; there wasn't anything there but the runway. We weren't going to walk back to town, so I headed back to the private airstrip.

The strip was pretty short, maybe a thousand feet. I greased it on and rolled up to the little parking spot and tied down. There were nine planes sitting around, waiting for their owners, all Super Cubs, making the Cessna 206 look like the big bully on the block. All the canvas-backed Cubs sat with their noses pointing to the sky, while the Cessna sat level and a foot taller.

Looking through some birch trees and across the road we could see a big building with a deck in front. People were standing on the deck, gawking at us. Beside this building were little buildings, cabins and old rundown shacks. As we walked across the road, I noticed Café, Bar, Post Office and Laundry signs on the bigger building. Music could be heard through an open door. As we stepped on the deck, one of the guys came forward, staggering as he moved. All had angry glares directed at us and three of the guys had pistols on their sides.

I had learned a long time ago that the best way to handle drunks was to strike first. Both Leo and I weren't in the mood for any bullshit and weren't going to take any.

The drunk said, "That airstrip you just landed on is closed to everyone but the locals." My cowboy hat and boots must have tipped him off that we weren't local.

Stepping directly in front and six inches away from the man, I asked if this was a government regulation or *his* regulation. It caught him off-guard; he thought we would cower to the odds. Before he could answer we pushed past the crowd and into the bar.

The building was one room with a bar and café on one side, a washer and dryer in the back and a Post Office beside it. Sitting down at the bar, we ordered hamburgers. The music kept playing, but movement had stopped. Looking into the mirror in front of us showed every eye in the place fixed on us.

It was Friday evening, and all the miners had come to town to wash down the week's dust. This was the spot to be in, the place was packed. Slowly people turned their attention back to drinking and dancing. It was amazing that half of the people had pistols on and rifles were standing in corners. Evidently no one trusted anybody. I told Leo that this was a place we didn't want to stay in very long. He needed to find out about the trapper and then get the hell out of here.

Leo started asking people about the trapper we were looking for but no one would give him a straight answer. Everyone was closed-mouthed.

Sitting down the bar from me was a gal with a boy about ten years of age beside her. I don't believe I had ever seen a rougher-looking woman in my life. Most of her teeth were missing and she was about 150 pounds overweight. She wore dirty jeans that were held up by orange suspenders and a work shirt that smelled and looked like it hadn't been cleaned in months. The kid sitting next to her started whining about something. A meaty hand knocked the poor boy off the barstool and to the floor where he lay crying.

I had to bite my lip to keep from saying something to the woman. This was one place where we had to be careful about what was said. Everyone was looking for a reason to start a brawl with the two outsiders, and a fight in this place could be disastrous.

Leo walked over to this lady, I use that word with hesitation, and sat down beside her. I couldn't believe my eyes. He bought her a couple of drinks and they started talking. I couldn't hear their conversation but knew Leo was doing his best to get the information we needed. I noticed guys were starting to huddle together and stare at us while they talked. My instincts told me it was time to go, so

I walked over to Leo and told him so. He said he'd be at the plane shortly.

I was glad to get outside and get a breath of fresh air and didn't waste any time getting to the plane. That place was trouble and we didn't want to be on the receiving end of it.

It wasn't long till Leo showed up and said he'd found out the whereabouts of the trapper. The deck at the bar had filled back up with guys, and they were giving us the evil eye. I fired up the 206 and we departed Central without any problem.

Even though it was 8:00 p.m., the sun was still high in the sky. It seemed like it was early afternoon but my body was telling me that it had been a long day. We headed for our last stop of the day, Circle Hot Springs, which was only about ten miles away, so the flight would be short. As we flew Leo told me what he had found out about the missing trapper.

About a week earlier the guy had been shot in the head. He had been dealing cocaine to the locals and must have made a bad deal. The last time he walked into the bar someone blasted him. Everyone knew who had done the killing but no one was talking. Even the feds had been around asking questions. That was the reason no one talked to us; they thought we were undercover agents!

We arrived at Circle Hot Springs and buzzed the lodge as my map said. The buzz let people know we needed a ride from the airstrip. I guess I didn't do a good enough job the first time because no one came out of the building. I made another run. This time I flew a few feet above the ground directly at the lodge, pulling straight up seconds before impact and missing the building by mere feet. This got results. People came running out the front door and headed for the vehicle. The strip was about one mile away and by the time we landed our ride had shown up. We loaded our gear into the van and headed back for the lodge.

The place reminded me of the town on the old TV series, Gun Smoke, with a big lodge at the end of Main Street. There was a hot springs beside the lodge. The room we rented was neat and clean, but we had to share the bathroom at the end of the hall. There was a nice café in the lodge where I cooked us a big steak for supper. Everyone was at the saloon. A sign at the cash register said to cook your meal and pay your bill here. So I paid the till and took my change. Most of the place operated on this honor system.

Leo headed for the bar and I headed for bed. It seemed like I had been awake for a week. We had come a long way since this morning, now I needed some shuteye.

The wind woke me from a sound sleep. A storm had moved into the area overnight. As the hours went by the wind grew in strength. As we drove to the plane I told Leo we would give the weather a look, but doubted we'd get very far. We departed, but the wind and low clouds made it impossible to fly, so we turned back toward Circle Hot Springs. Minutes later we were back on the ground, and it was great to be sitting on something solid and not in the bumpy air. Leo didn't care if he ever got back to Anchorage, but Alan needed me at the mine.

The lodge was a big vacation spot for the people of the Fairbanks area. Everyone was very friendly. One elderly gentleman had flown in from Nenana for his yearly vacation. His weekend companion was a beautiful 22-year-old girl. Slender and tall, this was the type of girl many a lonely miner dreamed about. Why was this girl with the older guy, we wondered? For the next two days the same scene played out, except for one difference. The poor guy was getting weaker and weaker each time I saw him.

The next afternoon I was sitting in the café when this older guy came down the stairs and staggered over to the table. Falling into the chair, he looked close to death, pale and breathing hard. He said, "That girl is going to kill me! She just won't leave me alone." He swung his head around looking for his attacker. Then he continued, "I've got to find a place to hide. Don't tell her you saw me."

I had a big laugh, but he was completely serious. Shortly after that the gal showed up hunting for her man! She was simply gorgeous, a rare find in that part of the country.

During our short stay at the springs I got to know the guy. He told of his life adventures in Alaska. His present job was flying fuel to all the small villages using a Piper Cherokee Six, which was filled with plastic fuel tanks. He was so proud of his plane that he wanted to show it to me, so we drove over to it and found it parked next to ours. It looked a mess, like it hadn't been washed in a year. The end of the prop resembled a saw blade, where chunks as big as dimes were missing. The plane was his pride and joy, so I lied and told him how great the plane looked.

I also heard the real story about his young, beautiful companion.

She was from an escort service in Fairbanks. This guy's friends had hired her for his 65th birthday. What a gift!

I wondered if his friends ever found out if the old guy got their money's worth out of the deal. It looked to me like he got more than they had bargained for.

My plane was low on fuel so I purchased some from the lodge at $4.00 a gallon. It was stored in five-gallon cans, which concerned me because there was always a good chance for the fuel to become contaminated with water when in plastic containers. But I didn't have much choice, so I ordered 30 gallons of fuel to be delivered to the plane the next morning.

The weather improved overnight, making it a good time to leave. I was getting anxious to return to the mine and was up early the next morning and went to the plane to check out the new load of fuel. The man from the lodge had already poured it in the plane. When I checked the tanks for water I drained ten gallons of contaminated fuel and water. Each tank has its own drain, and with water being heavier than gas, the water ran out the drain.

So I drained and waited, and eventually all the water was removed. But now I only had enough fuel to get to Fairbanks, if I flew as straight as possible.

Soon we were up flying again and it felt good. The weather along the Steese was still poor. The mountains and higher spots along the highway were still covered in clouds, so we headed cross-country. The clouds and fog hung low, forcing us to scud-run up the bottom of a valley and squeeze into the next. A couple of times we were forced to retrace our flight path and try a different route.

I knew the general direction of the highway east of Fairbanks, but after an hour and a half of zigzagging I started to wonder if I wasn't a little lost and glimpsed the fuel gauges every few seconds. With great relief, the highway finally came into view.

I strained to see the smoke that had plagued us on the first landing, but to my surprise the wind had blown it away. I didn't have enough fuel to be flying around looking for the airport, so asked for a straight-in approach. I had only five gallons of fuel left in the plane. With both tanks full again, we left Fairbanks and headed toward Anchorage where Leo needed to be dropped off and I needed to get a planeload of groceries.

I had only been gone five days, but I missed everyone. I had to do my low-level flight past the Matanuska Glacier on the way back to the mine. Low glacier fog forced me to fly dangerously low, causing concern and pressure, but this time I smiled as the white ice slid by the right wing. It was great to be home!

The landing at the mine strip was actually fun. I stepped out of the plane and took in a lung-full of crisp mountain air. If this was what the saying 'high on life' was about, then I had it. I was home.

Everyone wanted details of the trip and got a good laugh about the old gasoline hauler and his young girlfriend. Alan was disappointed to hear that there weren't any mining claims available up north. He was counting on them for the next year.

More of Shorty's lies were being discovered daily, so Alan wanted to fly to Anchorage to have a face-to-face talk with him.

Melvin's eyes opened wide as quarters as Alan told him that he wasn't going to give Shorty any more gold. He tried to argue about the decision but Alan shut him up when he said, "That little Bible-thumper lies to everyone he talks to. The Idaho boys aren't even on his leases and he wants part of their gold. They could have died up where he put them. Two miners downstream have already been forced to give up, all because Shorty is a damn liar and a crook. He might have gotten away with lying to other people, but he won't get away with it scot-free with me."

Melvin knew that he'd better not defend his partner-in-crime with Alan in his present state of mind. One wrong word and he and his whole family would be gone.

Alan told me that Melvin's daughter, Devlyn, was turning into a big problem. Her fiery red hair, playboy-body and white teeth would melt the heart of any lovesick miner. The last thing we needed in camp was a young girl creating jealousy among the workers.

The extra people in camp meant that beds had to be shared. One crew slept while the other worked.

The camp had been living on caribou meat and the supply was low. Tony wanted to shoot another, and the next day we found a fat cow for camp meat.

As we talked, Tony walked to the stove to get coffee. I noticed a slight limp as he went. I asked him why he was limping.

He slowly limped back to me, sat down and said, "I stepped on a nail three days ago. I didn't want to worry anyone so I kept it to myself."

I was out of the chair and taking his boot off in a second, knowing he had diabetes and had a problem with sores healing. The bottom of the foot was black and swollen. The nail had gone into his heel, and yellow puss ran out as I pushed around the wound. He didn't even flinch, not wanting to show me how much it hurt.

I said to Delores, "Look at this mess! I'm taking him to the doctor right now." She looked as worried as I did. He needed to get to the hospital. Delores packed his clothes as I cleaned the sore the best I could.

Fifteen minutes later we were in the air and headed for Providence Hospital in Anchorage.

XI
FAMILY

Tony had one arm over my shoulder as we walked into the front door of the emergency room. The pain that he had been hiding from everyone now showed excruciatingly on his face.

I filled out the usual paperwork and in minutes a doctor was examining Tony. It had only been a couple of hours since I had cleaned the wound, but the bottom of his foot looked blacker and more swollen than ever. The size of the blackened area had doubled and puss was oozing out of the small hole.

The doctor said, "I don't like the looks of this, we need to open the bottom of the foot and clean out all the infection right away."

The look on Tony's face told the story. He was scared to death. I followed the doctor into the hallway and explained Tony's healing problems. His biggest concern was if the nail had penetrated the bone, Tony could get bone poisoning. If that was the case, and not stopped immediately, he could lose his foot.

I paced the floor, waiting for the surgery to end. The doctor finally showed up and said, "Almost all of the infection has been removed. The nail had punctured the bone of the heel, so I had to scrape it. I want to keep him in the hospital for a couple of weeks. The hole needs to heal from the inside out. In order for it to do that, he will need a lot of antibiotics and a real clean environment."

I waited for Tony to wake up, and then explained what the doctor had said. Tears came to his eyes, but there wasn't anything we could do now. I knew he thought he was letting the mine down, so I said, "Enjoy the time while you're here. You'll have all these cute nurses feeding you and giving you baths. Get that foot healed. We're going to need you back at the mine when your foot is better."

I told him I'd bring Delores in the next day. I loaded the plane with oil for the Caterpillars and bought a load of groceries then called Brandt's to see if any other miners needed gear from town.

There was one message. Jackie, Alan's wife, and their two boys, Joel and Levi, would be arriving in Anchorage on a 5:00 p.m. flight. The message said not to tell Alan; it was to be a surprise.

The plane was loaded to the ceiling with supplies, so I would need to fly it to the mine to empty it before returning for Jackie and the boys. Everyone listened as I relayed the story about Tony. Alan and Delores had worried themselves sick while waiting for me to get back with the news.

Delores thought it would be great to have Alan's wife at the mine to help. Since Jackie would be at the mine, Delores decided to go to Anchorage now, instead of tomorrow. She'd been slaving at the mine since day one. Not once had she been able to come up for fresh air. This would give her time to relax, take care of Tony and visit Anchorage.

As we were getting ready to depart Delores said, "Devlyn has been flirting with some of the guys. We just about had a fistfight here yesterday. I don't think Jackie is going to like her in camp. What do you think we should do?"

The answer was easy, "Get rid of her."

As long as Melvin was needed in camp it was impossible for Alan to get rid of anyone from his family, so I would take it on myself to do the dirty work.

I found her sleeping in the small cabin and said, "Devlyn, we don't need you here anymore. I'm bringing Alan's wife back with me. She'll be here to help with the chores, so you need to pack your gear and be ready to leave in ten minutes."

Devlyn was fit to be tied. For her, being in a mining camp with a lot of miners was like having control of the world. She couldn't pass up an opportunity to flash her big blue eyes or sway her hips to get everyone's attention. If she stayed, Alan and I were sure she would create a lot more problems. In a mining camp a female problem could get someone shot.

She didn't like being taken out of the camp and pouted all the way to Brandt's. As she turned to walk away, she flipped me off. I stared at her and wondered how in the hell her parents could let her act the way she did. There was more going on than meets the eyes.

I dropped Delores off at the hospital and raced over to the International Airport. The plane was just unloading and Jackie and the boys looked great. We were from the same town, had grown up and gone to school together. It was exciting to see someone from home. The two boys had a thousand questions as we drove across Anchorage, heading for the airplane.

The usual spot I tied the plane down at Wilbur's had been rented to someone else. It didn't take long to find a new tie-down spot at Bill's Aircraft Repair, which was located on the other side of the field. This meant having Jackie drop me off at the plane, then she would need to drive the pickup on the highway around to the other side of the airport, leaving the pickup at the new spot. I explained the route she would need to drive.

She understood the directions so I started the plane and received a clearance to taxi across the active runway to the other side, after crossing I turned on the taxiway and taxied east to the new spot. The radio keyed and the ground controller said, "There is a pickup on the taxiway." He wasn't talking to anyone in particular.

Then he called, "Cessna 101, there is pickup behind your plane that seems to be following you."

I thought," *It couldn't be!* "Making a slow S-turn made it possible to see behind me. Just as I thought, Jackie was right behind. I keyed the mike and said, "Merrill ground, this is Cessna 101, that pickup belongs to me. Evidently the driver got my directions mixed up. She's following me to my new tie-down spot."

Driving anything but an airplane on the runway or taxiway is a big no-no, but the controller laughed it off and made sure I would tell the driver where she went wrong.

Jackie turned three shades of red as I explained the last few minutes' proceedings. We had a good laugh when we departed for the gold mine, with the boys' faces glued to the windows, as I became their tour guide.

I pointed out the glaciers and then the sheep on Sheep Mountain. This was the wilderness their dad had been writing them about. Their wide eyes and continuous smiles relayed their feelings. But before landing at the mine, we made a stop at Brandt's for fuel for the plane and hamburgers for everyone after Jackie realized she was the cook for the night.

We were enjoying our part of the meal at Brandt's when someone came into the room. I had my back to the door, but by the look on Jackie's face I could tell it was something unusual.

As I turned to see, Devlyn stepped forward. She was made up like a queen, with a tight mini-skirt and skin-tight sweater. She wiggled toward me and said, "Where's Alan?" Then she sat on my lap before I had time to stop her.

Jackie's face went stone cold.

As I lifted her off my lap I said, "Jackie, this is Devlyn." Devlyn reached her hand out but Jackie was too shocked to move.

I walked Devlyn to the door and said, "What the hell are you doing?"

She replied, "If you think you can get rid of me that easy, you're wrong! Just thought I'd give your wives something to think about."

When I sat back down at the table Jackie said with a higher than usual voice, "That was Devlyn? Alan told me she was seventeen and fat."

All I could say was that she was a troublemaker and Alan had gotten rid of her because of that. As we flew toward the mine I hoped Alan wasn't in too much trouble.

Although Jackie was appalled at the living conditions, she settled right in. The hardest thing for everyone to get used to was the constant rain and lack of sunlight. Everything was always soaking wet.

It was interesting to see this city girl go from clean clothes daily to not even changing out of her full-length nightgown. It was the warmest thing she had and that's what she was going to wear.

Over the next week Jackie would go to town and shop while I ran supplies. The boys sat on their dad's lap as he ran the machine. It was the happiest I'd seen Alan for a long time.

The day finally came that I had to take them to Anchorage for their flight home and bring Delores back to the mine with me. Tony's foot had healed some, but he would need to stay at least a couple more weeks before returning to the mine.

The flight was leaving at 6:00 a.m., so we flew in the night before. Tears ran down Alan's face as I loaded his family into the plane. It was hard for him to let go, knowing he wouldn't see them again for months.

Normally I didn't have any problems finding a place to sleep while in town. If I couldn't find a room, I'd roll my sleeping bag out on the floor of the plane. But now I couldn't find a place for Jackie, the boys, Delores and myself. I had checked everywhere, except for one place, the Kobuk Inn. This motel was in the worst part of town and frequented by working girls.

They did have a room with two large beds and asked if I'd need the rooms all-night or just for a couple of hours. I explained the conditions to my passengers.

All agreed it would be better than nothing at all. Everyone snuck down the hallway headed for the safety of the room. Big black men leaned against the walls and stared as we went by. Each one had a baseball bat in their hands.

The room was filthy. When Jackie pulled back the covers to see if the sheets were clean a hundred curly black hairs lay everywhere. But we had no choice. Everyone did his or her best not to touch anything and we were glad to leave the place the next morning.

It was sad watching the three of them walk away, but in one week my wife and son would be here. Jackie worked herself half to death at the mine, scurrying around doing job after job. She would be missed, but Delores had a flair for making everything taste good. The miners had been counting the days for her return.

Tony's foot had been healing slowly. The doctor told Delores he probably wouldn't ever go back to the gold mine. But for now we decided to keep that news from him.

We let Tony know that I would be in town every couple of days to see him. Everyone felt bad to leave him in the hospital without one of us there.

He said to me, "You make sure you're careful with the plane." For Tony to say anything about the plane was unusual. He must have sensed something.

XII
A NIGHT LOST IN THE WILDERNESS

With the outline of the western mountains appearing as towering sentinels, I gently lifted off the airstrip. What was fear earlier in the season was now only apprehension. The everyday flights had turned this small part of Alaska into my home.

Hours of flying down narrow creek bottoms or around formidable snow-capped mountains gave me a good knowledge of the area. Any possible emergency landing spots were etched in my memory. Up until now I had managed to find a way to get back and forth from Anchorage most of the time. There was comfort in knowing that I would be the only one flying in the foggy conditions.

The weather service made it a practice to wait for my call to let them know how the weather conditions were in the pass. I would hear them repeat my explanation of the weather to other pilots waiting to get through.

I often wondered if I actually knew what I was doing or if I'd just been lucky.

So with the little bit of patience I could muster, I'd ease the plane forward in the bad weather, trying to leave enough room and time to back out of dangerous situations, knowing complacency could be a killer.

I departed the mine, and as I gained altitude and turned the corner I could see the weather in the direction of Chickaloon looked terrible with a dark gray cloud-cover that descended to the ground. This type of cloud formation usually indicated a weather front had moved into the Matsu Valley. Wind out of the south would push the storms north and plug the valleys up like a cork in a bottle, usually making flying down the valleys impossible.

I called Anchorage weather on Saw Mill Remote and they confirmed my thoughts. "Cessna 61101, weather in the Anchorage area is IFR, Airmet Charlie in effect, high winds to 50 knots from the south with mountain obscurement. VFR not recommended. Frontage passage would be around 3 p.m. local time."

Every time I called the weather people they would repeat, "VFR not recommended," meaning flying in and around the mountains wasn't a good idea. If I listened to them I would never fly. On a completely blue-sky day they would give the same message, "VFR not recommended."

The clouds looked a lighter gray to the west, indicating the weather might be more favorable. I had used this mountain route a couple of times, but because of its distance from any civilization and lack of suitable landing spots, I used the Chickaloon Pass whenever possible. At least it had a road in case of emergency.

Not wanting to fight the fog and poor visibility, I turned right and climbed with the creek, heading for the headwaters of Caribou Creek. Near the top the creek narrowed to a stop. I either had to turn around and go back to the mine or turn left and squeeze over Chitna Pass, which led to a narrow semi-straight valley that eventually would bring me out of the mountains around Hatcher Pass. The outlet of this route was low and usually would get me under the bad weather and into the valley. I decided to take a look.

The wind rocked the plane as I slowed my speed. I could see it looked lighter miles ahead down the canyon, which I believed to be the other end of the drainage. The clouds lowered and the wind intensified as I eased the big Cessna along.

Caribou moved in unison as I passed 100 feet overhead. There were no trees, only brush and low grass, which the wind blew as rolling waves.

I was about halfway down the valley when the wind and rain hit the plane like a tornado. Forward visibility faded, forcing me to strain out the side windows for ground clearance distance.

My thoughts went to the fog at Chickaloon; right now it would be appreciated. The narrow valley was acting like a wind tunnel, forcing the wind to increase as it narrowed. The visibility went to a quarter of a mile. I had seen enough, it was time to turn around.

Then I remembered that on a previous flight I had seen a small airstrip somewhere in this area. It was maybe 800-feet long, just right for a Super Cub or maybe even a Robertson-equipped Cessna 206. As I started my turn back and squinted out my left window I glimpsed the small airstrip through the sheets of rain. Landing there and waiting the storm out would be a better option than getting beat up going back to the mine.

I fought for control of the plane as I circled to have a better look. It was worse than I remembered, tire-width wide, with rolling humps and puckerbrush three-feet high running down both sides. A better name for this landing spot would be a CAT trail.

I turned a short final as the rain hit me in a torrent, forcing me to slip the plane sideways to see the runway. Steady power adjustments were needed to keep the plane headed toward my anticipated landing spot. At times the gusty wind seemed to stop my forward motion.

The wind had increased to the point that power was needed to get to the runway. The wheels slipped down in-between the brush and then contacted the ground. A spray of mud off the tires slammed the bottoms of the wings.

For a few seconds I fought the rudder pedals for control. Being anything but dead center meant running into the three-foot high brush and being stuck without help to free the plane. In mere seconds the plane came to a stop. My 20-knot ground speed had shortened my rollout to a hundred feet.

The wind on the ground was blowing at least 50 knots, making the plane rock as if I was still in the air. Adrenalin flowed as the plane lifted uncontrollably from the tornado-strength winds. I stared forward into the darkening sky, trying to see the monster that was attempting to bring an end to my plane and me. I could hear the big gust of wind before it hit. As it rocked the plane, I ran the engine, hoping the big prop would help stabilize the plane.

After what seemed like an hour, the wind let up slightly. I needed to get the plane tied down. I pulled the mixture and the engine wound to a stop. Although I was swaying back and forth, the plane sat on all three wheels.

Reaching for my survival gear, I dug out my tie-down ropes, and fearing another big gust, jumped out and tied the rope around the brush and the other end to the wing struts.

I couldn't have gotten any wetter if I'd jumped in a lake. The wind made the rain sting with its driving force. The stronger gusts would make the plane bounce, so I stayed in the front seat, just in case I needed to start the engine to help again.

What I thought would be a couple of hours turned into darkness. My thoughts went to my family; I hadn't seen them for months.

Ryan, my nine-year old, was the pride of my life. My wife had never wanted me to come to Alaska, which made our parting uneasy. But now, stranded in the middle of the Alaskan wilderness, tears filled my eyes and I yearned for their comfort.

Mother Nature pounded the plane with wind and rain all night. At times I thought I was going to lose the battle. The plane would jump with each gust. I could hear the roar of the wind as it raced toward me, making me feel like I was on the worst spot of the planet. Darkness swept down like a hammer, and loneliness and despair overwhelmed my soul.

I was at the mercy of the elements. This land had fought me from the start; maybe this would be the night it would win. It was a 50-mile walk to get out of these mountains, not an option that anyone would enjoy. No one knew where I was. I was on my own.

I prayed to God, asking for help.

Around 4:00 a.m. the wind slowed and the rain stopped. For the first time in 16 hours I relaxed. I had a small survival stove along, so I heated some water and had the best-tasting cup of coffee ever. I felt renewed with the arrival of the morning light. The clouds had lifted and blue sky shown through. It definitely was time to get back in the air.

I had only used a hundred feet to land, so didn't need to and couldn't if I wanted to, taxi back. The plane had wiggled itself into the ground so I pushed on the struts to get each wheel out of its mud hole. The departure was a piece of cake.

The airplane was made to soar like a bird, not be tied to the ground like a horse. I continued down the narrow valley, which led me to the Matsu Valley. The weather toward the mine looked dark and scary.

Boy was I glad to be back in the air! I felt like someone had just lifted a thousand pounds off my shoulders. What a rush to be up and moving. I had just spent the longest and loneliest night of my life and was looking forward to a good hot breakfast.

Tony was doing fine and his foot was healing, but he still needed to be in the hospital for a couple more weeks. He was so excited to see me. I snuck him a McDonald's burger. He smiled as he quizzed me on all the happenings. He told me Leo had stopped to see him and said he was returning to the mine.

I had to bite my lip as he said, "You tell everyone I'll be back in just a few days."

I hoped he was right, but I knew better. That was his biggest goal, to get back to the mining operation so he could help.   The flight back through Chickaloon was smooth and clear. As the saying goes, if you don't like the weather in Alaska, just wait a few minutes. It will change.

XIII
LADIES OF THE NIGHT

I had run the big CAT all night and was looking forward to Delores's ham and egg breakfast with hot coffee to warm my cold, numb body and refresh my mind. The old swamp buggy reminded me of a slow-moving bug as it swayed its way out of camp and headed toward me. Alan and Tim were taking over for the day shift. While Tim checked oil levels and greased both machines, Alan informed me that Leo was at Brandt's and coming back to the mine.

It was good news; Leo was a great asset and could take some of the workload off of Alan and also give Tim a little break. He'd been working 20-hour shifts.

I also knew that Leo's appearance meant Melvin would be a short-timer at the mine. Over the last few days he and his wife had hardly left their cabin. Ever since I'd forced Devlyn to leave, they would hardly talk to anyone. Leo and Melvin hated each other, and it was time to get rid of the freeloader.

I believed that once he was gone Alan would have one less thing to worry about and less gold would slip through the cracks.

Leo was sitting in the cafe when I arrived. He'd taken a fancy to Devlyn and had been visiting her while her mom and dad were away. He smiled and waved as I stepped into the building. I immediately noticed that he looked terrible. "What the heck is wrong with you?"

He replied, "I've been at Devlyn's house for the last three days and she just about killed me! I guess I'm not man enough to satisfy that redhead." As I laughed he continued, "Over the last three days I've learned alot about Shorty and Melvin. She said the two of them have been scamming miners for years. Shorty finds people from outside the area and talks them into mining his claims. He gives them this exaggerated story about all the gold and how easy it is to find.

"That's not all," Leo continued, "Devlyn said that she was brought to the mining camp for a distraction, giving Melvin a chance to steal as much gold as possible before the miners went broke or Shorty told them to leave. And get this," he continued, "She said that her dad encouraged her to flirt with the miners and that a couple of miners got in a fight over her two years ago. One of them was shot."

Leo's story answered a lot of the questions for us. We had been lied to from the very start. But one thing for sure, Shorty and Melvin had run into the wrong miners this time. We wouldn't just leave peacefully.

Eldon Brandt walked up and informed us that Shorty had left his place and headed for the mine a couple of hours earlier and to keep an eye out for him. Even Eldon knew what kind of person Shorty was.

We didn't think he'd show up in our camp, but who knew? Alan needed to hear what Leo had just learned, just in case Shorty drove into camp.

As we flew toward the mine Leo and I had second thoughts about telling Alan. We were afraid that if Shorty showed up right after Alan learned of the deceit, someone might get hurt.

Shorty was probably checking up on the Idaho boys. Little did he know that he was in for a big surprise. The boys were just waiting for him and would make it clear he wasn't welcome anymore.

On short final to the mine airstrip I could see two guys standing at the other end, the young Idaho boys. Leo had lit a cigarette and just laughed as usual when I told him to put it out. Things were back to normal.

I had been hauling food and supplies for the boys since the day they first showed up. Our hearts had gone out to them, so the flights had been free, since they didn't have any money. I asked, "What do you guys need?"

Both of them just stood there and kind of stared at the ground. The older boy finally got brave and said, "We want you to ah, ah, well kind of find us, well you know, find some girls that will come to our mine." His face turned redder and redder as he talked. "You see we're real tired of being alone, and we have gold to pay them."

I looked at the gold he held out in his hand. He had nuggets the size of quarters! I was flabbergasted and asked, "How long have you had that gold? I've been flying you all summer free and you had gold all that time?"

"No way," the boys replied, "we just started finding gold last week."

I felt a little better when they said that. "Let me understand what you want. Find two girls that will come to your gold mine for a couple of weeks."

They both nodded their heads in unison. The younger one said, "Take these nuggets with you and tell them there is a lot more gold just like this." As he handed me two $500 nuggets he said, "This bigger nugget is for you for finding us the girls. There's another like that when you show up with them."

I didn't want anything to do with the girl idea until he handed me the big nugget. Just then I remembered that I needed to go to town for groceries and might as well make a little extra money to help pay for the trip.

They also wanted me to pick up a new floating dredge and handed over a few more nuggets to pay for the thousand-dollar gold finder.

Leo said, "Shorty's supposedly around the area. Have you guys seen him?"

Both boys smiled and the older one replied, "He drove into our canyon this morning. I guess he didn't like the bullets ricocheting off the rock walls all around him. The last thing we saw of him was the back of his swamp buggy bouncing downstream almost out of control. We're pretty sure he won't be back."

Back at the mine, Alan and Delores laughed as I told them about the wish list for the Idaho boys and how they had gotten rid of Shorty. Alan rolled the new nugget around in his hand and smiled at me. I knew exactly what he was thinking—no more free flights.

Leo walked me out to the swamp buggy and said, "I think I'll tell Alan what Devlyn told me."

I replied, "You'd better tell Melvin what you have learned and give him time to leave before you say anything to Alan. I don't think it would be good if he were around. Alan might tear his head off."

Leo agreed that would be wiser and shook my hand goodbye as I headed for the plane. It was great to have him back.

So I left to get groceries, buy a dredge, see Uncle Tony and find a couple of lovelies that would be willing to spend some time with two love-sick miners.

The boys watched as I started taxiing to the other end of the runway. Then I stopped the plane and motioned for the boys to come over. As the older one stuck his head in the opened window I asked, "Does it matter what they look like?"

He replied, "As long as they are female, it doesn't matter!"

As I flew toward Anchorage I thought about the boys from Idaho. Shorty had somehow talked them into coming to Alaska to mine his claims. They were young and naive, but probably no more so than we were. The ground that he had put them on wasn't even his. With our help the boys had survived up to this point. I just hoped they knew what they were doing when it came to having working girls in their camp. And I was more than a little surprised to see all the gold they had found. At least it was the end of the free flights for them!

Tony was doing well and was anxious to get back to the mine, but the doctor said, "That foot just doesn't want to improve. We can't take any chances. As slow as it's healing, I doubt it will be healed by winter."

The mining company traded the gold for the floating dredge and in an hour I had all the groceries in the back of the plane. Now all I needed was to build up my courage and go find a couple of friendly girls!

I wasn't sure that finding personal entertainment for other miners was part of my job description, but the thought of another big nugget changed my outlook. So I headed for Fourth Street to give it a try. Every corner had a couple of girls selling their wares; it was just a matter of finding the right corner.

The first girls I talked to said that I would have to make my deal with the guy who was sitting in the white Cadillac down the street. That sounded a bit scary, so I passed on those two and moved on to the next corner.

I literally got laughed off of that corner. The girls thought I was a little crazy asking them, a couple of city girls, to go into the back country. I then realized that this was going to be tougher than I thought.

As I walked back to the pickup I noticed a gal standing all by herself. I approached her and explained the situation. As she teased me about wearing a cowboy hat in Alaska I pulled out the two nuggets. Her eyes widened as she noticed the yellow gold.

Now I had her attention and talked fast. "These two nuggets are for you and they're yours the minute we depart Merrill Field. The miners told me to tell you that there is more." I didn't have to say anything else; the shiny gold had made her mind up for her.

She said she had a friend who would love to go to a mining camp.

I guess I forgot to tell her that the camp consisted of only one tent, no running water, except in the ice-cold creek, lots of grizzly bears and two miners young enough to be her sons.

We agreed to meet at the airplane in two hours. As I waited I wondered how old the girls were, 40, maybe 45, I thought. Well, the boys didn't give an age limit!

I took the spare time to wash and clean the plane, the first time in a month. The old workhorse looked like it had been in mud-bog races after weeks of takeoffs and landings in the muck. Cleaning the underbelly would be a major undertaking, so I left that project for another day.

When the girls showed up, I couldn't believe what they were wearing. They both had on makeup, mini-skirts and high-heeled boots. I explained that it rained every day at the camp and that most of the time everyone wore some sort of rain gear, and that the mud was always about six-inches deep. I didn't want to say too much, though, for fear that they would change their minds.

They listened intently and for a second I thought I'd lost them. But in short order they returned dressed in the oldest clothes they owned. With their new backcountry outfits, they looked more like moms than working girls.

It made me wonder what the Idaho boys, who were probably 19 and 20, would think about these older gals.

I got them situated, received my clearance from the tower and departed Merrill Field for the mining camp. I was always glad to get out of the air traffic rat race that was constantly around Anchorage. Planes were always going in every direction and there were always special departure routes that had to be used. Once I reached Palmer I relaxed a little and enjoyed the scenery.

The gal sitting beside me held out her hand. I knew exactly what she wanted. I reached in my pocket, pulled out the nuggets and placed them in her hand. *These two were astute businesswomen.* Both girls smiled from ear to ear, even though they were a little nervous about flying. I calmed them down, and they enjoyed the scenic flight through the mountains.

The two brothers were waiting for us when we landed. I made the introductions and it looked like they were going to get along just fine. Both boys glowed red and stuttered through their words as they met their new companions, then made plans to come and get the new dredge later.

I didn't think gold mining was on their minds at that moment. It was quite a sight to see them holding hands as they walked away. I had to wonder how shocked the girls would be when they first saw their new accommodations.

The next day I had to fly to Brandt's for supplies so thought I would check up on the boys and their new acquaintances. From a mile away I could see that something was wrong. It looked like a Boy Scout leader's nightmare! The tent and supplies were strewn everywhere.

I saw a big black object and immediately knew a grizzly was in the camp. As I circled I saw the two guys and girls on a hillside above the camp, waving their coats and trying hard to get my attention.

I later learned that the four of them had been in the creek below when the bear had wandered into their camp. Their rifles were in the tent. The only thing they could do was retreat to higher ground and watch the demolition of all of their earthly possessions.

Because there were no trees or other tall hazards in the area, I tried to buzz the bear out of the camp, which was in the bottom of a long, narrow canyon, and my only option. I slowly climbed upstream, then turned downhill and descended to within 50 feet of the creek with the canyon walls inches away. It was hard to keep my eyes on the bear as the brush shot so closely by.

The marauder had stopped his rummaging and was now standing on his hind legs looking in my direction. He stood his ground as I charged straight toward him. He had been king of the mountain for a long time and didn't have to give way to anything. I looked him straight in the eye; he glared back and cowered down as I passed over and then he turned to look at the large, noisy intruder.

I climbed for altitude and turned back over the camp. He was still there, but his full attention was now on me. The second pass went the same as the first. Only this time the bear turned and ran, then stopped, and stood back up to confront his attacker. The bear had moved up the hill and was slightly above the plane.

With my speed at 130 knots, the closure rate was alarming. I turned straight at the bear, which dropped back to all fours and charged. He was brave and cunning, but all his years of ruling everything around him hadn't prepared him for this. His giant paw swung at the plane as I raced by, then he turned and ran. Now I had him on the move.

On the third pass, I flattened the pitch on the prop, which developed a high-pitched deafening noise that speeded the bear's retreat. He ran down the mountain, turning every few minutes to see where I was, before resuming his retreat. On each pass he would rush the plane, forcing me to gain altitude to keep from hitting him, and then cower down as I passed over. On the final buzz the bear sprinted into a brushy area a half-mile from the camp.

Everyone waved as I turned to fly over for the last time. The next day the younger boy showed up in camp looking for fresh supplies. We loaded him down with all the groceries he could carry. He never mentioned the girls, whom we were dying to question him about, but thanked me for getting rid of the bear. He left camp with a big smile on his face and a hop in his step.

The next day my wife and son were arriving. I hadn't seen them for months and was anxious to get to town. Alan was going to go along and have a big talk with Shorty. He had taken as much as he could, and it was time to have a heart-to-heart discussion. Then he was going to stay in town for a few days with his dad.

As we drove up to the plane we could see smoke coming out of the old cabin. This usually meant someone was waiting for a ride to town. The girls ran out to us as we checked out the airplane. Now they were looking their age with matted hair and filthy-dirty clothes. Neither had taken a bath since I'd last seen them.

They wanted to catch a free ride to town on my next flight. I explained there wasn't any such thing as a free flight.

Both girls talked at once; they were anxious to get out of this wilderness and back to town. "One of the boys threatened to kill us if we didn't give them back their gold," yelled the older gal. "We have gold and will pay whatever it costs to fly to Anchorage right now."

The flight was uneventful, but the girls' body odor burned our noses all the way to town. As they walked away we couldn't help but wonder what happened at the Idaho boys' camp.

Alan knocked on Shorty's door, with no response, so he knocked again. The door held tight as Alan pounded on it. This moment had been a long time coming and he would make sure he got his point understood.

I leaned on the hood of the pickup and stared at the house. A small movement of the curtain in the side window gave evidence people were inside. I said, "There's someone in the house, I just saw him look out the window." Alan gave one last slam on the door.

The door opened slowly, Shorty stepped out and shut it behind him. Evidently someone must have told him that Alan had figured out his scam. By his body language, I could tell Shorty didn't want to face Alan.

Alan pointed his finger at Shorty and said, "You have been lying to us since the very first day. There was no sluice box, gold isn't lying around waiting for people to pick up, and Melvin has turned out to be your puppet. I've paid you fifty percent of the gold till now, but that's the end of it. There won't be any more gold for you. Do you understand what I'm saying?"

Shorty was going to speak when the door behind him opened and his son Jimmy stepped out. Jimmy was about 30 years old and maybe 170 pounds. In his hand was a ten-inch screwdriver. He immediately pointed the screwdriver to within an inch of Alan's face and said, "Don't talk to my dad that way!"

David and Alan

I stepped toward the action knowing Alan wouldn't put up with Jimmy for a second, and all I could think was, "Good night, Irene." Maybe I could ease the tension. But as I expected, Alan wasn't someone to be intimidated and wasn't one to talk when threatened. In a flash his fist connected with Jimmy's forehead.

The first thing to hit the ground was the back of his head. The whites of his eyes shone; Jimmy was in dreamland.

That was that, Alan said what was needed, and talked with his fist as to the seriousness of the situation. Alan didn't feel good about punching Jimmy, but he was relieved to have told Shorty the way it was going to be from now on. I dropped him off at the hospital and hurried to the big airport, the anticipation of seeing my wife and son built as the big jet pulled up to the terminal. Ryan blasted down the ramp and sprinted to me, almost running me over. We had been inseparable since he could walk. With his long legs and a face full of freckles, he looked older than his nine years. In Montana we had spent our spare time shooting bow and arrows or exploring the high mountains. Now he looked like he had grown three inches.

Noreen's smiling face shown through the crowd. We had met when we were still in high school and married at the age of 19, soon after Ryan came along. This was our first separation, and it sure was great to have them both with me again.

As I hugged Ryan I thought back to his first cross-country race when he was in the first grade. He sprinted from the bus to tell his mom that there was a race at the school. All the neighboring country schools were bringing their racers to his school and he wanted her to take him back so he could race. He ran up to the kids lined up at the starting point and blended into the crowd of runners.

He looked down the farmer's field at the finish line a quarter-mile away. The gun fired and he was off at a full sprint, leaving the pack behind. At the finish line he slowed to a stop.

A man standing there yelled, "Keep going!" and pointed to the next corner of the field. Ryan sprinted to that corner only to be told to go to the next corner where the race had started. He finally found the finish line. He won the race by a quarter of a mile.

Noreen had always been scared of airplanes so I gave my best piece-of-cake answers when she wanted the details of the upcoming flight to the mine. Ryan teased his mom about her fear as we loaded the plane. We departed Merrill Field and headed across the open water. In the distance stood McKenzie Point. Noreen kept her eyes focused straight ahead, too scared to look down at the cold water below.

The window latch on my side window had been broken since we'd bought the plane. If I bumped it accidentally the window would blow open. It wasn't dangerous, but the sudden rush of air was a little frightening. As I turned to answer Ryan's question, I bumped the latch and the window slammed open. Noreen screamed, her face turning white and yelled, "Take me back to Anchorage, now!"

That wasn't an option; she was going to the mine. Ryan pointed out the new scenery and smiled from ear-to-ear as we flew toward the mine. Noreen stared straight ahead.

The clouds had lowered enough to force me to fly slowly and change course constantly. Caribou Creek was covered with low clouds and fog. I strained to see any openings up Alfred Creek; the remaining five miles to the mine was going to be real nerve-racking. I was doing my best to be smooth with the controls, but as the clouds grew thicker I was forced to lower my elevation.

With two miles left to go, the fog descended into the top of the trees. Smoothness left my mind as I banked the plane sharply to turn around. Noreen held her eyes shut as I leveled out and headed back the way we came. I had one option left and not one I used often.

Where the fog touched the trees I could drop down into the narrow canyon the mine was in. When I turned around, I looked up the bottom of the steep narrow canyon; it was clear of clouds.

Ryan laughed in delight as I dropped into the narrow ravine. The speed was 60 knots as we stood the plane on its wings at each sharp turn. The veins stood out on Noreen's neck; she was at the end of her rope.

I said, "Just one more corner and we'll be on the ground."

Mud and water splashed in every direction as the plane touched down. Noreen uttered a low scream. Ryan hit me on the back and yelled, "Alrighta!" He was so excited he could hardly talk. The rain pummeled the top of the plane as we taxied back to the tie-down spot and shut the engine down.

For the first time in an hour Noreen turned her head and spoke. "You're crazy!"

Ryan had a hundred questions as we drove the old swamp buggy toward the mine. Everyone was glad to see the two of them.

I wasn't surprised to learn that Leo had run Melvin and his wife out of camp. He had told him what we had learned about Shorty, and in the space of five minutes he was gone.

Although Melvin had helped us get the mine going, it was done under false pretense. The whole time he had been at the mine he'd refused to do any physical labor. He was one of the laziest guys I'd ever been around, except when it came to finding or stealing gold. I was sure the attitude at the mine would change for the better now. The mistrust had made the place very unpleasant.

Two days later, the two Idaho brothers showed up in our camp, and they weren't a bit happy. Half-jokingly we inquired about the success of their venture with the two girls. It was not a good subject and they said, "They were real friendly at first, but that changed quickly."

It seems once the girls had the boys interested, they paid dearly for anything and everything. A kiss cost the boys each a small nugget. As new adventures played out, the cost increased. The girls held out for more gold and finally were able to acquire almost all their gold with one big final romance. The boys got what they had been wanting from the very start, but at great cost.

With the gold gone, the girls' friendly ways evaporated. About this time the boys woke up to the scam and kicked the girls out of camp, which is why they showed up at the airplane. They didn't mention anything about threatening the girls.

The brothers knew that their summer's work had been almost totally lost and were feeling pretty stupid. They only had about six more weeks left of the mining season in order to replace the gold they had so easily parted with.

The younger brother asked some questions that at the time didn't seem strange but later would have meaning. He wanted to know how many miners were on the creek below our camp and what kind of work hours they kept.

Then they left our camp and headed upstream. The boys had learned a very expensive lesson. The two older working girls had really taught the true meaning of the phrase, "The school of hard knocks!" The boys had learned that surviving in the Alaska wilderness meant more than just carrying a pistol. Not all predators were the four-legged kind.

We were still in the cookshack laughing about the boys'

misfortune when a caravan of equipment rounded the corner above camp, the noise of the machines echoing off the canyon walls. We watched as the new equipment rattled by, each piece being bright yellow. We had been hearing that a big mining operation was headed in to mine the hot spot where we were hoping to find a lot of gold in the next couple of weeks.

Our first reaction was to run the intruders off, but we just stood there in disbelief as they stopped a quarter of a mile downstream at the very location that had been promised to us. By now we realized that promises were made to be broken, and up till now every one had been. Shorty was still up to his devious ways.

In the morning Ryan and I would fly to Anchorage to get Alan and fill him in on the latest news. Our chance to make up for all the lies and bad luck lay in the ground right where the new miners were setting up.

"You're crazy!" played over and over in my mind. Flying with low visibility or in turbulent conditions always generated a lot of tension. But ever since the very first day I had departed Merrill Field in the 206, I'd struggled to survive. Noreen was right, one wrong decision or unforeseen weather condition could be disastrous.

I had let the pressure of keeping the mining operation functioning cloud good reasoning. I told myself, "I'm not immortal." But almost every day I had pushed my life to the very edge of disaster and definitely past the point of good sense. I didn't have the right to do that to my wife and son. I had to pull back a little. If it meant changing the timing for hurried-up flights, or waiting for better conditions, that's what I needed to do. Somehow I had survived until now, but if I kept pushing, that could change in an instant.

XIV
THE MAFIA CONNECTION

As Ryan and I taxied toward the end of the runway for takeoff, Shorty's swamp buggy drove by and headed downstream. He stared straight ahead, not wanting to look in our direction.

After Alan's direct discussion with him and Devlyn's explanation of her dad's and Shorty's devious practices, he wanted nothing to do with us. I'm sure all he wanted now was to get the Montana boys off his claims and hunt for his next victim.

We departed to the north. Ryan had a million questions as I flew toward a valley where I'd seen a lot of caribou. "I want to see a grizzly! Where are the caribou?" On and on he went.

"Just watch over that ridge, there are usually a lot of caribou in the next valley."

We both stared forward looking for any sign of animals. As we floated over the ridge they came into view, shaking their heads from the tormenting flies and lowering them for a bite of grass as they moved.

Ryan pointed at the animals and peered with wide eyes as I descended to 100 feet above the landscape.

The front of the large herd stopped as they eyed the large and noisy bird that was coming straight at them, then parted to get away from the intruder, splitting the herd in two. Then they blended back into one as we made a slow turn to look back at the awesome sight. Thousands of animals covered the landscape. I'd seen a lot of animals before, but nothing like this.

One more low pass parted the giant herd again and then we turned south toward Anchorage. Both of us sat in silence and watched the caribou move in our minds' eyes. It had been the sighting of a lifetime.

All Alan could say was, "It doesn't surprise me when it comes to Shorty." He looked out the side window all the way back to the gold mine. We had talked a lot about moving the operation down to where the new miners were setting up their operation. Now it was too late.

We glared down the creek with hatred. The new miners were making noise and finding our gold. It was the main topic of conversation, and grew in intensity for the next couple of days.

Because I had the ability to fly to town and get away from the mining operation, I could see a change in everyone's attitude. This change forced me to become the constable and peacekeeper at the camp. Alan's mind was on finding gold at our mine, not thinking about the miners below us.

Now all the attention from everyone else turned to the other gold mining camp. As the days went by, talk of running the other miners out became more constant. I didn't think that would happen, but everyone's attitude was getting kind of scary. I smoothed things over constantly to keep trouble from starting. It didn't help both that the other miners had new equipment and drove by daily, heading to the highway for supplies, without bothering to stop to introduce themselves. I had to remind everyone that it was hard to know what Shorty had said about us.

I had heard that gold mining could bring out the worst in people, now I was starting to see it. We were finding gold, but our old equipment was worn out and there wasn't enough gold in the creek. A cloud of despair lingered over our camp, slowly suffocating the spirit and fight that had given us the willpower to start this grand adventure in the first place.

Alan was reluctant when I told him I was going to walk down to the other camp and introduce myself. With the present mind-set, I thought it was the only way to fend off a physical confrontation. I heard that the Mafia owned the new camp. Although we had dismissed the rumor, the last thing anyone wanted was a problem with any crime boss.

Not knowing what I was getting myself into, I walked away from our camp somewhat hesitantly. I could see a swamp buggy from the other camp coming up the creek. It stopped right in front of me and a short round-chested guy introduced himself.

He said his name was Tom and he had been hired to run the mining operation that had just come in a few days earlier and they were having trouble getting their operation going. I told him I was headed to his camp, and would be happy to see if I could help them in any way. The camp consisted of two big tents, one for cooking and one for sleeping. No toilet or washing facilities.

They had a new sluice box that was sitting high and dry. Twelve guys peered at me as I walked around the camp. Three said that they had mined gold all their lives and knew everything there was to know about gold mining.

It turned out all the hired hands had lied about their experience level. They had been hired on at a high hourly wage, and thought they could bluff their way through. They didn't have any idea how to service the heavy equipment or how to operate it.

The foreman was now in a panic—he had misled the owner of the mine, who he affirmed was affiliated with the Mafia out of Chicago. The owner had spent hundreds of thousands of dollars getting equipment and supplies to Alfred Creek. Shorty had set up the operation for the Chicago owner. Tom, the foreman of the new mine, had never met the moneyman personally. He was now in fear for his life, and rightfully so.

I spent the next couple of hours explaining the little I knew about mining, servicing and running the equipment. Their new D8K Caterpillar had ten times more power than ours. I set the box for the camp and explained how to dig and push the overburden up to the sluice box, purposely not telling them how to high grade the ground.

The camp was so disorganized that I didn't think they would be mining very long. Just maybe we might end up down there yet. In the meantime, if they removed any overburden for us, that would be good.

I really doubted they would find much gold. Their camp was a mixture of misfits, who had the ability to talk, but had not run equipment or mined gold. I also understood their fear of misleading a guy who solved problems permanently.

The news about the Mafia Camp was a big hit in our camp. Our minds had led us to believe the camp was getting rich, and from our gold-nugget hole.

Being from Montana, we had a hard time believing that the Mafia had moved in next door and we really didn't care who was there. We just wanted them to leave. It didn't matter whom or by what name they were called, being in an Alaskan wilderness put everyone on equal footing.

The next day I flew into Brandt's Texaco with Tim. He had been working double shifts and Alan rewarded him with a real shower and supper. The big, burly guy worked without complaint and gave his heart and soul to the operation. He could operate a piece of machinery like a doctor performing surgery.

But taking him to Brandt's also had a hidden agenda. He worked so much he didn't take the time to keep clean. His ever-present smell got to the point that we couldn't handle it anymore. He hadn't taken a bath, shaved or changed clothes for weeks.

Although I had heard all the complaining, I worked an opposite shift. But when his odor lingered in the bunkhouse for hours after he left, I knew it was time to get him to Brandt's for a real cleanup.

Tim complained from the minute we departed the camp until I walked him to the shower at Brandt's. I made sure he had clean clothes and soap with a bristle brush before he entered the shower room. I had no sooner sat down and ordered burgers than Tim walked into the café and sat down. There was no way he could have gotten clean in two minutes, his hair wasn't even wet and I was pretty sure there were things growing in his beard.

With a forceful tone I marched him back to the shower and threatened him with me handling the scrub brush. We would have mutiny back at camp if I returned with Tim anything but squeaky clean. This time I stood next to the shower curtain, making sure the cleaning job was done right. The threat of a 30-mile walk back to camp got the job done. As hard as I talked, he refused to shave or cut his hair, but at least the big chunks of food were cleaned out of the six-inch beard.

We had just sat down when Mary Brandt came up and handed me a note. I was supposed to call some guy in Chicago. Getting notes from other miners was common whenever I landed at Brandt's because they had the only telephone in the area.

I made the call. The person introduced himself and said he was the owner of the new mining operation. Shorty had told him his camp was right below ours and that I was available to fly him from Anchorage to the mine. He explained that he had hired a local pilot to fly for his camp, but he wouldn't be available for a couple of weeks. Would I pick him up at the Anchorage International Airport in two days? It was more of a demand than a request, so I thought I'd better set him straight right away.

I replied, "I fly for the Montana camp and the plane belongs to it. If you need me to fly for you and if time permits I would be happy to help out. The flight to and from the mine will cost $300."

I was surprised by his courteous reply, saying he would pay whatever price was required.

I told him that I had been to his camp, and everything was going fine. He was pleasant to talk to, not at all what I expected. I agreed to pick him up in Anchorage on Wednesday.

That night Alan and I discussed Mr. Mafia. We both agreed that we would go beyond what was customary to be nice. His new equipment was what we needed, and if his operation failed, maybe we could make a deal to use it.

As we were talking, the door to the cookshack swung open. The younger Idaho boy jumped into view. He was so out of breath that he couldn't talk. After a couple of deep breaths he yelled that a bear attacked him up on the airstrip. According to his story he managed to shoot the bear with his revolver, but the injured bear had chased him all the way to our camp. In a second he had his shirt off and showed us the wound, one long deep gash that ran from the top of the shoulder to his shoulder blade. Noreen and Delores dressed the wound as the young man filled his mouth with food.

Alan and I grabbed our pistols and my hunting rifle and slowly searched around camp for the wounded bear, then drove to the airstrip to check on the plane. The last thing we needed was a wounded grizzly walking around. The pelting rain made it impossible to find any sign of the bear.

That night everyone slept lightly, listening for strange sounds. The only one who got a good night's sleep was the wounded boy. He left our camp early the next morning like nothing had happened. We all agreed that there was something real strange about him. What was he doing out in the middle of the night, strolling around in a bear-infested wilderness?

I departed the airstrip early on Wednesday. Everyone was anxious since it had been a week since anyone had seen Tony. He was ready to come back to the mine. His foot had healed considerably, but the doctor said that he needed to remain in the hospital one more week. While I was in his room the doctor agreed to let Tony come back to the mine under one condition. The nurse would show me how to remove all the gauze out of the incision, then disinfect the opening and reapply clean gauze. With great effort the infection had been stopped.

The doctor walked me out of the room and told me that going

back to the mine was against his better judgment. The infection in the bone of Tony's foot had been real bad and he couldn't guarantee it was all gone. But all Tony wanted to do was go back to his gold mine operation, and after weeks of persistence from Tony, the doctor agreed to let him go. In one week I could pick Tony up. He smiled from ear-to-ear when I gave him the news.

I completed my usual grocery shopping and laundry, then drove to the International Airport to pick up my passenger. Being a little early, I sat down to people-watch. It was amazing to see all the different types of people: tall, short, fat, and skinny, people from all national backgrounds, each one with a story or dream.

One guy even had a pair of ladies nylons on his head that hung down over his shoulders. Two black women walked along his side and hung on his arms. They both had on mini-skirts and high heels, and looked like they were ready to party. I wondered what his story was as I kept watching them. They got closer and closer. He had a sign in his hand, and when he got close enough for me to read it, I was surprised to see my name. These were my passengers. I walked up and introduced myself.

After we picked up their luggage I explained about the flight and told the girls that they should change their clothes to something warmer and buy some rubber boots. My explanations of the weather conditions at the mine went unheard. "We're only going to stay one day, so we'll be fine with what we have on," the boss replied. He wanted to fly to the mine immediately. I never did figure out the nylon thing and thought it wouldn't be wise to ask.

The air was rough and every time I hit a bump the girls would let out a scream. As I got closer to the mine the weather got worse and my passengers got quieter. It was raining hard when I buzzed his camp. I circled it once to let them know they had someone to pick up and then headed to the airstrip for landing. The whole time the girls were whining about the conditions and rough ride. I thought to myself, just wait a few minutes; things would get worse.

As we touched down mud flew off the wheels and hit the bottom of the wings with a big bang. Both girls started screaming again. I couldn't take my eyes off of the little bit of runway I had left but managed to get the plane stopped before the end, then turned around to see what everyone had been yelling about.

Nothing unusual had happened, just a grizzled-looking pilot with a muddy airplane landing in the middle of God-Knows-Where. I couldn't see what the problem was, but the wide-eyed stares and fearful looks confirmed what I thought. My passengers were scared to death. I'm sure the girls thought that if there was a hell, they had found it.

As I taxied back to my tie-down spot the rain pounded the top of the plane. The misty fog lifting off of the tundra and blowing across the runway gave the surrounding hills a ghost-like appearance. Three inches of mud and water made finding my tie-down ropes difficult. All three of my passengers were completely dumbfounded. The temperature was in the low forties and both thinly clad dark-skinned girls were turning blue.

I put on my hip boots and rain gear and told them that I had tried to warn them about the conditions. I dug out a couple of old coats from my survival gear. Both girls still trembled, probably more from fear of death in this wilderness than of the cold conditions. I explained that the weather was like this lots of the time and that they'd better toughen up.

Their ride was probably about an hour away so I suggested that they come down to our mining camp and wait there. I drove the old swamp buggy up as close to the plane as possible and loaded my supplies into the backseat. The old buggy had McDonald Douglas DC3 tires, which put the bottom of the old Dodge pickup four feet off the ground, making the old war-horse able to roll across mud swamps and water holes. It was slow going, but always got us to our destination.

The girls made a dash across the mud to the swamp buggy. They tippy-toed as if that would keep the mud out of their four-inch heels, then hiked their skin-tight skirts up to their waists. After three tries I walked over and lifted them into the rig. All this time the boss sat quietly. The three of them were soaked to the bone.

Curly hair hung limp over their faces. The ride to our mine was slow and as we crawled up and down steep hills the girls screamed with fear. Both girls yelled and cussed at the boss as we rolled into our camp. All they wanted to do was go back to Chicago. They weren't happy campers.

Delores got everyone a hot cup of coffee while the girls backed up to the woodstove for warmth. After a few minutes the heat cooled their tempers. The girls told us they had no clue such a miserable place existed. What they didn't know was that their camp was more primitive than ours. No one said anything, letting them enjoy the moment.

The boss said, "Shorty called me with stories of a lot of gold on his claims." We all looked at each other, knowing exactly what he was going to say. "How's your camp doing? Is there as much gold as Shorty said?" he asked.

This was Alan's chance to finally get one up on Shorty. He replied, "We're finding some gold, but our equipment is so worn out that we can't dig enough dirt to find the gold. Have you ever heard this statement: 'Lots of gold, easy to find and easy to get out of the ground'?"

The boss's eyes grew larger as he thought about where he had heard the last thirteen words.

Alan continued, "Finding gold in this creek is not as easy as you were led to believe."

The swamp buggy from his camp rolled into ours. Both girls had warmed up and didn't want to leave the heat from the woodstove, and with a lot of complaining finally loaded into their taxi. The boss put $300 on the table and walked to his swamp buggy.

I was amazed that he would spend so much money on a project about which he knew so little. Then I thought about our prior knowledge. We hadn't known much more than he did. He would need a ride back to Anchorage the next day to catch his return flight to Chicago. I said, "Under the present weather conditions, flying will be impossible." I was trying to stall him a few days so I could pick Tony up and take Noreen and Ryan to Anchorage to catch their flight home.

The weather didn't let up for the next three days, but was good enough to fly to Brandt's to pick up supplies. Ryan was my copilot. When we arrived at the plane, caribou stood all over the runway. Ryan sprinted after them and then returned with a smile a mile wide. I said, "The funny thing about caribou is they usually circle back to the spot where they started."

The young cow he'd just chased ran back to the other end of the airstrip. It was the same animal I'd been dodging for the last couple of weeks. No matter how many times I buzzed her, she would stand like a statue until I taxied up to her after landing.

Ryan started to fidget as we gazed at the animal. I said, "Go get her!" Ryan was off in a flash, running halfway up the mountainside and then came back. We lifted off just as she came back onto the runway. I told Ryan, "If she's there when we come back, we'll have caribou for supper." All I got for a reply was a big toothy smile.

The usual route to Brandt's from the mine went around Syncline Mountain. Almost every day I would see a pair of full-curled rams hiding in a small draw near the top. I told Ryan to look for animals, making bets who would see the first one. His head was stuck to the window as we approached the rams' hideout. From a mile away Ryan spotted the two sheep. Their white coats shone bright, surrounded by all the dark grass. Ryan was so excited he could hardly speak.

When we flew back to our mine airstrip, I buzzed the young caribou again. She stood her ground in the middle of the airstrip and didn't flinch as we passed over. She wouldn't move and showed absolutely no fear of the plane. We landed and I slammed on the brakes to keep from hitting her. She still stood her ground. I told Ryan, "Caribou for supper!"

After we tied down the plane, I pulled out my hunting rifle and shot her between the eyes. Eventually she would have caused a wreck. Ryan gutted the animal; we loaded the carcass into the swamp buggy and took it back to camp. We had the meat cut, wrapped and in the barrel freezer in two hour's time.

The Mafia camp had been building an airstrip for their pilot. He would show up when it was finished. The foreman of the mine had been driving up daily, hoping I could fly the boss and the two black girls out. He said, "Those girls are driving us all insane. Everyone wants the three of them gone."

On the fourth day the clouds cleared and my passengers showed up moments later. The girls had on old coveralls and hadn't fixed their hair or applied makeup. Not one word was said on the flight to town.

I dropped them off at the big airport; the boss paid me for the ride and showed me the five ounces of gold found at his mine. He seemed to be happy as I watched him walk away with his former friends. I believe his friendship with the girls had ended at the mine.

Heads hung low as Noreen, Ryan, and I walked to the gate for their flight home. The time they had been at the mine had flown by in a flash. Noreen had worked hard; helping out anywhere she was needed. The flight to the mine had scared her so badly that she had feared the flight back to town the whole time she was there. I was sure she hadn't enjoyed one moment, but Ryan loved every second. He explored and flew everywhere with me. Now I was without them again; tears flowed as they walked away and disappeared. I planned to be back in Montana in two months, which seemed like a lifetime. "I promise I'll be careful," I mumbled to their retreating forms.

As I drove to Providence Hospital tears continued to stream down my face. I was alone again and already missed them.

Maybe Tony could come back to the mine a couple of days early. His eyes sparkled as he gazed down the hall, waiting for me to appear. It had been almost a month since the surgery, and his antics had been driving the nurses insane.

I spent the next four hours being shown how to create a sterile environment, which meant putting on a new paper gown, rubber gloves and wearing a mask. Then came the hard part. They wheeled Tony in and the nurse had me remove the old bandage, then with tweezers pull all the gauze out of the incision. The piece I removed was eight feet long. The hole in the bottom of the foot was still enormous. I could look in and see tendons and ligaments.

I had no idea it was that bad. The nurse said that they could stuff 20 feet of gauze in the open wound right after the surgery. The incision needed to heal from the inside out and had healed a lot, but it would still be months before it completely healed.

When the foot was bandaged, I talked to the doctor. Tony was so excited to go, but after the shock of seeing his foot, I didn't think he should go back to the conditions at the mine. The doctor agreed with me, but Tony's only wish in life was to get back to his family. The doctor said, "Maybe you can talk him out of going."

The sadness in his face hit me like a rock when I told him I didn't think it was a good idea to leave the hospital. Tears rolled down his face. It was more than I could handle. He promised that he would stay on his crutches and out of the mud.

Tony double-timed down the sidewalk and to the pickup, crutches and all. The doctor made it clear that I was to bring him back immediately if any infection showed up.

That night we had a big reunion at the camp. I had picked up a couple of bottles of wine and two large pizzas. We laughed and joked half the night away and teased Tony about stepping on the nail; it was a hell of a way to get out of work! We didn't want to hear about being waited on in the hospital and getting sponge baths from the good-looking nurses.

Tony's appearance brought life and joy back to the camp. He was so excited; he couldn't quit hugging everyone. I sternly said, "No one will clean the foot but me. Any mud or dirt will cause the infection to return. We can't be careful enough."

Tony promised to stay off the foot and to let everyone wait on him. Knowing Tony, that was going to be the hardest part.

The pressure of the mining operation made it difficult for Alan to enjoy anything. But having his dad back brought a smile to his face, the first I'd seen in weeks. Later that night he told me that his dad's return was bittersweet. Tony was back at the mine with us, but the foot hadn't healed after over a month in the hospital. Neither of us expected Tony to be at the mine much longer. But for the time being, it was great to be together again.

XV
A BUSH PILOT NAMED WILD DICK

The next week I flew to Anchorage daily for supplies. After making the promise to be careful, I made it a habit to buy extra supplies and made sure there was plenty of oil on hand, giving me a little headway with the urgency of flights.

The one thing no one had control over was a breakdown of one of the big machines. If a part were broken on the big Caterpillar, the whole operation would be at a standstill, which forced me to fly no matter how terrible the conditions. These flights intensified the steady shake in my hands.

Operating the machinery and the daily flying hadn't given me much time to think about things to come. But over the last few weeks I noticed the weather in the mountains around the mine seemed to be deteriorating. The nights were getting colder, creating more fog and forcing me to retrace my flight path on almost every flight. The mountain winds grew in intensity, making the flights very uncomfortable.

Tightening the seat belts kept me from hitting my head on the ceiling. The worsening flight conditions made envisioning upcoming flights nerve-racking, and gave me a continuous ache in my stomach.

The Mafia camp had finished their short airstrip, but I hadn't seen any sign of a plane on it yet. They were bulldozing dirt through their sluice and finding some gold but not much, according to their foreman. He showed up in our camp with a couple of ounces of gold and was so excited he bounced off the walls.

We were glad for him. A lot of effort and money had gone in to get to that point. But we all knew that if that were all the gold they had found, the Mafia operation probably wouldn't be in business for long.

The thunderous noise of an airplane propeller brought me out of the cookshack. The plane blasted overhead at 50 feet, rattling the walls of the canyon as it passed. Either someone was in trouble or the pilot was crazy, the later turning out to be the case.

The airplane only missed the steep walls by feet as it maneuvered downstream and then disappeared out of sight at the next turn. We listened for a crash, but never heard anything. Evidently the pilot wanted to be in the canyon. I figured it must have been the Mafia's pilot showing up for work.

Their airstrip was around the corner and out of sight from our camp. The echoing of the airplane's engine confirmed that the plane was making an approach. No one in their right mind would land on that short runway unless he was getting paid a lot of money! It was only about 500-feet long and constructed out of the top of an old tailing pile. The downstream end of the strip was 50 feet up from the creek. I was glad it was he and not I.

The pilot's name, Wild Dick, was printed across the tail section of the plane. The plane was a brand-spanking new Cessna 180.

Dick was the craziest pilot I had ever been around. The first time we were on the ground at Brandt's together he acted like I wasn't even there. That was fine with me. From the very first time I'd heard the guy bragging while eating lunch, I had him pegged as an egotistical idiot.

We would pass in the air or on the ground and ignore each other. But that was soon to change. He didn't like the idea that I wouldn't give him any sort of respect.

To prove his importance, he would see how close he could get to my plane while in flight, then buzz our camp so low that we thought he was going to blow the roof off the cabin.

I had just departed Brandt's when the Cessna 180 appeared in the windscreen of my plane. In seconds he would have slammed into the plane! I pulled back on the control yoke and turned left. The 180 slid by under my left wing. Dick's arrogant smile appeared as he passed by. The maneuver to keep from colliding put me in an inverted attitude. I fought to get the plane back to a level flight and then scanned for the crazy bastard that just about put both of us in the ground. He was nowhere in sight.

That night I drove down to his camp to have a big discussion with him. He was as arrogant as ever with all the miners standing around to see what would happen. I immediately got my point across, "If you ever come near me again, I'll hunt you down and break your neck! You stay away from our camp and me! Do you understand?"

As Dick stepped back through all the miners, he laughed and said, "If you can't take the pressure, get the hell out!"

I'd made my point and turned to walk away and said, "You've been warned."

For a few days Dick didn't buzz our camp. Evidently he'd taken the message to heart.

We soon learned that Wild Dick would disappear completely with not even his camp knowing where he had gone. The foreman from the Mafia camp drove to our camp and asked me to look for him.

I didn't like Dick, but the people from his mining camp were really concerned about their pilot. Since he was supposed to be back at a certain time and hadn't shown, they thought he'd gone down in the mountains. Besides, the foreman was willing to pay for the flights during the search.

I scanned the mountains and valleys as I headed for Brandt's, not seeing anything that resembled a wrecked plane. Dick wasn't at Brandt's either, but maybe Eldon had seen him.

He said, "Dick was here a couple of hours ago and then departed to the north. He was so drunk he could hardly walk," pointing in the direction Dick had flown. Then he continued, "Wild Dick has been floating around here for years, picking up flying jobs with any miner who didn't know him. As far as I know, every job ended up with Dick getting fired. His drinking problem really cost him."

Eldon went on to explain that once Dick started drinking he didn't know how or when to stop. He would get so drunk he'd lose all sense of reality.

That was the way I found him at the Eureka Lodge. His plane was on the airstrip, in the middle of the runway, not tied down, which was a must in the windy conditions that prevailed in the area. He was sitting at the bar, seemingly without a care in the world.

He swung around and straightened up as I walked across the room toward him. "Your boss is worried sick about you and has hired me to find you. He doesn't know if you are dead or alive."

The last thing Dick wanted me to do was tell him anything. "I don't need anyone looking for me, especially a cowboy from Montana!"

The conversation wasn't going anywhere and was going to end up in a fight if I stayed, so I said, "I'll tell your boss where you're at and your condition."

As he slid off the stool he said, "I don't need any son-of-a bitch talking for me."

He staggered toward me and clenched his fist to take a swing. I sidestepped as he went stumbling by, hitting the floor with a thud. He was pulling himself up along the wall as I walked out the door, then crossed the parking lot to the plane. This guy had some major problems and I didn't want any part of him.

I departed Eureka to the north, making a slow left turn heading for our airstrip. As I looked out the side window I saw Dick stagger to his plane. The second he got in the propeller turned and the plane roared north off the airstrip. I lost sight of him as he turned behind me.

This drunken fool had something stupid in mind! Whatever it was, I was sure it would be focused on me, so I pushed the power up to the top of the green arc to optimize my speed. I wanted to be back on the ground before this crazed pilot, Wild Dick, could catch up with me.

As I made a straight-in approach, I strained looking for caribou on the strip. Ordinarily I'd circle, making sure the runway was clear, but now my sixth sense told me Dick was near. I relaxed slightly, rolled to a stop, thinking that being on the ground was safer.

Boy, was I wrong! The wheels of the Cessna 180 filled the windscreen, missing my plane by inches. I scrambled out from under the wing as he shot by the second time. He was so close I cringed back as his wheels missed again.

Instinct brought me back to the plane and my sawed-off shotgun. He was going to wreck our plane and kill himself! The gun was loaded with nine shot, not enough to bring him down, but definitely enough to dent some metal. I hurried from under the wing, scanning the immediate area for the plane. He was flying away and down the valley. I walked around the plane to see if he had done any damage and was amazed to see no dents. Furious, but thankful, I drove down to tell the foreman about his pilot. "If Wild Dick shows up, we're going to have a man-to-man talk."

I picked up groceries for the Mafia camp for the next few days. They still hadn't seen or heard from their pilot. Then, on a flight to

Anchorage I noticed Wild Dick's 180 sitting on their airstrip. I knew I would receive a message shortly saying they no longer needed my services. As much as I loved to fly for anyone who needed me, I didn't have time to be running around for them on a regular basis. I calmed down and decided not to confront Dick.

From that time on, whenever I was in the air, I would keep an eye out for that Cessna 180. He started buzzing our camp every chance he got, but stayed away from me. The guy would blast down the canyon, skimming the ground and walls. The sharp rattling noise the long propeller made would startle everyone out of a sound sleep.

His crazy pranks started to get on everyone's nerves, including Tim's, who wanted to go rip Wild Dick's head off.

Alan calmed him down, saying, "We need to concentrate on mining, not some dense pilot."

The flights to and from Anchorage had turned into misery. The weather fought me at every corner, making it impossible to enjoy any part of the flights. The tension grew, expanding in the pit of my stomach before each departure. I put this anxiety on myself; Alan knew the demands of flying. All he would say was to get back as soon and safely as possible.

I tried to tell myself to slow down, just a little, and enjoy what I was doing. Up to this point, my earlier near-death experiences had filled my thoughts with impending danger. But the mine was now fully operational. We had done everything that could be done to continue in the gold mining operation. It was time to clench our teeth and keep working, hoping for a miracle or a honey hole of gold.

The ice-permeated mountains south of the Glenn Highway reflected shades of aqua-blue light, changing to dark green as I soared by. Each valley had its own glacier flowing down to the deepest draws of the lower valleys. The sun penetrated the ice of each canyon, blasting its own distinct shade of bluish-green ice back to my eyes. Only Mother Nature could orchestrate such a brilliant light show.

As I flew over our airstrip looking for animals, I noticed a man standing near my tie-down spot. It was Wild Dick. I hadn't talked to him since his perilous buzz jobs, but this was as good a time as any. I had never met anyone as arrogant and pompous as this guy. It was strange to see him without his airplane, like a goldfish out of his bowl.

As I walked up to him he stepped back and said, "My airplane got run over." The statement brought me to a stop. He rambled on, "One of the stupid miners backed over my plane with the front-end loader and the tail's flattened!"

My anger waned completely. I got the complete story as we drove to the Mafia camp. He had tied his plane down as usual, at the north end of the airstrip. The big rubber-tired front-end loader had rolled completely over the tail section of his plane.

He was right, all I could say was, "Holy shit!" From one foot in front of the tail feathers and back everything was as flat as a smashed pop can.

Even after all the rude behavior, my heart went out to this crazy bush pilot. I had to bite my lip to keep from laughing out loud, thinking of the poetic justice of it all.

Dick went over to the camp, giving the boss time to tell me that all the guys in his camp hated the guy. He couldn't prove it or wouldn't try, but thought that the running over of the plane wasn't an accident. It was someone's way of getting rid of him.

Without his wings, Wild Dick's attitude made a complete turn-around. Now he needed help, so he treated me like I was his long-lost friend. He wanted to know if I would fly to Willow, which is northwest of Anchorage, and pick up replacement parts. Alan and I talked it over and decided that if he paid in advance we'd do the job. The next day I dropped No-Tail-Feathers Dick off at Willow. He would have all the parts there in three days.

Three loads later I had all the replacement pieces to the mine. He must have stolen parts off a bunch of wrecked planes, each piece having a different faded color.

Old Dick, my new best friend, was pretty resilient. Replacing a complete tail section was supposed to be a tedious and exacting job, but not for him. He taped, drilled and glued together all the pieces. It looked like a wreck waiting to happen. The horizontal stabilizer hung at a precarious angle. The trimwheel was non-operative and the tailwheel had been strapped to the bottom of the plane.

I said, "You're not really going to try and fly this?"

"You're damn right I am," barked Dick. The nice guy from last week was fading away and the old Dick was starting to resurface. He said, "Your straight and level flying was the most boring thing I have ever done. If I had to fly like that, I'd quit altogether!"

Any pilot with half a brain wouldn't fly the repaired plane. But, if I had to, I would have been as gentle as possible, trying not to stress the plane in any way. Not this guy! Wild Dick started the plane, roared to the other end of the runway and took off like a rocket, pulling the plane into a near-vertical climb and then pushing over to a near-vertical descent. This crazy maneuver ended with everyone running for the creek bank and belly-flopping for the ground! As he went by me, he flipped me off and smiled disdainfully.

This guy hadn't grasped a thing about humility or responsibility. Dick wasn't ever seen again. Everyone was glad to be rid of the obnoxious pilot. But I, for one, still kept an eye out for Wild Dick.

XVI
WHO'S STEALING THE GOLD?

Working with and mining gold was a great experience. I had read stories and heard that gold mining could turn a person into a crazed lunatic. Gold Fever was only a saying, we thought. But evidently someone had the fever.

At one time or another I flew for every miner on the 40-mile creek. Everyone started or ended up at Brandt's, so if any rumors were drifting around, that would be where I'd hear them. Almost all the miners said someone was stealing gold out of their sluice boxes.

Tracks left from an intruder would show up during the night. Stealing gold in Alaska was like stealing a horse in Montana, a hanging offense to a vigilante.

Our camp was operating 23 hours a day with one hour for maintenance on the machinery. With all that activity we had noticed a few tracks around the sluice, but had no real problems, yet. That would soon change.

A lone miner five miles downstream said he had a two-legged intruder, "The damn robber was sneaky and fast, but not as fast as old Betsy." I knew Betsy to be his doubled-barreled shotgun. He explained that he'd heard some noise down at his sluice box and finally found what was making the noise. A man was bent over his sluice, stealing gold.

It was two in the morning and he didn't get a good look at the robber. There was no evidence of blood, but he had scared the hell out of him! He asked me if I would keep an eye out for any suspicious-looking people around his camp. By this time, everyone looked suspicious.

Tony's foot was doing better. I disinfected the opening and applied new dressing daily. He had managed to stay off the foot and used his crutches most of the time. But I still had to remind him that it was a long way from healed and to stay off it.

I noticed he was making a lot of trips to the outhouse. Sheepishly he told me that he had taken a gout pill from one of the workers, thinking it would help heal his foot faster. He was paying for the discretion now. Over the next three days he made hundreds of trips to the outhouse. He had a case of the runs that wouldn't quit. The many trips produced a one-footed print with three-inch deep crutch marks on each side, the strangest looking tracks I'd ever seen. I even had to dig a replacement toilet; he'd managed to fill the old one up!

Our first outhouse.

A new meaning to the phrase 'wide open spaces'.

The modern day version.

The next evening the camp had just settled down for the night when a blood-curdling scream came from the cookshack. I rushed out with one leg in my pants and rifle in hand, thinking a bear was in camp. To my surprise Tony was sitting at the kitchen table with head bowed. Delores was cursing at him and kind of smacking him on the head to get her point across. Their bed was a mess.

From what I could tell, Tony was making a run for the toilet, but his timing had been off. Control not what it used to be, the pressure had won out over fortitude. He had sprayed most of the bed Delores was sleeping in. As I left, Tony looked at me and smiled, winking a laughing eye.

I picked up my usual supplies in Anchorage, departed Merrill Field and headed back to the mine. The winds buffeted the plane, making it almost impossible to fly. I lowered my elevation after leaving the highway and turned up Caribou Creek. I hoped being down by the ground would make the flight a little smoother, and was just about ready to turn up Alfred Creek when I saw movement on the gravel bar ahead. Closer examination revealed a person crossing the wide gravel creek bottom.

This was the area where the lone miner had his camp. Maybe this was the gold thief. I turned the plane toward my fleeing adversary. I could tell by the way he ran that his pack was heavy, swaying from side to side.

It wasn't my habit to bother people with the plane, but with this guy running for the trees, I thought I'd better get a good look. Only anyone up to no good would run from a plane. It was obvious from my flight path that he wasn't going to quite make the trees. I bore down straight as an arrow toward him. There would only be one chance to get a look at this guy, and I'd better make it close.

From 200 yards away I could see the man had a long gray beard, an old coat, and a wooden backpack with a rifle slung over his shoulder. He must have realized he wasn't going to make the safety of the trees, and in an instant he skidded to a stop, swung around, pulled the shotgun off his shoulder and aimed it directly at me. It was alarming to be looking down the working end of a shotgun! The end of both barrels looked as big as baseballs.

I glimpsed his face as I shot by and flinched back unconsciously, trying to duck the unseen bullet. Our eyes met for an instant; I saw the eyes of a serious man. I didn't know it then, but those eyes would haunt me in the future.

I thought I heard the report of the rifle, but never felt the impact of a bullet. I hunkered down in the seat and looked away as I put the plane in a steep bank to the right, putting distance between us. I scanned the gauges; everything seemed to be performing as usual. A thorough inspection of the aircraft revealed nothing. I concluded he must have been the gold thief.

Leo had found a hot spot on the creek a mile above the airstrip. It was on Indian ground, or ground that wasn't open for mining by white men. With the money situation getting bleaker as the days went by, Alan decided to make a two-day run to the off-limits ground.

We would move on a Friday afternoon and work the area until Sunday night, then get back to our camp before anyone flew over and spotted us on the forbidden ground. We thought no government agency would be working on the weekend. It was a risk we hoped would pay off.

Immediately we had complications. The boulders in the area were as big as our D8 Caterpillar, making a lot of work to move them out of the way, and slowing the operation to a crawl.

I made a fast flight to Anchorage to get a load of oil for the machinery. On the return I flew over our new mining location. The swamp buggy was gone, the Caterpillars sitting still. I figured the whole crew had decided to drive back to camp for lunch. The operation was unattended.

To prevent theft of gold from the sluice box, we would run about five inches of water down the sluice. This made it impossible for anyone to steal gold. The sparkling gold reflected brightly from the water, but its weight made it impossible to grab.

Our airstrip was right on the other side of the new location, so I let down as I passed over. As I looked down I thought I saw someone kneeling behind the big D8 CAT. If there was someone there I didn't want him to know I'd seen him. I continued straight ahead and landed, then drove down to our camp where everyone was accounted for. We all arrived at the same conclusion, gold thief.

Leo and I jumped into the swamp buggy and headed back to the mining operation. We slowed to a crawl as we rounded the last corner, giving us full view of the sluice and machines. Someone was working the D3 Cat and trying to shut off the water that fed the sluice box. The thief was so intent on his job that he didn't see us drive up behind him.

There was no surprise on his face at all when he finally noticed us. Evidently, he had done this before. He was calm as a cucumber, in no hurry, and stood up pulling his pistol out of the holster, holding it up to show us that he was armed. He then stepped to the ground and walked up the creek and away from our mining operation.

We didn't have any guns with us, which was probably a good thing. We just sat there, stunned by his blatant attitude and watched the kid walk away. It was the younger Idaho brother.

The last time we had seen him, he had rushed into the cookshack claiming a grizzly had attacked him. At the time we thought something was real strange about his story. After Leo and I talked about it, we came to the same conclusion. The one long wound the boy said the grizzly made was probably a mark left by old Betsy.

Leo and I headed for the camp to let Alan know what had happened. We decided that I would fly to Glennallen again and report the incident to the State Troopers. Glennallen is a little village that sits on a high plain in the Copper River drainage, 60 miles north of the mine.

I told the trooper what had happened for the second time. He replied, "Listen young fellows, I have three deputies to cover this whole area. If you or any miners catch your gold thief, I'll back you, whatever happens. What I'll do is deputize you."

I believed he was saying we would be justified if the thief was killed, and said, "We don't want anything to do with being a deputy. But if we have any more problems, I'll give you a call from Brandt's."

He wished me luck and we departed for the plane wondering what would happen next.

The miners were on their own. From that point on, everyone wore a pistol to work. It was hard to relax, especially during the night when someone could shoot the operator while he was running the machinery. The camp's atmosphere turned gray. Strange footprints were showing up in the mornings.

Grizzlies were one thing, but human trespassers were scary. An animal only wanted food, but there was no end to what a deranged Homo sapiens mind could do.

Every once in a while my sixth sense would kick in, and the hair on the back of my neck and arms would stand straight up. I knew eyes were watching me; the feeling would get so strong that I would back the CAT into the middle of the creek bottom, turn out the lights and wait for the feeling to subside. I figured that with the lights out, he couldn't see me any better than I could see him. I always felt like someone was looking at me from afar, watching and waiting for a chance to get to our sluice box.

Delores had me buy a ten-pound beef roast. She wasn't going to cook it for a couple of days, so I put it in the bottom of the freezer barrel. Not wanting to take a chance on the roast thawing, I removed all the wrapped caribou meat and put the beef roast on the bottom, then stacked the frozen caribou back on top.

When I went to get the roast two days later, it was gone. The thief had to have removed the caribou meat to get to the beef roast and then put the caribou packages back in the barrel. He must have watched me put it there!

I made a circling search around the camp, finding at least three sets of footprints that didn't belong to anyone in our camp. This unseen danger alarmed everyone, making us wonder if the thievery would turn to something more serious.

The next day the older Idaho boy walked into camp. He said his brother had been gone for a couple of weeks. The younger boy hadn't recovered from losing all his gold to the prostitutes and said he was going to get all the gold he needed. The older boy had spent a week looking for him, but after not finding him went back to mining. He thought maybe his brother had gone back to Idaho.

This boy strained to keep his composure; his brother could be dead as we spoke. I didn't want to build more anxiety, but to do the right thing I had to tell him. "Leo and I caught your brother trying to steal gold out of our sluice."

His facial expression showed his concern. "You're sure it was my brother?" he asked with an 'I don't believe you' look.

"It was your brother." I filled in the details of how we saw his brother and told him that all the miners were having theft problems.

I said, "I saw a stranger trying to hide from me in the lower part of the creek the other day. I assumed he was the one stealing gold down there." I hoped this information would ease his worry a little. But we all knew if his younger brother had enough courage to steal from us, he'd probably steal gold from everyone. I decided he'd heard enough bad news, so didn't tell him what the trooper told me to tell all the miners.

The tracks around camp didn't show up for a couple of days, then were spotted again. There were more than just one person's tracks. One set of tracks belonged to a man with a 15-inch foot. During the day the thieves would case our camp from a distance and then move in under the safety of darkness.

The older brother wandered up and down the creek for a couple of days. I suggested he tell all the miners what his brother was up to. Maybe this would help keep him alive. If a man didn't want to be found in this wilderness, it would be easy to keep hidden.

Two days later the older boy and I flew up and down the creek. The possibility of seeing his brother was almost zero, but by this time he was almost in a panic, worried sick for his brother's safety.

A man out alone in this dangerous country would have to be half crazy. The chance of a grizzly bear killing him wasn't his worst problem. In his new profession, a bullet carried more weight than a bear.

XVII
LIFE AND DEATH RESCUE

It was another of the continually cold nights, the frigid air seemed to bite harder at exposed skin as the fall season approached. This wind started its journey south from the North Pole, mixing with the cold temperatures as it penetrated our deep little canyon, turning the whole area into an icebox. Even though the date said it was still summer, this invisible enemy would turn faces bluish red.

Leo and I had worked the machines as hard as possible, hoping the extra effort would pay off at the next day's cleanout. The CAT strained, blowing black smoke as Leo slammed into a rock taller than it. A boulder that big usually had a lot of gold under it. The five-ton rock as big as a house sat firmly on the bedrock. The creek had been mined eight years earlier, but only by manual labor, not with heavy equipment. Rolling the giant pebble one-quarter turn would give us access to the gold beneath it.

For the first time I didn't have gravel to feed the sluice. While Leo dug out around the boulder I decided there was time to go to the cookshack and get hot coffee and just maybe a chocolate-chip cookie. It didn't matter what time of the night, Delores and Tony made sure we had coffee and cookies.

Tony started to get up as I entered the kitchen. "Go back to sleep, don't get up, I'm just getting coffee and heading back down to the sluice," I said.

He wanted to be so useful and never complained about the night intrusions. Both he and Delores didn't realize how important they were to the whole operation. I considered them the lifeblood that bound the camp together.

Leo was across a little draw and I couldn't get the swamp buggy any closer, so I turned the rig toward him, lighting the ground all the way to the CAT. The giant rock dwarfed the big machine sitting beside it. I blinked the lights, which meant come and get it. He waved and stood up while taking off his earmuffs.

As I poured a cup of warm coffee a movement behind the

machine grabbed my attention. My mind second-guessed my eyes as I stared into the darkness. Did I really see something move behind the machine? The image moved again. My body froze like ice, not wanting to believe what my eyes perceived, a grizzly, moving toward Leo. I vaulted out of the rig and yelled, "Grizzly, grizzly!" waving and pointing frantically. Leo showed no sign of seeing me. "Oh shit," I said to myself.

The light from the swamp buggy shone directly in his eyes. I jumped in front of the rig. Now the light was shining around me and toward Leo, enabling him to see me. As I waved and pointed behind him, he waved back, thinking I was waving him over. He stepped out from under the canopy and onto the tracks. My heart vaulted into my throat. I dashed to the front seat and grabbed my pistol, then jumped back in front of the light and waved the pistol like a madman. The bear stood 20 feet from Leo. It lifted its nose and sniffed the air; it hadn't detected him yet.

The silver-colored hump glistened as muscles flexed. Leo pulled his earplugs out. The bear moved toward the machine and into the darkness. I waved hysterically; the pistol meant something was really wrong.

Leo reached over and grabbed the lever that shut the engine off. After removing earplugs all noise is amplified. The bear was close, but how close? I had Leo's attention now his eyes were on me. Instantly he hit the ground running, digging up dirt as he sprinted the 50 feet to safety.

I believe he would have set some kind of a record. It looked like he floated across the uneven terrain.

When I quit laughing and Leo got his breath back, he said, "What the hell was that weird noise?"

Between breaths I said, "A grizzly just about bit you in the ass. It was right behind the CAT!"

His eyes were still the size of quarters as he said, "As soon as the noise from the CAT stopped, a heavy breathing and low growl scared the hell out of me!"

Leo's survival instinct brought him to me. "How did you get across that ditch so effortlessly?"

We both laughed as he said, "What ditch?"

The big bear wandered out in front of the machine. His back was as tall as the four-foot blade. He looked pretty harmless from our vantage point. I hoped this bear never came into camp, his size and hair-raising look would put the fear in everyone. The clear plastic around the cookshack and thin plywood walls of the bunkhouse would provide zero protection.

I admitted to Leo, "When that bear was moving toward you, it was one of the most helpless feelings I've ever had."

Not wanting to take a chance that it was hiding behind a bush and ready to pounce, we drove the D3 Caterpillar to his CAT. Our heads swiveled from side to side the rest of the night. We both had images of a savage beast climbing over the metal tracks. My shotgun rested across my lap and I didn't notice the cold wind for the rest of the night.

Daylight broke with clear skies, but it would be hours before the heat of the sun entered the narrow canyon. Alan and Tim arrived and started dismantling the sluice for the cleanout. Spirits around camp were always better on cleanout day with the fruits of our labor producing shiny, yellow gold. Seeing a unique-shaped nugget for the first time was always exciting. These illusive rocks lay in the ground for millions of years, to be seen for the first time by us.

Ham and eggs were on the plates when we entered the cookshack. Tony's eyes glistened with anticipation as I conveyed the night's adventure. After a pot of coffee, both of us started to feel warm again. I told Tony, "Make sure you keep that shotgun close, never be without it." He had grown up in Montana and knew about grizzlies.

Tony would wake us up in two hours, not wanting to miss the cleanout. Besides, it wouldn't be right not to help put the sluice back together. The more hands the faster the job got done. Then it was back to pushing gravel. The process played over and over every three days.

We stepped out of the cookshack and saw the Mafia's swamp buggy coming toward us. Any sound in the canyon created an echo that rebounded off the steep walls and made it impossible for anyone to get by our camp. I walked down to the creek and toward the vehicle. Whoever it was, he was in a hurry. He drove straight toward me, jumping out of his rig and talking as he approached.

The guy was in a panic, taking deep breaths, saying, "One of the workers was riding on the ladder of the front-end loader. While crossing the creek, he fell off and got run over. Can you fly him to town?"

I couldn't answer fast enough. "Get him up to the plane!"

"He's broken up so bad that we don't dare move him. Fly down to our strip."

The thought of landing on that airstrip was like getting an electric shock. A shudder ran through my body.

The man continued, "The tires ran completely over him, crushing his legs and hips. He's barely alive and needs to get to the hospital immediately!"

The short Mafia airstrip.
Life and death rescue of a near death miner.

I wanted to say, "Get a helicopter," but knew that would take hours. Their first thought went to the 206 because its cabin was big enough to accommodate the injured man. They were right. The big cabin would make it possible to put him in without bending him. I needed to talk to Alan.

Alan's reply was, "It's your decision. You were up all night and need to rest. Spend the night in town. I won't expect you back until tomorrow evening. Be careful."

I wasn't sure that was what I wanted him to say, but for the first time Alan wanted me to have some free time in town. It was nice of him to say so.

Alan trusted my decision, knowing that any accident with the plane would be devastating for the operation. Up till now I had pushed the envelope to the limit and had survived by the skin of my teeth. Many pilots have died doing exactly the same type flying.

The man departed with the knowledge I'd be down to his airstrip shortly. My mind reeled as I drove up to the plane. Could I handle it? Could the plane handle the short strip and then depart with a load? Over the last two months my knowledge of short, muddy airstrips had grown. I could remember every landing and takeoff, the difficulties and also the mistakes. All this stored wisdom flashed in my mind's eye, replaying like a video. I knew exactly what I needed to do. Could I blend all this knowledge into one thought?

Five-hundred feet long, plenty of length. I'd landed on a lot of short, muddy strips and stopped easily within 500 feet. The problem was, I always had more runway to use in case I didn't get stopped. This airstrip left no room for error. As I flew over the little strip, I asked God for help. "Please, dear God, help me to remember, bring all wisdom I've gained to the front, give me strength and perfection to do this right."

Wild Dick had used the airstrip for a couple of weeks. I knew he'd complained about the strip's poor condition, but managed to get in and out without wrecking. That scenario played in my head. But the difference between his plane and mine was substantial.

The Cessna 180 was smaller and more nimble. It also had a tailwheel that made the plane more maneuverable for rough, rocky conditions. The Cessna 206 acted more like a one-ton truck; it could haul a lot heavier load, but didn't have near the maneuverability. I stared down at the hair-raising airstrip, hoping the modified wings would give me the edge needed to get the injured man to town.

I made a slow pass down the creek, checking out the airstrip. The uphill end of the airstrip was level with the creek bottom. The lower end stopped 30 feet up from the creek and wasn't much wider than the plane's wheels. The miners had flattened out the top of a tailing pile and called it an airstrip. A closer look at the airstrip confirmed what I already knew; it was the worst excuse for an airstrip I'd ever seen.

The miners from the camp were all gathered at the end of the runway. For an instant, I thought about flying to Brandt's and calling for a helicopter. That thought left as fast as it arrived. The injured man would probably die if he didn't get medical attention soon. I knew I could do this job.

I flew downstream a couple of miles, then made a slow descending turn that ended with the plane being lined up with the runway. I wanted to purposely be a little low, which would help produce the slower airspeed needed to get the plane stopped. As the distance to the end of the airstrip closed, I altered the power continuously.

Looking up to the end of the runway confused my senses. My soul said, "Blast the power on. Save yourself while you still can." My mind repeated, "Adjust power, keep lined up, we can do this."

The closure rate speeded up. All of the sudden I felt too low. My touchdown spot disappeared over the hill. It was now or never. The Continental engine roared to life and maximum power ballooned the plane. The stall horn blared as the surface of the runway reappeared. I'd climbed just enough, missing the rocky tip of the gravel pile by a couple of feet.

The edge of the hill disappeared under the nose of the plane. Without thought I pulled the power off, causing an immediate drop. The plane slammed onto the runway. Continuous jockeying of the rudders and brakes kept me somewhat in the middle. The edge of the runway was only a few feet from the wheels and the creek bottom 30 feet down.

Rocks flew off the wheels as they grabbed for solid ground. The plane finally slowed to a crawl and I took a much-needed breath. The realization that I had landed put a slight smile on my face, even though my senses were at maximum, and an adrenalin-induced shake grabbed me like a vise. I told myself to relax; I still had to get off this airstrip.

I taxied to the end of the runway and shut off the engine. The injured man's fellow workers swarmed the plane. We turned the plane around by hand and lined it up for takeoff. We slowly eased the near-death miner into the plane and slid him up beside my seat. I had removed the copilot seat, which left the cabin empty except for my seat. One man would go along to take care of the injured man. He sat with his back to my seat.

I wanted to walk the length of the runway, but after looking at the injured man decided against it, his glazed eyes and skin coloring giving me new urgency. I started the engine and gawked down the narrow airstrip, focusing on the job of getting all three of us into the air.

I knew that once the power was added I would be totally committed. Trying to abort would mean sliding over the end and down to the creek in a twisted heap. This was going to be a scary and dangerous takeoff.

I pushed the throttle lever to the stop and applied brakes to keep from moving, then adjusted the mixture to get the perfect gas-to-air mixture, producing maximum power. Then I frictioned the throttle lock, knowing I wouldn't pull the power off no matter what. The engine roared at full power, the plane vibrated and fought the brakes that were holding it back. All the instruments showed everything in the green. It was time to go.

I relaxed the pressure on the brakes and the plane surged forward. The concentration and workload to stay centered on the runway made it impossible to look at any gauges. The wings were starting to gain lift, but would there be enough to fly before I ran out of runway?

Keep the wings flat, I told myself, not wanting to produce unwanted drag. With about 200 feet of runway left I applied twenty degrees of flaps. As the flaps and ailerons lowered, the weight of the plane moved from the wheels to the wings. It was now or never; I applied backpressure on the control yoke. The stall horn shrieked defiantly. As the wheels rolled over the edge, the plane settled toward the creek below. More backpressure stopped the descent. The airspeed shot upward, producing more needed lift to climb out of the creek bottom.

We made it! The controls responded sluggishly, but the plane was flying. I relaxed slightly as we headed down Caribou Creek. It had to have been more than luck to survive that takeoff and landing.

I looked at my sick passenger. The expression on his face told me he was in a lot of pain. Unseen bumps rocked the plane, producing painful moans. At Palmer I called Anchorage Approach Control and conveyed my medical emergency. The radio stayed busy as they moved other planes in the area out of the way. Merrill Tower cleared me straight to Runway 26.

The ambulance waited beside the tower and in a matter of minutes my injured passenger was on his way to Providence Hospital.

After tying the plane down in our usual rented spot I staggered to the pickup, feeling like I'd just gone five rounds with a grizzly bear. The tension of the last couple of hours and lack of sleep put me in a coma-like state. As I lay on the seat of the pickup, I thought about the day's events, wondering about my decision to fly the injured miner. I finally decided it was right. We'd survived.

I thought for a few minutes about going back to the mine. But Alan had offered, and I would take him up on the offer. For now I was going to get some sleep on the seat of the pickup.

The pressure drained from my body as sleep hit like a rock. No one could see my smile fade as sleep turned my world quiet.

A loud banging brought me out of my coma. The sun was shining in and had warmed me way past comfortable. Now, as I sat up to see what was making the noise, I felt nauseated from the deep sleep and being overheated. The guy who tied his plane down next to mine looked in the window with a sheepish smile.

I stepped out and said, "Hello, what do you need?" I had talked to him earlier. His name was Barry, a hunting guide, who hunted at a place called Jacksonville.

As I walked around his airplane he explained that moose-hunting season had opened a few days earlier, which seemed early to me. In Montana hunting season opened in late October.

He wanted to know if I was interested in flying to his camp to fly out a load of moose meat back to town. "I'll give you a quarter of moose and buy your gas for the one load."

I thought about it for a few minutes. An hour's flying for a couple of hundred pounds of meat and fuel. I didn't need to be back to Anchorage till the next day, so why not? I agreed to the terms. He backed up his pickup to the plane and loaded the 206 to the ceiling with supplies.

He hadn't mentioned hauling supplies to the camp, but it didn't matter. I was going anyway.

I departed Merrill Field behind the Cub, and followed him to his base camp. He paid no attention to any standard departure, which was important around the Anchorage area. From his heading I could see he was going to fly through the control zone at the International Airport, illegal without permission. I radioed departure and told them a flight of two would be passing through. They had no conflicting traffic and cleared us. I didn't know what I'd do if they had refused the entry. Barry wasn't on the frequency that had been agreed upon.

The half-hour flight turned into an hour. We crawled through the air at a snail's pace; with Barry never answering my radio calls, forcing me to match his slow speed.

The area northwest of Anchorage was covered with stunted black spruce. Willow marshes surround open meadows filled with moose standing belly deep. The big bulls' horns reflected sunlight from miles away. It was a completely different world than the mountains where our mine was located. Creeks and rivers fanned in every direction. An occasional cabin lined rivers and lakes.

We passed over the Yenta River, the Yenlow Hills and then started a descent toward a narrow canyon. Looking ahead I could see four buildings, and leading to the buildings was a giant airstrip, which looked to be a mile long. I landed behind the Cub and taxied to the buildings. As I stepped out, four guys walked up to the planes and introduced themselves.

They were all teachers from Anchorage, and quite upset with Barry. From what I could tell he had flown them in to hunt. Two of the teachers had shot a couple of giant bulls. When they told Barry about the moose, he had told them that he would go to town to get some help. That was two days ago.

My mind started to wonder, *Was I the help?*

The teachers had tried to retrieve one of the bulls and a grizzly had run them off. They were too scared to see if the grizzly was still there. That was about when we landed.

The area surrounding his camp looked like a great place to hunt. Rolling hills with short yellow bunch-grass and willow thickets made a perfect spot for moose. As I walked down the airstrip, the guide and hunters argued.

Not wanting to be a part of the argument, I explored the camp. From all the old rusted equipment lying around, I figured Jacksonville to be an old gold mine. All the grizzly tracks on the airstrip caught my attention immediately. There were so many that it was hard not to step on them as I walked.

The hunters had gone back into the building, so I walked up to Barry. He said, "I'm going to fly down and see if a bear has bothered the moose kill, would you like to go?"

After watching this guy fly from Anchorage, I wasn't sure I

trusted him. But his Cub had backseat controls, so I could fly it, if need be. We departed and leveled off at 200 feet.

He explained, "My son and I have cut trails from swamp to swamp. Then the hunters drive three-wheelers to each swamp until they spot a moose. It works great except for one problem, grizzly bears. They seem to find almost every kill, especially if the meat is left there overnight."

If a bear found a hunter's moose it usually would pee all over it, eat as much as it could and then hang around until all the meat was consumed. The grizzlies would also use these trails. Barry spotted the gut pile from the moose that the bear had taken. We circled looking for the bear.

Over a little hill and about a hundred feet from the kill spot lay the bear. Under him was a mound of dirt full of the remains of the moose. The moose was his to keep; no person in his right mind would try to take that moose away from him.

The second moose was right where the hunter said it was going to be. We couldn't see any sign of any bears, then headed back to the airstrip. The light of day faded and the darkening skyline created eerie reflections. We all sat in the main shack and discussed the plans for early the next morning.

I volunteered to take Barry's 16 year-old son and quarter the moose before Barry and the hunter showed up on a big track machine. When they arrived the meat would be ready to haul back to camp.

I slept in a little log cabin down by the airstrip. The one-foot square windows made sense to me, especially when I saw all the fresh bear tracks around the little building. That night I slept with my shotgun as a bed partner.

The next morning brought fog as thick as pea soup. The boy and I left on the three-wheelers. The kid knew exactly where we were going. We eased up and down hill after hill, crossing three swamps, which in Montana would be called meadows. Each one had two or three inches of water that seeped up as we rolled across them. As we got closer to the moose kill in the meadow I started to get more concerned. I realized that with the fog we wouldn't be able to see the dead moose until we walked up real close. We stopped across the meadow from the moose and shut off the machines.

There was absolutely no noise. Everything was deadly quiet. My sixth sense kicked in, the hair on my body stood up. Something was watching us, but I couldn't see what. The fog drifted between the moose and us.

I whispered, "I think I see the moose," and pointed toward a faded black object that was low to the ground. I strained to focus on the object, then caught a movement in the mist. The fog cleared, turning the black object into a very big grizzly.

The bear growled, shook his head in disapproval, then charged three jumps toward us before returning to the moose. He paced back and forth, bouncing on his hind legs as he moved. Then he stood up on his hind legs to get a better look. The black beady eyes strained to see the intruders.

He went back to all fours, turned and bit the moose right above the shoulder. He stood back up with the thousand-pound moose hanging like it was a deer. The hunter had told us the moose's horns were 60-inches wide. This was a big animal and the bear had half of it in the air. He then dropped the moose and started charging at us.

I had a three-inch magnum shotgun in my hands with slugs in the chamber. Enough firepower to handle this animal, but the last thing I wanted to do was shoot a bear. The outfitter's son had a 30/06 rifle.

As the bear loomed closer I could see that he had very little hair. My eyes went to tunnel vision, the world around me becoming non-existent. All focus and attention zeroed in on the bear. It grew larger as the fog cleared and he closed the distance. One hundred feet in front of us was a small draw that the bear would have to cross.

I whispered, "When he comes up our side of the draw, start firing." A wounded grizzly could cover a lot of ground and would be extra mad, so it would be a big mistake to let the bear get too close. I took aim with the shotgun. The bear would be on our side in seconds.

He slammed on the brakes right before the draw, sliding to a stop, then stood up on his hind legs, popping his jaw and shaking his head in defiance. The massive bear looked down at us, giving me a good look at his enormous size. I'd seen a lot of bears, but none even close to his size or so ugly.

I whispered, "Hey bear, hey bear!" All this time I was slowly backing up. I didn't know exactly where the boy was but figured he was right beside me. The bear turned and lumbered back to the moose. This gave us the opportunity to escape. I turned around to tell the boy to run for the three-wheelers, but he was nowhere to be seen. I hardly remembered touching the ground as I retreated. Now I knew how Leo had felt a few days earlier.

The boy thought the bear had killed me. The outfitter ran out in great relief as I rolled to a stop in front of the cabin. The kid was still so scared he could hardly talk. I sure couldn't blame him, still shaking a little myself. We loaded into the big track machine and headed for the moose. It was slow and noisy, but more than a match for the bear.

When we arrived the bear was gone. He had buried most of the meat and urinated on top of the pile. We tied a rope around the antlers and pulled the moose to the surface. There wasn't much left to salvage, but we took what we could and headed back to the cabins. It was noon and I needed to get back to town soon. Barry said the meat that I would haul to town was in a shed out in back, pointing to a building I hadn't looked in.

When I opened the door I was shocked. Hanging from the rafters were dozens of quarters of moose meat. I didn't even ask where all the meat came from. Hunting season had only been open for a couple of days. We loaded the plane with moose parts.

Two of the teachers wanted to go to town with me and insisted to Barry they were going. After a little arguing Barry said it was all right. I listened to the heated conversation and wondered why they needed his permission. The long runway made the heavy plane take off easily.

I was glad to be away from that guy. I didn't know what was going on with all the moose meat, but knew it couldn't be legal.

The teacher sitting beside me started digging around in his pocket then looked at me and pulled out a badge. A quick glance produced the words, Federal Marshal.

Immediately I wondered if I had done something illegal.

The marshal explained that government had been watching Barry for years. I had dropped into the middle of a sting operation. He went on to explain that this guy had been guiding big game hunts illegally for years and had always stayed one step ahead of the law. They had been in his camp undercover as teachers and now knew exactly what he was doing. He was killing moose, hanging them in the shed and killing grizzlies as they came to investigate. Then he sold grizzly parts to the black market and probably also moose meat.

They had a great fear of the guy and now, thanks to me, had managed to get out of the camp alive. The stories went on all the way to Anchorage. I landed at Merrill and taxied to my tie-down spot, wondering if I was going to be able to keep my moose quarter.

It wasn't long until an Alaskan State Trooper's pickup pulled up to the plane. They loaded the meat into the pickup, leaving one hindquarter.

The Marshal said, "We might need you to testify, but I doubt it." I gave him all the information that he needed to find me. We shook hands and they drove away.

The Mush Inn had a freezer to put the moose meat in. Then I bought a shower and drove over to Providence Hospital to see how the injured miner was doing. He was in intensive care, but was awake. I was shocked to see a bodycast from toe to neck. The nurse said he would spend months in the cast and wasn't sure if he'd walk again. He said he was grateful to me for bringing him to town, then closed his eyes. I walked out of the hospital with tears in my eyes.

As I drove to the plane I thought about the over-exaggerated stories Barry had graced us with all evening. The whole time I was around the guy I had a bad feeling about him. It sounded like he was going to get what he had coming.

Life at our mine would take a big change in the next few days. Just maybe we might be back for another year.

XVIII
PARTNERS WITH GANGSTERS

The sound of machinery echoed up the canyon. Leo and I stepped out of the cookshack to see what was making all the noise. A caravan of machines crawling like worms was headed up the creek and stopped just below our cabins.

The machines belonged to the Mafia miners. Tom said that the boss had pulled the plug and was giving up on finding any more gold. He had spent a lot of money and didn't have much to show for all the effort.

We'd all figured they wouldn't be here very long anyway. Our equipment was completely worn out; his new equipment was exactly what we needed. If we could strike a deal with the boss, just maybe we might have a successful season after all.

"Do you think the boss would be willing to lease the equipment to us?" Alan asked.

The foreman replied, "He might, but all I want to do is get out of this hellhole. This whole operation has been a losing battle from the start and now the boss wants my head."

Alan continued, "Mom and Dad have cake and coffee in the cookshack. Stay here until we have time to talk to your boss. If we can strike a deal, maybe you won't be in trouble."

He smiled at us and said, "Good luck."

Alan and I flew to Brandt's. After a couple of tries the boss answered the phone. Alan said, "We see that you're pulling out of the gold mine. How would you like to lease your equipment to us for the rest of the season?" Alan talked fast. "You have already spent the money to get the equipment to the mine. It won't cost you anything to leave it with us, and with your new machines maybe we can find a lot of gold."

Alan gazed at me with a blank look on his face as the boss talked. Then he said, "That sounds good, that's right. Whatever you want to do, OK? We've got a deal. Goodbye." He hung up the phone and sat down.

I asked, "What did he say? What did he say?"

"You won't believe this. We can have the machines for the rest of the summer, under the following terms. We pay for all the maintenance, oil and diesel, and then split any gold that is left. That's it. He's going to send two guys here to watch over his interests. Can you believe it? We have new equipment!"

Both Alan and I were in a daze as we flew back to the mine. The new equipment would give us a better outlook for the rest of the season. We felt like we'd done everything that was possible with our old machinery. Now, who knew what lay ahead?

Tom and the guys that worked for him were more than glad to fly out of the gold mine. I shook hands with Tom and said goodbye.

He looked at me and said, "I have something to tell you about the Idaho boy." He frowned at me for a second and then turned and walked away and said, "Just forget it."

"What's up?" I asked.

He looked at me for a second, shook his head, then walked around the corner and out of sight. I followed him and watched as he got into his pickup truck. As he drove by he shook his head again, then drove onto the highway and disappeared. I stepped into the café wondering what he was going to tell me. By his actions I could tell something was wrong.

Dan, one of the pilots I'd buzzed at the party at Gunsight Mountain Lodge, was sitting across the room. He swung around and glared as I walked across to the Post Office area. My patience with him was at the breaking point. He seemed to be getting bolder and bolder, and a confrontation was inevitable. We were going to have a heart-to-heart talk real soon.

I had one message, which said, "Sending two guys to watch over my interests, arriving August 3, 1:30 p.m., Alaska Airlines, Flight 2314. Their names are Jim and BC."

I looked at my watch. I had four hours before I needed to be in Anchorage to pick them up.

All the new equipment was blowing smoke as I passed over for the landing. Everyone was acting like kids in a toy store. The new D8K pushed anything that was put in front of it. I pleaded and begged, but couldn't persuade Leo or Tim to let me try out the new machine. Alan drove the 955 front-end loader and cleaned out below the box, it was the perfect machine for the job. The camp had new life, with everyone wearing a big smile. No matter how hard I talked, no one would give me a turn on any of the machines, so I walked to the cookshack to clean Tony's foot.

The hole had healed to the point where I could only get about three feet of gauze back into the incision. I cleaned the foot daily and reminded Tony to use his crutches. Reminding him of hospital life was usually enough to keep him off the foot.

Delores and Tony decided they wanted to go to Glennallen for supplies. I would drop them off at Brandt's and then go to Anchorage to pick up our new Mafia guests. Leo had enough of working at the mine and would fly with me to town. He'd never liked the fact that even though he was older than Alan, Alan was the boss. I dropped Leo off and drove over to the International Airport to wait for my mysterious passengers.

I sat on a bench and held a sign that said, "BC and Jim". A tall, bald guy in a black suit was headed in my direction. He stood out like out like a fox in a henhouse. The person with him had a cape over his suit. I thought to myself, what could these two guys want in Alaska? As I watched them I noticed their eyes reading my sign. Then they looked at me and turned in my direction. I thought, *'it couldn't be!'*

"Are you the Montana miner?" asked the big guy.

"That's me," I replied as I stood up to shake their hands. Neither gave any indication they had seen my hand. The tall man said, "I'm BC and this is Jim. We're here for one thing, to watch out for our boss's interests." They turned and walked before I had time to say anything. I already disliked them.

We squeezed into Alan's Ford Courier pickup. The three of us fit like sardines in a can.

All they had was one small bag each. Both of them stared straight ahead, not saying a word. I thought I'd better warn them about the weather conditions at the mine, saying, "It rains all the time and we've had a few snow showers. I recommend we stop at a store and get some winter clothes for you guys."

Jim, the smaller of the two, replied in an arrogant tone, "If we need your advice, we'll ask for it."

That was all I needed to hear. We'd soon find out how tough these boys were. We departed Anchorage and headed for the mine. The wind had picked up, making for a roller-coaster ride. The clouds lowered, and the wind and rain pummeled the plane as we turned the corner leaving the highway at the glacier. A big gust slammed the plane, causing the right wing to drop violently. BC yelled, "Are we going to die?"

I laughed as I looked at the tough guys, both looking like spiders holding on for dear life. I replied, "This is the good part, wait until we get closer to the mine."

It was a little rougher than usual, but pretty much the norm when weather systems rolled in from the coast. I made sure my recovery to level flight from the wind gusts was a little slower than usual. The cabin of the plane was dead quiet as we rocked and bounced our way up Alfred Creek.

By the looks on their faces, I was sure my passengers thought their lives were ending soon. With each gust of wind the plane would jump and jerk, generating moans from my passengers. I yelled, "Don't throw up in the plane! There are plastic sacks behind the seats, use them."

As I dove over the hill and floated toward the end of the runway, both guys screamed out in fear. I'd forgotten to tell them that down through the fog and rain laid our destination. They sat in shock as I taxied back to the tie-down spot. Rain pummeled the plane as I stepped out and pulled on my hip boots and raincoat.

BC cried in disbelief, his eyes wide with shock, "This can't be real!"

As they stared I said, "I tried to tell you about the weather. See the swamp buggy over there? You have to get in it, the mine is two miles downstream."

I had to smile as they tippy-toed to the swamp buggy and awkwardly pulled themselves up into the cab. Both guys stared at their penny loafers, now covered with mud and slime.

The not-so-tough guys shivered as we rolled down the creek and hung on for dear life as we crawled up and down the steep embankments. Even though they had answered me abusively in town, I felt I now had their attention and asked, "Have you guys ever been to a gold mine before?"

With shaking teeth BC replied, "I've never even seen snow before." I wondered where they had come from.

Jim leaned forward from the backseat and said, "I hate bears, there aren't any bears around here, are there?"

I laughed. *Boy, was this going to be fun!*

Alan was waiting for the Mafia boys. Both of them shivered their way into the cookshack and leaned over the woodstove. I introduced them and told Alan I was headed for Brandt's to pick up his mom and dad. As we walked to the swamp buggy, I relayed the story of the last two hours. Both of us laughed out loud at our new tough guys.

Alan exclaimed as I started to drive away, "You can't believe how much the new equipment has upped our production!"

Tony and Delores hadn't arrived yet, but that was all right with me. A shower and hamburger would make the wait more comfortable. I had just sat down when I heard Dan and Blacky's familiar voices. It was hard to ignore them as they got increasingly louder. Dan had pushed me to my limit a couple of hours earlier. They had been rude and obnoxious since the day I arrived.

Almost every time I showed up at Brandt's they would be seated at the bar whispering as they glanced in my direction. A couple of weeks earlier I'd heard that Dan had yelled at a Japanese tourist that had walked too close to his plane. I was waiting for the right opportunity to let this guy know what I really thought of him, and this looked like it might be the time. I sure would have liked to have Leo around, just to even the odds, but it wasn't absolutely necessary.

As the booze flowed they got louder. Even though I was sitting with my back to the pilots, I was starting to understand the remarks, but didn't make any indication that I had heard anything.

With no reaction from me they got tougher and more assertive. There had been a few other people in the bar, but now they had retreated to the back room, not wanting any part of the inevitable.

The sliding of a barstool brought me to my feet. I turned around and saw that Dan had cut the distance to me in half. He staggered as he came. His eyes squinted with hate and bore a hole through me. He was out for blood. Just the right amount of booze and Blacky by his side had built his courage past caution.

To his surprise, his enemy was coming at him. His swagger turned to stagger as he assessed the situation. This wasn't supposed to happen. The booze-impaired mind couldn't stop his forward progress. Dan clenched his fist as he started to pull his arm back and yelled, "You've had this coming for a long time. I'm going to...."

Dan slammed onto the top of a table and bounced to the floor. The table and chairs went crashing in all directions. The whites of his eyes indicated that he was in another world for the time being. My fist had caught him just above his eyes.

I turned my attention to Blacky. He stood up and took two steps toward me.

My ten years of holding onto a chainsaw had produced a legendary vise-like grip. As Blacky's hand came forward I grabbed the backside of it. He pulled back, and I squeezed with all my strength. A pop and something giving under my grip made me release. Blacky went to his knees in pain and held his injured hand with the other. The fight was over. I must have broken a bone.

I walked back to my table and sat down, making sure I could keep an eye on the boys. The fight was gone from both of them. Blacky helped Dan up and they staggered out the door, never once looking back.

Tony and Delores showed up and we loaded the plane. Tony wished he had been there to see the action and made me tell the story a couple of times. They'd had a good time in Glennallen. I told them about the two Mafia guys showing up.

I wasn't sure what the fight with Dan and Blacky meant. But there was one thing for sure. They both knew that I wasn't taking any more of their crap.

XIX
HUNTERS FROM THE OUTSIDE

The Mafia boys moved right into the bunkhouse like they owned it. They spent almost all their time inside one of the buildings because of their fear of grizzlies, and never walked down to the sluice box. As darkness closed in they would stick closer to the bunkhouse, thinking a bear was hiding behind every bush waiting to pounce on the first victim that walked by. The tough boys thought that once it got dark, the only safe place was in the bunkhouse. The only time one of them would go to the bathroom at night was when they could talk one of us Montana boys with a rifle into going along.

Actually, all of us took a pistol or rifle with us after dark. The bears that wandered around camp kept everyone on high alert. Their tracks were left in the mud, but the ever-increasing signs left by two-legged intruders were what scared us the most. Someone was out there watching us; I could feel it almost all the time now. But up till now, the only sign left behind was footprints.

Tony had managed to find the Mafia boys some warmer clothes, although the pants on seven-foot BC ended right below the knees.

While cleaning gold they would stand over our shoulders, not helping, just watching our every move. When the gold was cleaned, sized and weighed they would take their boss's share and head to the bunkhouse.

I had talked Tim into letting me take his shift so I could run the new D8K. It was such a joy, all the levers and gauges worked, and the power was overwhelming. The big 12 x 5-foot blade would have gravel rolling over the top of it as I pushed the monstrous pile of gravel to the sluice box. This was exactly what we had needed from the start.

It had been another long and cold night. The chilling message was in the air that winter was getting closer, which gave us an urgency to work every hour. It wouldn't be long before the creek started freezing, indicating the beginning of the end of the mining season.

The surrounding mountains started to take shape as the dark night let go of its grip to the morning light. The new visibility made the air feel a little warmer and meant our shift was over. Alan and I drove up to the cookshack where Tim was waiting for us.

As I walked in I said, "That new CAT has three times the power as the old one. I'll bet we pushed a thousand yards through the box." I knew hearing that would push Tim as hard as he could go on his next shift.

"Let's go to work," said Tim, anxious to prove that no one could dig and push as much overburden as he could.

As Alan and Tim went out the door Tim said, "One of the hands from the California camp stopped by and said his boss wanted you to pick him up at Brandt's around lunchtime."

I had flown for this miner before. He had come up from California to make his fortune and evidently was doing all right. I told Alan I'd make the appointment as they loaded into the swamp buggy and headed back down to the sluice box.

This was my opportunity to get a shower and hot breakfast at Brandt's. I departed a couple of hours early, anticipating ham, eggs and hashbrowns.

The steamy water beat on my body until parts started looking like prunes. Then I savored every bite of the fabulous breakfast. Delores was a great cook, but the café-cooked breakfast was hard to beat.

With a full belly and clean clothes I sat relaxed, my eyes drooping almost closed. My body was telling me that I hadn't slept all night. Half-dazed I got up and walked down to the plane, hoping to get a little sleep before my passenger arrived. I opened the two big doors on the cabin of the plane and unrolled a sleeping bag that I kept there just for times like this. As I lay down on the floor of the plane, darkness hit me like a club.

Way off in the distance I could hear the sound of voices. The sounds slowly grew in intensity and brought me out of my zombie state. I slowly opened my eyes, hoping it was just a bad dream. It wasn't, two guys slowly came into focus as they walked toward me.

My first thought was, *what the hell are they wearing?* Bright hunter orange, head to toe. It almost hurt my eyes. Did they look out of place! But they definitely had a purpose in mind as they made a beeline toward me.

I lay in the back of the plane, hoping they'd go away, but had no choice but to listen to these two talk energetically about their hunting trip.

They asked, "Do you know Bob Pearce, the famous guide and pilot we've hired to take us caribou hunting?"

I stared at both guys, not knowing what to say.

"Are you Bob?" they asked.

Still a little bewildered, I said, "I'm sure not your guy, but I've heard of him." I didn't want to tell them that I had seen their pilot/guide in the bar. Many times I'd seen him so drunk he could hardly walk.

They were ready to go hunting. One guy said, "We've been saving for this hunting trip for years. This is our life-long dream." He explained that they had made arrangements to meet their guide at Brandt's Texaco. It had taken them 60 hours to drive from California to Brandt's. Their pilot would fly them to a hunting camp and pick them up a week later.

"Did you send any money to your guide?" I asked, thinking they may never see him if they sent all the money.

"We're smarter than that," said one of the hunters. "We only sent him half, $2,000."

Sleep was out of the question, so I walked them down to the lake where their pilot would arrive. We had been sitting on the dock for some time discussing the area and their upcoming hunt, when off in the distance I heard the faint sound of an airplane.

"I think I can hear a plane, it's probably your pilot," I said. The plane finally came around Sheep Mountain and into view, heading straight for us. As the plane came closer I could tell by the sound that the engine wasn't running well. I glanced at the hunters to see if they could hear what I heard. Both guys were smiling from ear to ear, so I thought it best to keep my thoughts to myself.

The pilot flew directly over us. The engine problem seemed worse and for a second I thought it might quit. Even from the ground I could tell that the outfitter's floatplane was a piece of junk. It had holes everywhere and pieces of wing fabric were flapping in the wind. The pilot made a nice smooth water landing on the little lake, then turned toward the dock and at an alarming speed raced to us.

The plane's floats hit hard; while still moving the pilot stepped onto the float and made a leap of faith onto the dock. Then he grabbed the wing and strained to stop the plane before he was pulled into the lake. Both hunters stared in shock at what they just witnessed.

The pilot turned around and asked, "Are you my clients from California?"

They both nodded their heads.

"Then grab this rope and hold the plane against the dock."

The image of this pilot would be hard to forget. Hair hung to his shoulders and hadn't seen a comb in weeks. As he talked it was hard not to look at his toothless mouth. I caught a glimpse of two, no, maybe three teeth. Two weeks of old gray stubble covered his face. His clothes were torn and dirty. My first instinct was to back away, not wanting anything to jump on me.

The pilot jumped back onto the float and grabbed a water pump from the plane. All floatplanes' floats leak a little, so a hand pump is kept handy. The pilot was now standing on the right float, which was sinking fast.

He frantically pulled the cap off the top of the float and pumped like a madman. As the float sank the right wing dipped closer to the ground. I was spellbound; realizing if he didn't get the water out soon the plane was going to sink. I asked, "What do you want me to do?"

"Get the hell back!" was the reply.

He pumped so fast I could hardly see his arm moving. Without missing a beat he looked at his hunters and said, "Hurry up and get your gear down here." They both ran for their rig.

For a second I wondered if they might drive away. I would have, but their enthusiasm was stronger than self-preservation. They backed their rig as close to the plane as possible and emptied their gear.

"You," the pilot pointed to the smallest guy, "Crawl way in the back, facing backwards."

The hunter wanted to protest, but slowly eased himself over the backseat and onto the floor of the plane. Normally a Super Cub carried two people, this pilot was going to try three. All I could see of the passenger was the top part of his face and head, which showed extreme terror as he looked out the back window.

"You sit there," the pilot pointed to the backseat. "Hurry up, we don't have a lot of time."

He was still pumping like a madman. The other guy gingerly lowered himself into the backseat, causing the plane to sink precariously lower.

The pilot ran to the hunters' gear, grabbed a handful and sprinted back to the plane. In one motion he threw the gear at the backseat passenger and pumped more water. Then he repeated the process until I could barely see the face of the second passenger, who was staring back in agony.

The guy way in the back had disappeared after the second armful of gear. I just couldn't imagine being on the floor of the plane, completely covered up and not able to see anything.

The pilot jumped into the front seat and fired the engine. The rough-running engine roared to life under full power and the plane moved sluggishly away from the dock. Tahneta Lake is a small lake that sits at an elevation of 3000 feet. I just couldn't see how the plane was going to lift that load, so I sat on the dock to enjoy the show.

A terrible thought entered my mind, *if the plane sank out in the middle of the lake, the passenger way in back would drown.* There wasn't any way possible for him to get out of the plane. The plane struggled to gain enough speed to get up on step for takeoff. The combination of weight and engine problems created an impossible situation, but the pilot wasn't one to give up easily. Around and around the lake he went. As he crossed his own wake, the plane jumped into the air momentarily, then splashed back down with a spray of water. On each pass by the dock the right float settled deeper into the water. In a few minutes the plane would sink.

The pilot must have known that, and raced toward the dock under full power. At the last possible second he pulled off the power. The plane sank as it crashed into the dock. The pilot/madman jumped into the waist-deep water, grabbed the pump and pumped feverishly. Then he barked at his passenger, "Throw that shit out!"

The passenger pitched everything he could onto the dock, with some of it falling back into the water. His face showed a combination of total shock and extreme terror. I retrieved the gear as the plane pulled away from the dock.

Away they went again, around and around. The weight reduction helped the plane stay airborne for three or four seconds before slamming back onto the water. Evidently the pilot learned quickly, because on the third pass he raced to the dock, jumped into the water again and pumped. He turned and yelled, "Unload all the gear!" The only things left in the plane were the pilot and two scared-to-death hunters.

I couldn't tell if the passenger in the back was still alive. He was pale white and had watery eyes. It was possible he'd had a heart attack. I stepped toward the plane to see if I could help. A *'get the hell back!'* look told me to stay away.

I'm sure the pilot thought the plane would sink if I stepped on a float.

All of the hunters' gear was now on the dock. As the plane pulled away, both passengers' pleading eyes looked at me and seemed to say, *we're going to die, please save us.* All I could do was shrug my shoulders in disbelief, which didn't give the hunters any comfort. The plane sped around the lake, with the engine coughing every few seconds. As it crossed its own waves it eased into the air, then dropped lightly back onto the water, before slowly lifting off again.

The shore was only a hundred yards away. The plane fought for altitude, then crossed the shoreline with inches to spare and skimmed the high brush as it flew down the valley. After what seemed to be three miles, the plane gained enough altitude to turn toward their hunting area, and then disappeared out of sight.

I shook my head in amazement. My thoughts were to jump in my plane and follow them. The way the plane was running I doubted they would get very far.

But it wasn't long before my passenger showed up and we were in the air headed for his camp. As I flew, I thought about the hunters dressed in orange. I could still see the look of terror in their eyes. I sure hoped they were going to have the hunting adventure they expected.

I landed at the miner's camp. The condition of his short and bumpy airstrip was terrible. I swerved and bounced to a stop. The airstrip was so rough it could easily wreck the plane. I would not land there again.

His dream of striking it rich had come to an end. He said he'd sold everything he owned to come to Alaska to mine gold. He'd taken the word of a local miner and leased some claims. There just wasn't the gold he was led to believe.

I said, "The guy's name wasn't Shorty, was it?"

He replied, "How did you know?"

The next afternoon I landed back at Brandt's to get supplies and check for messages. All the gear that had been on the dock was gone. Eldon said that the floatplane had returned and picked it up. The hunters must have survived their airplane ride.

I sat in the café and read a message. It said to call Tom, the old foreman of the Mafia camp. The end of the message said, "IMMEDIATELY." As the phone rang I couldn't help but wonder what was so important. Then I remembered he had wanted to tell me something when he left.

Tom answered the phone and I asked what was up.

The phone got real quiet, then he said, "Remember when I told you that someone was stealing gold?"

"Sure I do, why?" What was he getting at?

He continued, "First of all, you didn't hear this from me."

I replied, "Just tell me what you're talking about."

The phone went silent again and then he started in. "I was told from I don't know who, that a young boy was caught stealing gold out of a sluice box. He was shot and buried in the creek."

I was stunned. All I could think of saying was, "The younger Idaho boy?"

In a whisper Tom said, "You didn't hear it from me, but yes it was. I had nothing to do with it, but couldn't sleep thinking about his brother hunting for him. But it could be a lie." Then he added, "I'm moving out of the country." The phone went dead.

I hung up and slowly wandered back to the plane. I had a feeling something like this would happen. How in the hell was I going to tell the older brother that his brother might be dead?

In a somber state of mind I departed Brandt's headed for the Idaho boy's camp. I thought I'd better see if the older boy was still up the draw. If he was, I'd hike up to the camp the next day and let him know what I had heard.

The camp was gone. Evidently the older boy had left for home. As I flew toward our airstrip I wondered if I would ever see him again.

I touched down on the mains and then slowly lowered the nose wheel. To my surprise, it just kept going down, way past where the strut usually stopped the prop from getting too close to the ground. I held my breath as I added power to help raise the nose. Then I reduced power because the end of the runway was getting close, and eased the nose down. It finally clunked down on top of the tire yoke. I shut the engine off and stopped the plane.

Hydraulic oil ran down the strut, which meant the seal that held the oil and air in the strut was leaking. The prop was only inches off the ground. I couldn't fly the plane with the seals out. The end of the prop creates a vortex, which will suck rocks into the blades if they are too low to the ground. A dent the size of a match-head would ruin the propeller. The fix was a job for the maintenance shop in Anchorage.

The rain pounded the plastic roof as Alan and I sat in the little dining room of the cookshack. He was as shocked as I was to hear about the Idaho boy. BC and Jim had left for the bunkhouse to make sure they were in the safety of the flimsy building before dark, as darkness set in, the temperature dropped.

The endless noise of the machinery bounced off the steep walls. Tim and Bernie were working the sluice. The continuous noise got to be such a part of the mine that when the machines were shut off for maintenance it always felt like something was wrong.

The rain turned to slush as the temperature dropped, meaning winter wasn't far away. The deep canyon gave a new meaning to the word dark. With a low cloud cover and darkness, it was only possible to see a few feet. Our tough Mafia boys wouldn't reappear until morning.

Delores was in the cookshack getting food ready for breakfast. Tony kept the coffee cups full and shook his head in disbelief as he heard the news. I hadn't cleaned his foot for a few days; Delores had taken over the job. It had been almost a month since he'd returned from the hospital and it still wasn't healed.

As he moved around doing little jobs, I noticed he was favoring the foot. When he stepped up to the cookshack floor he grimaced in pain, and quickly turned his head away so I wouldn't see his expression.

"What's the matter with your foot?" I demanded.

He continued into the other room of the cookshack, acting like he didn't hear me.

Alan could see the look on my face and stopped talking. He said, "Dad, come in here and sit down so we can look at your foot." Tony slowly walked out from around the corner, with a sheepish look on his face.

"It's all right, come over here so I can clean your bandage," I said with a smile. I could see Tony was scared. He jerked back in pain as I eased the slipper off the foot. The bottom of the bandage was covered with a light-red colored blood.

As I slowly unwrapped the foot, tears rolled down Tony's face. He said, "I fell down the hill yesterday morning and poked a sharp stick into the sore. It bled for awhile. I didn't want to tell anyone, we have enough problems already."

"Oh, God!" I whispered as I looked into the opening. The stick had torn its way through the bottom of the foot, ripping open what had healed. Mud and pus drained out as I gingerly dabbed at the infected tissue. Dirt had been pushed behind tendons. There was absolutely no way I could clean the infected sore.

Tony clamped his teeth down and hung on tight as Alan poured warm water into the opening. Delores stood back in shock, unable to say a word. We all knew Tony was in real trouble. As hard as I tried, I just couldn't get to all the dirt.

There wasn't any reason to keep inflicting pain. His eyes were glassy and fixed directly on me as I poured a warm bottle of peroxide into the hole. White foam poured out as the cleaning solution ate away at the infection. Delores and Alan knew what I was going to say before I said it.

Tony moaned as I said, "We need to get you to the hospital. It's probably all right." I tried to not let him see the worry in my face. "But I think you need to get the foot checked in town. You have dirt in the wound that I can't get out."

Tony started to complain, but Delores said, "You walked around without your crutches, now you get to town with David and get the foot looked at. End of story." He wouldn't argue with her, and accepted the inevitable.

With the rain pouring down, the flight was put off until first light. Everyone was worried sick. Every few minutes I would wake up thinking about Tony. The foot looked as bad as ever and poison could set in. Minutes felt like hours. It might already be too late.

It was still pitch dark as I stepped into the cookshack. I couldn't sleep. "Is it time to get up?" asked Delores.

I replied, "It's only five, but I can't sleep. Daylight should start breaking in a few hours, just thought I'd get some coffee going."

"I can't sleep either," she said.

A minute later Alan walked in. He'd seen the light come on in the cookshack and couldn't concentrate on mining, so he shut the operation down, wanting to help drive his dad up to the airplane. We carried Tony from the swamp buggy and sat him in the front seat of the plane.

Tears flowed as Delores and Alan hugged him goodbye. Alan turned and said, "If he has to have surgery, come and get us right away."

Alan pushed the tail of the plane down and I put a small piece of wood between the tire yoke and the fuselage. As long as the weight of the fuselage was on the wood it would hold the prop out of the mud. Once airborne the strut would relax and the piece of wood would fall harmlessly away from the plane, at least in theory. I hoped it worked.

Tony and I sat on the end of the runway, waiting for a little more daylight. The heavy rains of the night had turned the airstrip into a caldron of mud and water. Fog hung over the top of the canyon. These conditions were going to force me to pull a Wild Dick trick, meaning, in order to stay out of the fog I would have to fly down the narrow canyon. Just maybe this would get me down lower in the valley where I hoped I could fly to the highway.

The small hill to the south of the runway was engulfed in fog. Taking off under these poor conditions was suicidal, but I knew Tony didn't have time to spare. Could I sneak down the narrow canyon? Once airborne, turning around would be impossible. I sat and stared at the fog, trying to let my sixth sense take over.

I wasn't feeling any sign of danger. The question lingered in my mind. *Was my ego-driven part of me saying I could do this, or was my concern for Tony the reason to take such a great risk?*

The second I lifted off I reduced power and leveled the plane. I kept the flaps at 30 degrees and turned down the narrow canyon. The lowered flaps would let me fly slower and make the plane more maneuverable. The fog grabbed precariously at the top of the wings. Forward visibility was poor, but I looked down at the creek to keep track of my progress. Flying into the fog in these mountains could be a death sentence.

We passed over our camp at 100 feet. I held the speed at 60 knots. As the hairpin corners approached, I eased the plane over to the far canyon wall, then made a coordinated turn around each bend of the creek. I had no horizon to help, but kept my eyes glued to the upcoming canyon walls. There wouldn't be a second chance to do this right. At times the canyon was only a couple of hundred feet wide. I'd lost track of how many sharp corners I'd made; it felt like at least 20 as the sweat ran down my face.

Caribou Creek had to be close; it was in a wide valley that I knew would give me more room to maneuver the plane. The fog seemed to be closing down. I slowed the plane slightly and lowered my elevation to the treetops. I peered through the fog; it seemed a little lighter ahead.

The fog hung dangerously above our heads as we turned down Caribou Creek. I relaxed slightly as we passed over a miner's camp that had an airstrip. At least I knew I could fly back to that strip if the flight conditions grew worse. I turned and looked back toward Alfred Creek, and it was hard to believe that we'd just flown out from our mine. The fog went all the way to the ground.

The bottom of the narrow canyon at the lower end of Caribou Creek was clear of fog, but it hung low and just above the rim. I circled, trying to get a better look down the steep ravine. Between the highway and us was another six miles of narrow hairpin turns. Or I could go back to the airstrip I'd just flown over and wait for better weather.

I looked at Tony, hanging on for dear life. He turned his head, smiled at me and said, "Let's go for it."

We eased into the canyon. Tony's face was pinned to the side window as he pointed out the vertical walls.

To remain in the canyon I used anywhere from 30 to 80-degree banks. The abrupt corners forced right to left banks, no leveling off between turns.

I'd flown this route many times with fog present, but never with the fog forcing me down to the bottom of the creek. The Glenn Highway was my lifeline. At least I could land on it if I had to. The fog pressed me down and the highway was still a mile away. I blinked hard and strained to see the craggy canyon walls through the murky weather, not daring to go lower.

The canyon was narrowing, which meant I was getting closer to the highway. In an instant we floated out of the confined chasm, crossed the highway and made a right turn around Lions Head. To my relief, the fog lifted as we floated by the Matanuska.

The rain and wind pounded us all the way to Anchorage, but at least I didn't have to deal with the fog. The fog could turn a young man into an old one real quick or worse yet, a dead one. I had Tony wait in the plane as I talked to Wilbur's about fixing the nose strut, then headed for Providence Hospital.

The fear showed on Tony's face as the nurse unwrapped the bandage. The doctor finally showed up and examined the infected foot. He immediately started numbing the incision and told the nurses to clean the foot. He told Tony he'd be right back after he talked to me. As we walked out the door Tony gave me a scared look and said, "Don't leave me."

The look on his face was almost more than I could handle. "The doctor just wants to talk to me, I'll be right outside the door. I won't leave you, I promise," I replied.

I explained to the doctor how Tony had re-injured his foot.

Then he said, "The foot is infected really bad and I'm not sure we can stop the infection this time. I think Tony needs to go back to Montana and work with his own doctors. At least if something happens, he would be with his family."

I wanted to say "What do you mean if something happens," but I knew what he meant.

He continued, "The bone in his heel has turned completely black. With his diabetes this could cost him his life. This is what I want to do. We'll clean the foot and pump antibiotics into him for five hours. Then you get Tony and his wife headed to Montana as soon as possible. I'll send along pills for the trip. They need to drive straight home. Tony should be all right until then."

The doctor shook my hand and walked away. "Thanks, Doc," I said.

Now I had to give Tony the bad news. I bit my lip as I walked into the room, trying not to show the bad news I'd just heard. Tony relaxed as I held his hand and explained what the doctor had said. He sobbed as I explained that the doctor wanted him to go home to his own doctor. "You're going to be all right. I think it's a good idea not to take any more chances with your foot. Besides, the mine is going to get real cold before long and just think, you'll be home sitting beside your warm fire."

My heart broke for Tony. He sobbed and held my hand. Tears rolled down his cheeks in a steady stream. I sat down and cried with him. I couldn't hide my feelings any longer.

Gold mining in Alaska had been his dream, and now it was over.

The realization of this drained the life out of both of us for the next hour. We held hands and stared into unfocused space, not knowing what to do next.

XX
SAD TIMES

Both Tony and I were resigned to the fact that he and Delores were leaving the gold mine. Wilbur's had fixed the nose strut; I was thankful for their speedy work.

The weather improved. The snow-capped peaks on the mountaintops reflected their fluorescent white colors. Never once had Tony or I wavered from our daily duties. We'd sped to Anchorage and then raced back to the mine, not wanting to waste time on anything but the mining operation.

I looked at Tony and his eyes were watery as he thought about leaving. I said, "The mountains are so pretty, what do you think about flying over them to see what's on the other side?" Earlier in the year I had to fly over them to get by some poor weather conditions. The sight into Prince William Sound was a memory of a lifetime.

Tony replied, "Sounds good to me, let's go." I turned the plane to the east and headed up Knik River. The muddy water in the river led us to the Knik Glacier. Looking ahead we could see the glacier meandering up the valley.

As the giant moved downstream, the ice cracked open, leaving deep dark fissures that seemed to have no bottom. The shades of blue went from black to translucent light aqua-green and adjusted colors continuously as the angle of sunlight changed.

The tree-covered mountainsides thinned as we climbed for altitude. I leveled the plane at 8000 feet, above all the mountains. Only the sabertooth mountain peaks protruded out of the top of the giant ice fields, the thickness of the ice on the top of these mountains must have been thousands of feet and millions of years old. This was the spot where the glaciers were born. The whole area turned to one enormous white glacier.

Fingers of ice extended down each valley like arms of an octopus. As they made their serpentine way, each extension would get its own name, but at the top they were one.

Off to the south we could see the expanse of the ocean, filled with a thousand islands and inlets. Ice rivers with dark stains paralleled their progress as the glaciers' lower ends cracked open and disappeared into the ocean. Icebergs that had calved from the rivers of ice dotted the expanse of Prince William Sound.

Tony and I flew down the Matanuska Glacier.

We passed Mount Goode and then turned north for the upper end of the Matanuska Glacier. Denmark Peak marked the turn down the glacier and toward the gold mine. The sight of all the brilliant ice colors reflected continuously as we soared down the prehistoric river of ice. I held the elevation at 100 feet and for the next 20 miles we peered out the windows at the craggy ice so close below.

I glanced repeatedly at the engine instruments. There was absolutely no place to land on the cracked glacier. Giant vertical jagged cliffs shot skyward thousands of feet above the ice on each side. I held my breath and talked silently to the plane, hoping the sweet talk would keep the old girl running.

I finally relaxed as I turned north on the highway and hoped the little side trip would help Tony forget about what would happen in the next hour. "I'll drop you off at Brandt's and then fly to the mine to get Delores and Alan. I should be back within the hour."

Tony argued for a second, but I knew that having him back at the mine would only make saying goodbye a lot harder.

He gave instructions all the way to Brandt's. "Take care of Alan, he's working way too hard. Help him make decisions; he'll listen to you. Make sure you eat good food." He was still doing his best to help out. Now he couldn't talk fast enough, knowing he would be gone shortly.

I fought back tears as I thought about losing him and Delores. I remembered Alan asking his dad about how he handled the rough air. We'd just gotten back from a terribly bumpy flight and Tony had replied, "I hate flying, but David needs my help buying groceries and doing laundry. I'll fly with him wherever he goes." That statement was proven true many times.

We'd had many harsh and uncomfortable flights but never once did I hear him complain. He put all the effort he could muster into helping the gold mine run smoothly. The appearance of the two of them pulled the mining operation together.

I helped Tony into Brandt's and told him I'd be back in one hour. Eldon and Tony were visiting as I left for the plane. I was glad he had company as he waited.

"Where's Tony?" asked Delores as she and Alan walked toward the swamp buggy. Both were worried sick. Showing up without Tony scared the hell out of them.

"He's OK, he's OK." Then I explained what had happened at the hospital and what the doctor had recommended. Fifteen minutes later Alan, Delores, and I were in the air and headed to Brandt's. Tony was all smiles as we hurried into the café. On the table were four cheeseburgers, fries and milkshakes. The second he'd heard the plane, he'd ordered supper for us.

I just shook my head in astonishment. Here was Tony, leaving Alaska with a life-threatening infection and still doing whatever he could. We spent the next half hour talking about the mine and what they suggested.

Both were worried about Leo. They wanted me to keep trying to get ahold of him.

Alan said, "With the Mafia equipment it looks like we will get enough gold to come back next year. So get that foot healed up. We're going to need you both back here then."

I wasn't looking forward to their departure. We helped Tony into the car. All four of us teared-up as Delores started the engine; I turned away to help lessen the pain. Alan didn't know if he would ever see his dad again. In a second they were on the highway and headed for Montana. We stared in disbelief as the car slowly drove out of sight.

An aching, empty feeling welled up in my chest. It felt like a part of me was gone and like a dream—just yesterday they were cooking and trying their best to keep everyone happy.

"Let's buzz them," I said. It was the only thing I could think of doing. We sprinted for the plane, fired the old girl up and departed down the highway. In a few minutes we spotted the car. From three miles in front of them I eased the plane down to the highway. When they were a quarter of a mile away I decreased our elevation to 20 feet.

Their faces shone brightly and hands waved out each window as we passed over. I rocked the wings up and down in a wave goodbye.

We sat in silence as the airplane headed toward the mine, absorbed in our own reflections and thoughts about the near future. Our mining luck had been horrible all summer with one problem after another. Lies, breakdowns, thievery and just plain bad luck put the odds of coming back near impossible. But our family wasn't one to give up easily.

During my free time, I would take the small Caterpillar and hunt the creek for more gold. Just below our sluice the canyon made a sharp left turn. On the inside corner of that turn I'd found a lot of gold. A pan of dirt usually held fifty flakes of gold, which was a lot for a shovelful of dirt. We'd been working toward this gold-filled corner all summer, hoping to get there before winter set in. But we still had a month of mining before reaching the honey hole.

I looked at Alan, who was staring off into space. I said, "The buzz job was a great sendoff, it sure made me feel better about them leaving. It kind of put closure on their departure."

He shook his head in reply. He was struggling with the departure of his parents.

I continued, "They'll be home in two days. He'll be in good hands, and at least we don't have to worry about them being at the mine. Winter is only weeks away, I think they left at the right time."

Alan nodded his head in agreement. The stare in his eye and lines on his face told what he was feeling. The possibility of losing his dad, business, and farm was getting closer with each passing day.

"I think we should move the sluice down the creek. We need to find a lot of gold quickly. That inside corner is full of gold."

Alan was trying to comprehend what I said.

"If we come back next season, it won't be working Shorty's claims. Let's jump to that hot corner. Maybe we can find a bunch of gold. Think about it, Alan. Why are we still here?

"I should have crashed a long time ago. Some of the takeoffs and landings were impossible. Why did I survive? We've had so much bad luck gold mining, most people would have put their tails between their legs and headed for home. You know as well as I do, that isn't us. Call it luck or whatever, we're still here and we have work to do."

As I talked the fire in his eyes reappeared. He looked at me with enthusiasm in his eyes and said, "Let's do it! We'll clean the sluice right now and move."

This was the Alan that drove to Alaska with me five months earlier, ready to undertake any problem. We both knew that Tony's dream was over for now. Even though he was gone, we were still here and had a job to do.

The minute we drove into camp Alan started barking orders. BC and Jim slothfully stepped out of the bunkhouse. Alan aimed a finger at them and said, "You two are going to do the cooking and cleaning from now on. We have three weeks left and you're going to work for your room and board or start walking."

Both guys stared at him in shock.

"Do you understand what I'm saying? No one is going to wait on you guys anymore. It's time to buck up or get out."

They took the demand as best they could. They didn't have a choice; these guys could barely find the outhouse. The chance of them walking out of this wilderness was zero.

Tim was surprised to hear that Tony and Delores were gone. He'd been running the big CAT all night and day and was elated to hear we were doing a cleanout, giving him time to relax. As our numbers dwindled he became more valuable. Bernie, Alan and I disassembled the sluice box. The speed of our work seemed to increase. All the fines were shoveled out of the bottom of the box and then we reassembled the sluice. The procedure usually took five hours; we did it in three.

Leo or Tim usually placed the big sluice for the next set. It was a slow process that demanded accurate maneuvering of the big CAT. The sluice was 60-feet long, constructed for a five-foot drop from the beginning to the end. The operator would cut the bedrock to develop the slope needed. The rippers on the back of the CAT would sever the hard rock apart.

Then the disjoined ground would be flattened for the sluice box, which was chained to the ripper on the CAT and dragged into place. A canal from the creek dredged to the top of the box and then a departure channel constructed below the box would eliminate the water.

I'd only set the box a couple of times. Tim was dead tired so I told Alan to let him sleep and I would set the box. I really didn't want to miss out on cleaning the gold, but it was more important to get the sluice operational. I had started cutting the bedrock when something hit me on my side. I looked down to see a rock lying in my lap. It was Tim, stepping up on the CAT and saying, "Get the hell out of here, this is my job!"

We smiled at each other; I gave him the thumbs up and cuffed him on the back. He gave me a jostle off of the machine and applied throttle. The guy worked 20 hours and slept two, ready to go again.

As I walked toward camp I thought about the effort Tim had put in all summer. At times he needed a bath and would eat more than his allotment at the table, but his energy and mastery went way beyond the call of duty. Bringing Tim along was a wise decision.

As I got closer to camp the white Dodge pickup pulled out and headed upstream. Having a rig leave toward the airstrip was unusual, unless I was in it. "Who's in the pickup?" I asked Alan as I stepped in the cookshack.

"Bernie quit, so I gave him the old truck for wages."

The kid had been a good worker, and was doing well, despite his dad. So now we were down to Tim, Alan, the two Mafia boys and me.

It took Tim most of the day to set the sluice in the new spot. Another immediate problem arose. With all the new equipment at our mine, our supply of diesel fuel was being depleted quickly. The most efficient way to get fuel moved to the mine from Brandt's now would be with the big front-end loader. Alan could rent a set of tires, the same set I'd used earlier and roll the fuel to the mine.

Alan headed up the creek and was out of sight in a few minutes. We figured the rubber-tired rig should be able to cover the torturous ride in half the time of the metal-tracked rig.

We were worried when Alan didn't show up. He was ten hours late, and although it was still rainy, the clouds had lifted enough to let me fly the trail to look for him. Neither Mafia boy wanted anything to do with the plane, so I departed the airstrip looking for my cousin.

I scoured every bend and then crossed over the top and looked down the thread-like trail. From the air the trail didn't look wide enough for any machine. I crossed back and forth over the trail, and finally saw the front-end loader sitting at a precarious angle near the bottom of the slope. On the first pass I didn't see Alan. My thoughts went to the worst-case scenario. Had he been run over? Where was he?

As I turned for a closer look I lowered my elevation and slowed my speed to 60. As I floated by I saw Alan sitting on the ground between the big tires. He raised his hand slowly and waved. At least he looked OK. On the next pass he waved his arm back and forth in a gesture that said he needed help. I headed back to the mine. Tim was better at fixing things, so we loaded the swamp buggy with chains and tools, and he left to give Alan a hand.

I pushed overburden for the rest of the day, then walked to the cookshack. They still hadn't returned. All night long I would back up, push the material forward and stare at the cookshack a quarter of a mile away. If they were back, the light would be on. I couldn't concentrate as night gave way to daybreak. They should have been back.

As I walked upstream toward the plane I could hear the sound of machinery echoing off the canyon walls. It had to be them. I almost yelled for joy as Alan rounded the next corner and stopped beside me.

Alan relived the story with us. "I made great time as I went up Alfred Creek and then turned up the gorge. But my progress slowed as the clay banks that the trail travels over turned to slick and gluey mud. I was forced into plowing the mud, one bucket-load at a time, all the way to the top of the mountain.

"The five hours it took to get to the top were spent shrouded in the clouds with almost zero visibility. I felt like a blind man feeling my way down an unknown street. I eased the rubber-tired machine over the top and started down the other side. The mud stuck to the big tires. The combination of the weight of the machine and slimy mud made it impossible to stop. My speed grew as the tires slid and bounced down the steep slope. I pumped the brakes and shifted into low gear, but it didn't help. In a few seconds I would have slid over the edge of the trail and rolled to the bottom, hundreds of yards below.

"Without thought I jammed the big bucket into the ground. This caused me to jump and bounce to a stop. So here I was, sitting on the steep hillside, with a mile left to the bottom. It seemed like it took a half hour to get my breath back. Then I carefully raised the bucket just enough to let the machine roll forward. When the machine slid again I'd push the bucket back into the ground and bounce to a stop. It took a couple of hours to reach the bottom.

"I loaded 2000 gallons of fuel into the tires and headed back toward the mountain. The second I started up the hill I spun to a stop."

With fresh hot coffee he finished the story. "I spent hours plowing the mud off the steep trail, but I couldn't get the tongue on the trailer hooked up to the front-end loader. I must have gotten into and out of the machine a hundred times, each time I moved it I hoped it was the right spot, but I couldn't keep it from sliding down into the tires."

He looked at me and continued, "When you flew over I was at my wit's end. The tires and machine had slid to the edge of the trail. If they slid any more at all, they would go over the edge.

"Tim looked so good when he showed up I could have almost kissed him. We hooked a chain on the tires and pulled them back on the trail. Tim blocked the tires from rolling and I backed the loader into place and here we are. I thought I was going to lose everything. Then I would have owed the boss an $80,000 machine. Sitting on that rainy mountainside not able to do anything was the most depressed I've ever been."

My heart went out to Alan. Five months earlier I'd spent ten lonely hours plowing in the same spot.

We built a small sluice for the first step in cleaning the gold. It was made out of 1 x 4 boards, nailed together. In the bottom of the sluice we positioned a rubber mat, bottom up. The mat had small squares that would grab the gold as it was tossed into the sluice. A four-inch hose fed water to the top of the little sluice. One cupful of fines from the big sluice was dumped into the small sluice.

Alan cleaning the fines and finding gold.

As Alan dumped the cupful of fines in the small sluice, the dirt and mud would rinse away, leaving yellow gold in the small squares. Every few minutes we rinsed the mat in a bucket of water and then replaced it in the small sluice. Any nuggets bigger than a marble would be handpicked out of the fines and positioned into the bucket of water. It was a slow process, but one that worked well.

The Mafia boys hovered around like hawks, watching every move. With all the fines cleaned, we ended up with the bottom of the bucket encased with gold. Alan cautiously dumped the gold onto a fine mesh screen, catching all the gold, while draining off all the water.

All four of us went to the cookshack table to separate and size the gold. The gold was sold by size, not weight. The bigger the piece, the more it was worth. This was the fun part, the bonus for all the hard work.

As Alan reached into his pocket he said, "You can't believe what I found in the sluice." He laid his clenched hand on the table and slowly opened it. A nugget the size of a quarter appeared, the second biggest nugget we'd unearthed, spherical in shape, one-quarter of an inch thick and polished smooth.

I grabbed it and rolled it in my hand. "How much do you think?" I asked Alan as I seized the weighing scale.

"Half an ounce." The scale read fifteen-penny weight or three-quarters of an ounce. Alan continued, "Since this is my gold mine and I'm paying all the bills, I'm going to keep the nugget!"

BC slammed his hand down on Alan's and said, "No you won't, we'll flip for the nugget!"

Over the last couple of weeks the Mafia boys had gone from disdainful to meek. But now, the look in their eyes told us that their former selves had returned. Flipping for the nugget was not going to be a debate. Alan looked at me and kind of shook his head in agreement. I dug a quarter out of my pocket, flipped it in the air and said, "Call it."

As the coin rotated Alan said, "Tails!" The coin smacked the table and then glanced off to the dirt floor. George Washington's profile showed from the shadows.

When BC reached for the nugget, Alan slammed his hand down on top of his and said, "Flip again, the coin stays on the table."

This time BC wanted to argue, but seeing Alan's ardent face stopped him short.

"Flip again."

I flipped the coin again. "Tails," said Alan. The coin arched into the air, floated for a second and then plummeted to the table. It spun on its side and for an instant the eagle displayed its spread wings. The nugget was Alan's. The pivoting of the coin slowed and in surprise I watched the coin flop onto the other side.

George's face slowly became distinct as the coin came to a stop. We had lost the precious nugget.

BC slid the nugget into his leather pouch.

Alan stood up and walked outside. The money from the nugget would have helped a lot.

I continued cleaning the gold. A series of screens sized the gold. Eventually I had the gold sized to dust, match-head size, pea-sized and nuggets. Total weight for the cleanout was 34 ounces. I split the gold in half and slid the Mafia boys their share. Each size of gold was put in its own glass jar and then stored in a box with a lock and positioned under Alan's bunk.

We didn't trust our roommates, so on the next trip to town I would put the gold in our safe-deposit box. For the first time in hours, I realized I hadn't seen Alan. He wasn't in camp, but I could hear the sound of the big CAT.

I was surprised to see that it was midnight. As I seized the shotgun and strapped on my pistol, BC turned over and said, "Where are you going?"

I replied, "I'm walking down to the sluice. My rifle is in the corner if you need it."

The petrified look on his face pretty well told me what he was going to say. "You're going to walk down there in the dark? What if a bear comes into camp?"

As I stepped into the darkness I said, "Just make sure you don't shoot each other!"

I examined all the bushes and dark spots with the flashlight as I walked down the creek. Although I didn't have much fear of bears, I sure didn't want to surprise one and have it attack.

It had been a long day for everyone. Tim staggered as he walked over to the little CAT. They had pushed a tremendous amount of gravel through the box, and both of them needed rest.

"Why don't you guys go to the bunkhouse and sleep until morning? I'll push overburden until you relieve me." Both guys agreed.

I handed Alan the shotgun and said, "Make sure you yell before you enter the camp. I don't trust those two idiots."

The first thing to do was dam up the water that poured through the box. Leaving the water running would wash some of the gold out. Because I was close by, no one would dare come around. With that job done I started pushing the gravel to the side of the canyon.

Back up and push forward, as usual the top three feet of gravel needed to be dug and pushed to the side. This would leave the last foot of gravel and bedrock for Tim and Alan to push through the sluice.

The steady vibration and movement put my mind and body into a hypnotic state, back and forth, back and forth. My watch said five o'clock. Where had all the time gone?

As I neared the edge of the flat creek, a strange feeling caused me to peer out into the darkness. I backed to the middle and the feeling subsided. The big machine rumbled and shook as it pushed another blade load of dirt. At about the same spot the weird feeling returned.

The sheer bushy bank was only 20 feet from the edge of the machine. The hair on my arms and neck stood up. Something was watching me.

I scanned the darkness looking for a bear or worse yet, a human. I'd had this feeling before but not to this magnitude. Maybe my mind was playing tricks on me. The feeling went away as I reversed to the middle again. I'd had enough, my sixth sense had been right all summer, now was not the time to doubt it.

Without lowering the blade I drove the CAT to the bank at an out-of-control speed. At the edge I ascended a small hill. The uphill attitude and bright lights of the CAT illuminated the hillside. I squinted at every bush. Something was watching me and it was right here in front of the machine. To the right I saw movement.

Immediately, I swung the big machine toward the movement, thinking I could make out an image in back of a bush. Then I saw it, two black beady eyes glaring directly at me. Seconds felt like minutes, and the eyes never moved. If it were a bear the eyes would reflect their green color. The object stood up and glared back; it was a man with a gun in his hand.

Then I remembered the eyes; I'd seen them before, sighting down the end of a shotgun as I flew by. The man sluggishly walked into the darkness. My hands shook as I backed the machine to the middle of the canyon. How long had he been there? He could have shot me and stolen all the gold out of the box. The box, maybe he'd been to the sluice! I rattled the CAT to the box and shined the light on it.

Reluctantly, I stepped off and into the light. Now I was a sitting duck. In the mud above the box were his tracks indicating he had walked through the now-dry channel that delivered water to the sluice, the same channel I had dammed up hours earlier.

The situation was not good. Many a miner had been shot over gold.

I opened the dam just enough to let water run down the box. If he came back he wouldn't be able to steal any gold. Then I went back to pushing overburden.

I relaxed as daylight broke over the eastern mountains. For the last three hours I'd managed to stay near the middle of the canyon bottom.

Alan and Tim showed up ready to go to work. They looked at the tracks around the sluice. As we discussed the problem I got the feeling he was watching us again.

.

XXI

THE MONTANA SPIRIT

I strolled up the creek, heading for the cookshack. While keeping my head facing forward, I shifted my eyes from side to side, from bush to bush. Somewhere in the canyon a concealed beady-eyed onlooker was glaring at me.

The strange and unnerving feeling had been with me for most of the night and had kept my mind at full alert. The constant tension made me feel a little nauseated.

The steep cliffs and patches of stunted spruce trees above the camp provided a thousand hiding spots. As I walked closer to camp the feeling subsided, leading me to conclude that the observer must have turned his attention to Alan and Tim.

The smell of bacon and eggs drifted down the canyon. At least the Mafia boys were doing their best to help. BC met me at the door of the cookshack with a cup of coffee. He wasn't Tony or Delores, but at least he was trying to fit in.

The eggs were a little burnt and the coffee way too strong, but that was OK, I didn't complain. If I were a gambling man, I would've bet this was the first time BC had cooked anything.

For the first time since the Mafia boys showed up, we sat and talked. BC was from Florida, unused to the cold climate, but I knew his face from somewhere. As hard as I tried, I couldn't remember where. Jim was from Mississippi, a high school dropout and worked for the boss ever since.

The story of the night intruder brought both guys to full attention. Dealing with people was their profession. Their eyes squinted and tightened as BC said, "What do you think we can do about this guy?"

I answered, "There really isn't anything to do but keep our eyes open and carry a weapon at all times. He had enough nerve to walk around the sluice box while I was only a hundred yards away. The one thing I know for sure is that he has a shotgun with two big barrels.

"I've seen this guy's eyes, he is a serious man. If he's willing to move around at night with all the bears, he's capable of anything."

Both BC and Jim agreed, and from then on they wouldn't go anywhere unless they were together. I laughed to myself. Two big burly men walking around like schoolgirls in a pack, safety in numbers.

I needed to fly to Brandt's to get oil for the machinery. If I had time I would see if the older Idaho boy had returned. Both of my new camp friends wanted to go along, but with someone lurking around camp I thought it better to leave them there.

I examined the airplane carefully, making sure no one had meddled with it, then departed. I skimmed the upper ridges of Syncline Mountain for the resident Dall sheep, and as usual they showed up in their customary hiding spot, a small ravine that hid them from all directions except from above. Their full-curl horns and white capes made them look dignified. They stood in defiance as I floated by.

The rains turned the airstrip at Brandt's into slimy mud. I didn't want to take the chance of getting stuck so I chose to use the highway. Flying at 200-feet elevation I checked the highway for traffic, then made a steep descending turn which lined me up with my unusual runway. The highway seemed narrow, but it was definitely long enough!

The tires squealed as they made contact with the pavement. I turned into Brandt's parking lot and taxied up to the restaurant.

As I stepped onto the wooden deck I could hear the engine noise of a couple of airplanes. I searched the sky and saw two new-looking Super Cubs pass overhead and then turn a base leg for Brandt's muddy runway.

I couldn't let them land without trying to warn them about the mud, so I ran down to the strip and waved frantically. Both planes had turned final, one a half-mile behind the other.

I was standing right in the middle of the touchdown area. The first plane continued on, coming straight at me. I waved, and with no indication of the pilot having seen me, walked off the runway and stood back to see what would happen.

The approach was perfect until the weight of the plane shifted to the tires. The big tires grabbed the sticky mud and instantly the tail of the plane raised into the air. If it went any higher, the weight of the aircraft would shift over center and the plane would fall over on its back.

The left tire smashed into the brush on the side of the runway. The drag created from the bushes made the plane swerve to the left and then roll off the narrow runway and out into the brush. Amazingly, the plane slid to a stop still on its wheels, facing away from the runway.

My attention turned to the second plane that was still lined up to the runway. Nobody would be stupid enough to try and land after what had just occurred, but apparently I was wrong. I stepped back onto the runway and waved. I was just ready to move out of the way when the plane's engine went to full power and passed over. I pointed toward the highway.

The first pilot stepped out of his plane with the whites of the eyes showing. He said, "What happened?"

I replied, "You're lucky that you ran off the runway. That sticky mud would have put you on your back. The brush kept the tires out of the mud."

"My plane doesn't look so lucky!" he squeaked out.

We turned to see his partner land on the highway, then taxi up beside the Cessna 206. As we walked to the café he explained that they had flown up from North Dakota and were going caribou hunting. "Do you know where there are any caribou?" he asked.

The second pilot walked up and said, "That was the first time I ever landed on a highway!" He was so excited he could hardly talk.

I asked, "Didn't you see me waving you off?" He just stared at me. "You weren't going to land on that runway after your partner's landing, were you?"

He answered looking at the other guy, "Did you have a problem?"

I wondered if just maybe they weren't one brick short of a load.

I pointed toward the grassy hills to the north and said, "There are thousands of caribou out there. The problem is finding a place to land. The grassy tundra looks usable, but it's not."

I could tell by their expressions that they weren't paying heed to my advice. "I would recommend that you find an old trapper's or miner's airstrip. Many planes have been wrecked or stuck trying to land on tundra."

Both guys were anxious to get into the café. The first pilot said, "Our Super Cubs are made to land almost anywhere."

I loaded the oilcans, taxied onto the highway and departed for the mine. My route of flight crossed Belanger Pass and then I turned down the upper end of Alfred Creek. Our mine strip was 15 miles downstream. As I glided by Horn Mountain I climbed to 6000 feet. Usually I was forced to fly low in the canyon because of clouds and fog. But with no clouds in sight my altitude gave me endless vistas of mountains after mountains, which seemed to go on forever.

My route would take me over the Idaho boy's camp and I wasn't surprised to see that no one was there. I now was five miles north of our camp and too far away for anyone to hear me. My thoughts went back to the strange feeling I had all night. A thought came to mind: *If I flew over the camp from the north our intruder wouldn't hear me approach and maybe wouldn't have time to hide.* It was a long shot but what the heck it was worth a try.

I floated over the top of the ridge right behind camp and leveled off 500 feet above the creek, then strained to see any sign of movement. It was hard to focus as I scanned, keeping one eye on the steep canyon walls and the other one looking for anything strange.

Everything seemed to be in the right place, but as I turned, something on the hillside just above the buildings didn't look right. It wasn't any kind of object, just a different color in the green forest. Whatever it was, it didn't belong.

Another steep left turn brought me directly over the object. I said to myself, *"What is it?"* The plane raced by the object that looked like a blanket. The next pass told me the same thing.

I aimed upstream and flew toward the runway. Normally I'd circle looking for caribou, but now I had a mission. I landed straight ahead, tied the plane down, ran to the swamp buggy and then drove as fast as the old rig would go to camp. I couldn't see the blanket from camp, but could see just about where I thought it would be.

BC said, "What's the matter?" as I stepped into the cookshack, strapping on my pistol.

"I saw where our intruder has been hiding. Watch that hillside for anything moving," I said as I sprinted out the door and disappeared out of sight in the brush and headed up the steep hillside.

I'd had enough of this guy. As I neared the spot I slowed to a stop, it was time to be cautious. I scanned each bush for the beady eyes. With pistol ready, I eased one step forward, scanned everything and stepped forward again, a tactic learned years ago while hunting with my dad. But the person I now was hunting might shoot back.

The last hundred feet took half an hour. My hands shook and arm hairs stood at full attention. My sixth sense was on maximum overload. The guy was genuinely close. I warily stepped onto the only flat spot I'd seen since leaving the canyon bottom and could smell the pungent odor of an unclean person. My head swiveled in every direction searching for the eyes that I could feel on me now.

Down below was our area, but now I was on someone else's turf. The grass was matted with a small fire pit still smoking slightly. He was gone, but not far away.

Slowly I eased back into the brush. Out in the open I was a sitting duck. My eyes darted, the guy was out there somewhere.

I'd hoped just seeing me leave our camp and heading in his direction might frighten him off. From his perch he could see our camp and sluice operation. It was the exact spot I would have chosen if I'd wanted to keep an eye on the operation. A small trail headed downhill.

Then I heard someone yell. Where was it coming from? Looking at our camp I could see BC pointing downstream and then heard him yell again. I turned to look in the direction and saw something move.

On a ridge, 200 yards away, a man was running off. In two strides he topped the ridge and disappeared out of sight. I stood for a few minutes, letting my nerves calm down. I had gotten real close and hoped I scared him, but I really doubted it.

I slowly followed the trail down the steep hillside, and it ended directly across the creek bottom from the sluice. The guy had to have been around our camp for quite awhile to establish the trail. Alan saw me come out of the brush and stopped the CAT.

I explained what I'd seen and just done. After hearing my story Alan said, "We're going to have to be real careful, especially with only one person pushing overburden at night, but if he was going to do something stupid, he'd probably have done it by now."

Alan was right, now was the time to be real diligent. Hard to tell how much gold the guy had stolen.

I said, "I'll get some sleep and relieve you guys about six." I couldn't feel the presence of the intruder; at least he wasn't in our canyon at the moment.

For the next three days the operation went smoothly. Alan and Tim bulldozed mountains of gravel through the sluice. For 12 hours each night I forced the big CAT to push the top three feet of boulders to the edge of the creek.

The day shift would catch up to my night's work, with the cleanout producing the most gold ever. Just maybe we might be coming back!

Tim volunteered to take half of my shift at the sluice while Alan and I cleaned gold. With that job done we stepped out of the cookshack for some fresh air. Snow fell gently to the ground, marking the near-end of the mining season.

BC stared in puzzlement at the flakes and caught one in his mouth. He was enjoying the moment, but Alan and I knew what this meant. It was time to start thinking about shutting the operation down for the winter. The date was September 1. We had been told that winter came early in the Talkeetna Mountains and that once the snow started we'd better get out before the passes filled up with snow.

Alan, BC, Jim and I sat in the bunkhouse discussing the plans to get all the Mafia's equipment moved to the highway. We wanted to use the new equipment for a few more days, but BC said, "The Boss said to get his machines out at the first sign of snow and that is precisely what we're going to do." Neither guy wanted to spend another day at the mine.

I didn't want to agree, but that was exactly what we had to do. It was too bad, we'd just started working the honey hole.

But no matter what we said, BC wanted out. After the enthusiasm of seeing the snow wore off, he realized the seriousness of getting out before winter set in. The discussion started to get a little heated.

Alan demanded that we use the equipment for two more nights, but both Mafia boys said absolutely and positively not. Alan had one ace in the hole, the airplane. "We either use the equipment or you guys can walk out."

The cabin went silent, then the building moved slightly. I said, "What the hell was that?" Everyone stared at me with a stunned look. The cabin moved again and this time I knew it wasn't my imagination.

Whatever pushed on the cabin hit the wall again and jarred the whole building. I sat up quickly and stared at the thin plywood wall next to my bunk. Slowly the plywood bent in.

I knew exactly what it was, a grizzly. I yelled, "Get out of here, bear!" Everyone joined in, then the cabin went silent. We all stood facing the walls, waiting for something to happen.

Then came a low mournful growl. The noise grew in intensity; the sound came from a big animal and it stood only ten feet away. The thin walls of the cabin wouldn't provide any protection. I whispered, "We've got company," as I reached for my hunting rifle. The shotgun was in the cookshack.

Instinctively everyone moved behind me and away from the wall. I opened the bolt of the rifle and jacked a shell into the chamber. I said, "Everyone yell!"

BC and Jim yelled with all their might. The noise they made should've scared any living thing in the area. It scared me! The cabin moved again. The bear moaned as he pushed on the thin walls. With the rifle aimed at the outside noise we moved against the far wall and pivoted as one as the bear worked its way around the cabin.

Everyone grabbed what they could and beat on the floor. I motioned to stop. Everything went dead silent again. Like trapped rats we listened, feeling helpless and scared. I asked Alan in a low voice, "Are you sure the shotgun isn't in here?"

The two Mafia boys shook their heads, too scared to say a word. I reached under my bunk and grabbed my 44-magnum pistol and handed it to Alan. We both followed the movement of the bear by the continuous low growl. Every few feet the bear would push against the building.

Jim yelled in a shrill voice, "He's going to come right through the wall!" I turned my head and glanced at the Mafia boys. Both stood holding their little two-inch barreled 38-pistols, hammers cocked.

"What the hell are you guys going to do with those little pistols? You'll probably shoot me in the back. Uncock those toys and stay behind me!"

There was nothing now, no sound at all. Everyone held their breath, waiting to see what would happen. Then the sound of the bear came around the end of the building, the end the door was on. Between the bottom of the door and the floor was a two-inch crack and the only thing holding it shut was a small spring. The door rocked inward as the bear pushed before moving back into place.

For few seconds there was dead silence. Then his long ivory-colored claws slid in through the small crack between the door and the floor. All the bear had to do was pull back and up and the door would open. I clicked the safety off and aimed the rifle at the door. Alan pulled the hammer on the big pistol. If the door opened at all, hell was going to break loose! I started putting pressure on the trigger as the door bent in. Seconds turned into minutes.

Then the claws were gone. Dead silence filled the whole camp. We listened and turned our heads looking at the quarter-inch plywood. BC whispered, "What's he doing?"

I shrugged my shoulders and said, "If the bear really wanted in, these thin walls wouldn't have stopped him."

We could hear the sound of the big CAT approaching up the creek Tim was headed our way. With all the lights on, he pulled up beside the bunkhouse. I slowly opened the door and peered out. There was no bear in sight, but tracks in the snow told the story. Tim had scared him off.

The eight-inch wide tracks vanished into the brush behind the camp. The snow around the cabin was completely padded down with his tracks. He'd been there a lot longer than we'd thought.

Tim was looking for his replacement. He'd just put in a long double shift and was dead tired. For the whole summer Alan had told him that the minute it snowed he could head home. With the excitement of the bear over, we went back into the bunkhouse to discuss closing the operation down for the winter.

As we talked everyone listened for any strange sounds. BC sat on his bunk with the small pistol sitting in front of him. He looked at me and said, "I don't appreciate your comments about my pistol."

I looked at him and was surprised to see that he was serious! I said, "All you would do with those small caliber pistols is wound a bear, then we'd have a real problem!"

He shouted back, "At least I could hit what I was aiming at, you couldn't hit anything with that pistol of yours with its nine-inch barrel and scope."

The pistol was definitely not one that a person would carry every day and kind of looked like a big dinosaur. But I'd shot it thousands of times. I was sitting at the back end of the cabin. BC sat at the other end, about 20 feet away. As I pointed at the wall I said, "I'll bet you five bucks that I can shoot that knot on the wall."

He looked at the knot five feet from his head. "The knot is only one-inch around, you can't hit it. I'll take the bet," he replied.

I grabbed the pistol, cocked the hammer and sighted through the scope. The explosion in the small room was deafening. The pistol recoiled up. I stared at the knot. It was gone.

"Give me my five bucks," I said as I walked toward BC. He was pinned against the wall as he reached into his pocket and handed over the money. The new hole in the wall was within arm's reach of him.

He looked at Alan and said, "I want to get the hell out of here and away from you Montana guys. You've lost all sense of reality."

I winked at Tim and Alan as I walked back to my bunk.

We lived with smell of gunpowder for the next hour, and the recent visit from the neighborhood grizzly still remained fresh in our minds. An open door would be an invitation for him to come right in and make himself at home.

The temperature dropped sharply during the night. Ice formed along the edge of the creek. There wouldn't be near enough water except during the afternoon hours to operate the sluice.

Now Alan had a tough decision to make. He'd made a promise to Tim. Tim had earned his flight to Brandt's and departure to Montana. He had been waiting for this very moment for a month. There was no way to stop him now; he was going home.

It was hard for Alan to finally say the words. It marked the beginning of the end of the mining season. "Tim, pack your gear, David will fly you to Brandt's." He was going to drive my pickup back to Montana.

Five minutes later Tim rushed into the cookshack smiling from ear to ear and replied, "I'm ready to go!"

While at Brandt's, Alan wanted me to see if I could get ahold of Leo and see if he would move all the equipment out to Brandt's. Any gold in the carpet would be his to keep. Under the riffles in the sluice was an Astroturf carpet that held real small pieces of gold. We hadn't cleaned it all summer and there could easily have been five ounces of gold in it. He also wanted me to call the Boss and let him know that we were shutting the operation down.

The oil on the dipstick dripped sluggishly. Usually if the oil dripped the engine would start. If not, I would need to preheat the engine. After a couple of tries the plane finally started. As the engine warmed, Tim plowed the six inches of new snow off the runway.

The clouds hung low over the mountains as we lifted off. Snow drifted lazily by the window and cut the visibility down to a mile. I didn't like flying in fog, but snow was worse. As we passed through intense snow showers, visibility would disappear completely. I immediately shifted my eyes to the instruments and out the side window to look straight down at the ground. I knew every bump and tree on this route, which helped me keep track of my location as we flew.

Finally my visibility got better as we scud run up Squaw Creek and then I eased the final mile into Brandt's. The runway was snow-covered so I used the highway and then taxied up to the front of the café. The last fifteen minutes of flight brought the shaking back to my hands. I was a long way from being back home in Montana and wouldn't let the Alaska environment claim another victim. Flying conditions had deteriorated drastically, now was the time to show restraint and exercise caution.

Tim was quite a sight. He hadn't shaved all summer, one front tooth was missing and hair hung down to his shoulders. An old cowboy hat and worn-out coat added to his rugged appearance.

"It should take three days to get to Montana. Take your time and enjoy the trip," I said to Tim. I was little worried. His appearance made him look like one badass criminal.

"You did an outstanding job this summer," I said as we shook hands.

Tim, a man of few words, replied, "It was quite a summer. I can't believe you survived all the flights in these mountains. Flying with you was the highlight of my summer. It was a pleasure working with you."

I watched him go out of sight. He'd performed all summer without complaint and did anything Alan had asked. He was definitely the guy I'd want on my side going into battle.

The Boss wanted his equipment moved out the next day. He would have three guys at Brandt's at 10:00 a.m. to be flown in to complete the job. He said, "Look out in the parking lot. Do you see a new motorhome sitting out there?"

I replied, "I sure do."

He went on, "Tell BC and Jim to drive it to Chicago. I'll expect them in a week. By the way, how much gold did I get?"

"I think your take was about 80 ounces and a three-quarter ounce nugget. It's beautiful, you'll love it." We said our goodbyes and appreciated doing business with each other.

Leo was in Anchorage. He had talked to Tony and Delores, who had made it home without any problem. Tony had spent another week in the hospital and was now in front of the warm stove.

I let Leo know that Alan and I were going to work the sluice for awhile. Maybe it would warm up and melt enough water to run the sluice.

He said, "Just give me a call when you want the equipment moved."

As I hung up I thought about Leo. I wished he'd stayed at the mine all summer. Leo was a lot of things, but most of all he was a real hard worker. With his help, we'd have found a lot more gold.

The wind blew snow across the highway as I lifted off and headed back toward the mine. The low visibility forced me to fly to the north. As I crossed over the pass that led down Alfred Creek I noticed something that really looked out of place. Whatever it was, it hadn't been there before. I turned toward the object to get a closer look and a Super Cub slowly came into view.

As I got closer I could see not one, but both of the planes. One was upside down and the other one had the landing gear torn off. They'd done exactly what I'd told them not to do. I circled looking for any sign of life, but couldn't see any. The two North Dakota pilots had bit off more than they could chew.

I descended slowly toward our airstrip. It was sad to think about leaving. The Mafia boys were packed and ready to go. Neither one was happy to hear that they had one more night at the mine. Poor Jim was so scared that the bear would return he wouldn't set foot out of the bunkhouse and hung onto my shotgun like it was a part of him.

Alan told the boys that the sluice had a day's worth of gold in it. If they wanted the boss's share, they would have to stick around and help clean the box.

"The hell with that, you can have it," was BC's reply.

The rest of the day was spent strengthening up the bunkhouse. We moved what we could from the cookshack because a big snow would cave the plastic in. That night as Alan and I sat in our plastic-covered dining room, dead silence blanketed the camp. The constant echoing that had been present all summer was gone, making the place feel like a morgue.

Instead of talking we whispered. Although this had been our

home for the last five months, now it seemed like a strange place. We jumped as a bright light filled the room and rushed outside. Streaks of multicolored light danced across the sky, turning the canyon into day. Instantly all the light melted away, returning the camp to pitch black. Alan gasped, "That was unbelievable!"

Just as quickly the light again blossomed across the heavens in pulsating waves and arcs that shot down toward the earth. Faded colors changed to bright green and deep red, flickering across the sky in continuous waves. Both of us stared in awe. The little valley turned to a faded moonscape as the light moved across the sky.

Throughout the summer the lights had tickled our interest, but now Mother Nature showed us her full glory. I heard the natives believe the Aurora Borealis is the highest level of heaven, where the dead dance. Now I understood what they meant.

The light show danced north toward the North Pole and disappeared over the mountain as fast as it had appeared. We stood in reverence for a while longer, then shuffled back to the cookshack. Neither of us said a word as I poured coffee.

The morning broke with clear skies and a 20-degree temperature. We departed the airstrip and landed back at the highway without a problem. I said my goodbyes to Jim and BC. They were gone in minutes. They had shown up looking and acting tough, but grew scared and timid. They were completely out of their element. Alaska had changed them completely.

I walked into the café to order burgers for Alan and me. Eldon sat down beside me and we discussed the season. "Did you know that the two guys from North Dakota wrecked their planes?"

He went on to explain that one of the guys tried landing on the ridge and in the process broke off one of the landing gears and bent his wing. His buddy tried landing further up the ridge and turned his plane over. Neither pilot got hurt, but they had a long walk out to get help. They had borrowed Eldon's pickup and headed to town to find a helicopter to lift the airplanes to the highway.

I told Eldon, "Alaska will bite your bacon if you're not careful." He nodded his head in agreement.

The guys the boss had hired to move his equipment were waiting to go to the mine. We departed immediately, knowing Alan was there all alone. After all the pressure he had been through, I didn't want to leave him alone very long. The continuous bad luck and the strain of keeping the operation afloat had taken a big toll on him mentally.

XXII
SOLITUDE

As we drove back to camp I saw a grizzly walking toward the cookshack. I couldn't see Alan so he must have been in one of the cabins. The bear disappeared behind the building as I turned onto the ramp that led to the buildings.

It was the same bear that had walked up behind Leo a couple of weeks earlier. I stepped out of the rig with my pistol drawn and yelled, "Alan, there's a bear in camp!"

The grizzly then came rushing around the corner of the bunkhouse directly at me. I yelled, "Hey bear, hey bear!" and waved my arms in the air. He slammed on his brakes, surprised to see a strange two-legged animal yelling and waving at him. My pistol was way too small for this giant bear. I stepped back toward the swamp buggy.

The bear turned direction in mid-stride and disappeared in the underbrush. I fired two rounds into the air and yelled again, hoping to scare him enough to make him think twice about coming back.

Alan walked around the corner and stared at me. "Did you see the bear?" I asked.

He shook his head and walked back into the cookshack.

The equipment operators looked astounded as I said, "There's your equipment." The closeness and sight of the grizzly hurried them on their way. They had the machines running and moving up the creek in minutes.

Alan was sitting in the same spot I'd left him in. "How ya doing?" I asked as I walked over to get a cup of coffee. The realization that all the hard effort put forth over the last year might have come up short and his family's dream coming to an end was devastating. The same vigor that had brought him to Alaska was now destroying him.

He had this vision of being a successful Alaskan gold miner. His soul was in a fight with his mind. It knew the truth, but the mind didn't want to give in to the inevitable. Tears ran down his face as I handed him his burger.

He said, "I did everything I could to make this a success. We needed two more weeks of hard mining. We're right at the honey hole and now the weather stops me. What else could go wrong? Could I have done anything else?" His heart was breaking. He shook his head. "What else could I have done?"

The whole thing wasn't easy on me either. At least I could get a logging job if I wanted. But I already knew that I would figure out a way to fly for a living if we didn't return for another season.

Alan could lose his dad's farm, he had sold his construction company, and worst of all, his dad could lose his life. Alan had bet his and his family's life work on gold mining in Alaska.

If we knew then what we knew now, things would've been a lot different, famous last words.

I replied, "Listen Al, no matter how this ends, just remember that you made it possible for your dad to come to Alaska and mine gold. All four of us trusted Shorty, we took him at his word. We just ran into a real scam artist, but all four of us made the decision to come to Alaska. Don't put all this on yourself.

"Ever since we were little kids that was all your dad could talk about, going to Alaska and mining gold. We both heard him say it a thousand times. I'd bet he wouldn't regret one minute of being here this summer. So hold your head high. Not many kids would make such a dream come true for their parents."

Alan didn't reply, he just stared at the ground.

As I looked at Alan I remembered back to the days when he and I had grown up. We'd played on the high school football team and basketball team as starters. But Alan's best claim to fame was his pitching ability. Although we were from Columbia Falls, Whitefish, a town ten miles away, invited Alan and me to play on their all-star baseball team. We traveled to Pincher Creek, a small town in Canada, to play in a tournament, with Alan pitching and me catching. He pitched a no-hitter in the championship game. From the years of playing together I knew he was a fighter. He would get through this moment, in time.

I said, "I think the ice is melted enough to work the sluice. Let's go to work."

It felt good to be back on the equipment. I pushed as much gravel to Alan as I could. This forced Alan to go full speed to keep up. It seemed to bring him back to the present. As the light of day gave way to darkness the water slowed with the dropping temperatures. The sluice box needed just the right amount of water to work and now we didn't have enough.

The camp seemed deserted as we started the fires for the night. We couldn't have been lonelier if we'd been on a deserted island. Somewhere around midnight a big blast of wind rocked the bunkhouse. Both of us immediately came to our feet. We'd had the grizzly in camp only a few hours earlier and it was still on our minds.

The wind blew the door open as I strained to look outside. It looked like we were at the North Pole. The area was in the middle of a full-blown blizzard. The mountains looked like a moonscape. The deep snow covered any sign of vegetation.

Alan and I looked at each other and had the same thought. "Let's get the hell out of here!" My fear was that I wouldn't get the airplane started.

We pulled the sluice box out of the creek and up alongside the bunkhouse. For the remainder of the day we cleaned the gold out of the gravel. The cold water froze our hands, turning them into icicles.

Around midnight we finally finished the outside part of cleaning the sluice. It had been a long, cold day. The blizzard hadn't let up and the snow was getting deeper and deeper.

As the time went on, Alan seemed to go deeper into depression. The summer replayed in his mind and put him into a trance. I was getting more concerned as time went on. When he quit answering my questions I knew that the sooner we left this place, the better it would be for him. He would be his old self, and a second later staring off into space.

The cleanout produced seven ounces of gold. We sized the gold and separated each size into its own jar.

After not saying a thing for two hours Alan spoke up. "Would you take this gold to town tomorrow and get the gold out of the safe-deposit box? Get the best price you can. I owe Eldon a lot of money and hope you can get enough to pay him off."

All summer long I had been worried about getting supplies and knew money was short, but I didn't realize that Eldon had let Alan charge the diesel fuel. "How much do you think you owe him?"

"Somewhere around $30,000."

A quick calculation told me that we had plenty to get Eldon paid off. "I think we have about 80 ounces of gold. Taking care of Eldon should be no problem."

The news seemed to feed a little life back into him. We spent that night talking about the summer events. Somewhere around midnight we wound down and drifted off to sleep.

I woke up shivering, the bunkhouse was freezing cold. Alan wasn't in his bed and the fire had gone out. I put my clothes on and started the stove. Immediately the barrel stove started throwing heat.

The wind had let up during the night, and it was snowing lightly. I sprinted to the cookshack. Alan was sitting next to the open door of the propane oven getting warm.

"Boy is it miserable outside," I said.

He never acknowledged I was even there. Evidently he hadn't slept all night.

"Are you OK?"

He never even blinked. I walked over and grabbed his shoulder. He jumped like he'd just been electrocuted, slowly turned his head and stared at me. Although he was looking at me, his eyes weren't focusing.

I sat down beside him and said, "I'm going to town, and I'll take care of all the gold, the pickup and get ahold of Leo about moving the equipment. All the kitchen stuff needs to be moved into the bunkhouse. Can you move it while I'm gone?

"I'll check on the weather forecast. If it doesn't look too bad, we'll get the hell out of here tomorrow. What do you think?" I asked.

"Be careful, the weather doesn't look very good. After everything that we've been through, we can't afford to have anymore bad luck," Alan replied. At least he was still talking.

The D3 started and I drove it to the airplane. The temperature was twenty degrees. After some hesitation the 300 horsepower engine came to life. While it warmed, I plowed the snow off the runway.

A strong north wind blew down the canyon. As I taxied toward the upper end of the runway, I saw someone running toward the plane. Who could that be out here now?

The guy sprinted straight for the plane, waving. As he got closer I could make out the shrunken face of the older Idaho boy. I opened the door of the plane, he tumbled onto the floor behind my seat and lay on the floor gasping for air.

"What in the hell are you doing out here?" I asked. The second I said it I knew the answer.

"I'm still looking for my brother. Have you seen him?"

I thought to myself, *Holy shit! He doesn't know.* I motioned him into the front seat and said, "We'll talk about it on the way to town."

As he slid into the right seat he said, "Would you drop me off at Brandt's? I've got to see if they have seen my brother."

"You're going to town with me, let me get us in the air and I'll explain," I said as firmly as I could.

We sat on the end of the runway. I wondered if this tail wind takeoff would be the one that would finally get me. I sat with the engine running, waiting for the wind to let up. I didn't want to be a statistic with only a day to go.

I soon realized that waiting wasn't going to make the takeoff easier. The wind rocked the plane continuously. It was now or never. I applied full power. The plane reacted immediately, rolling 200 feet and jumping into the air.

The strong crosswind shoved the plane toward the canyon wall, forcing me to apply down-wing into the wind to counteract the drift. "Thank God," I said to myself as the ground blizzard eased as we climbed.

At about the mountaintop level I eased into blue sky. The wind was strong but at least it wasn't bumpy. This would be my last flight to Anchorage. I was going to try and enjoy the ride, but then remembered who was sitting beside me.

Now I had to give the bad news to the boy, who was staring out the window. He must have known what I was going to tell him. He was skin and bones, all he had with him was a small backpack and sleeping bag. His face looked pale and he was still taking deep breaths of air. "Are you all right?"

"When I heard your plane start I was two miles away. I sprinted all the way until you saw me. Why are you taking me to Anchorage?"

I started, "What I'm going to tell you was told to me. Although it could be a story, I don't believe so. The guy that told me this was pretty convincing. He said that he had been told that someone was stealing gold out of a sluice box."

The kid looked at me with an agonizing stare.

"The person stealing gold was shot and buried in the creek."

"Was it my brother?" he asked pleadingly.

I took a deep breath, blew it all out and said, "He said it was the younger Idaho boy."

He turned his head and gazed out the window, never saying a word for the rest of the flight.

I taxied into my usual spot at Merrill, shut the engine down and stepped out of the plane. The boy slid out behind me.

He said, "I appreciate all the things you did for me and my brother." He shook my hand, turned around and walked away.

I sat down on a tire and reflected about the two boys. Both of them had a lot of salt just to show up in that wilderness. It was just too bad they had ever met Shorty.

I sold the gold at my usual spot. They gave the price I expected, knowing I'd probably be the last one bringing gold in until next summer. Our mechanic for the plane said we could leave the pickup at his place for as long as need be.

Leo didn't answer his phone, so I left a message telling him goodbye and that he could move the equipment right away. I sure wished I could have seen him one last time.

Then I drove over to the Flight Service Station to get the forecasted weather. It didn't look good. A cold arctic front had moved into the area and was expected to remain for some time.

I departed Merrill Field for the last time. The weather toward the mine looked terrible but it had been that way most of the summer. Why would it be any different now? The headwind made the flight back to the mine slow. I was surprised to see that the weather around the mine had improved greatly.

Alan hadn't moved from the spot I'd left him in. He said, "I've been worried sick about you, I just knew you had been in a wreck."

"It's going to take a lot more to get rid of me than a little weather."

We both smiled, realizing luck had been on my side all summer. I hoped it remained with us all the way home.

"The weather is going to get worse. I think we should get out of here while we can," I said.

"What do you mean, right now?"

"We still have five hours of daylight. If we both work we can have the camp closed up in an hour. Then we'll fly to Brandt's, pay Eldon and head for Montana."

The thought of heading home brought life back to both of us.

While I drove the machinery around and parked it for Leo, Alan loaded the bunkhouse with everything from the cookshack. We worked so hard and fast that we didn't have time to think about the past.

We took all the expensive gold equipment with us. Everything else went in the bunkhouse. With this completed, we nailed the door shut and wrapped the whole building with black plastic.

Then to make sure no animals got in the building, we wrapped rope around the entire structure. I told Alan, "We'll be back in the spring and move the operation to a new claim."

He replied, "With a little luck we might be."

As we drove up to the plane I told Alan I thought we were making a good decision to get out of the mine that day. The forecasted temperature might have made it impossible to get the plane started until spring.

We each kept our thoughts to ourselves as we loaded all the gear into the plane. We had 500 pounds of black sand. The sand was just about as heavy as gold, and took a different process to get the gold out of it. The plane was loaded all the way to the ceiling. Anything of any value was going home with us.

We took one last look around and then got into the plane. The ache in my chest gave away my feelings. This place had been our home for the last five months. This might be my last takeoff from the mine. As we lifted off, I turned down the creek for one last look at the camp. It looked lonely and abandoned as we both stared at our summer home. We sat in silence as we approached the highway at Brandt's. We taxied up to the café and shut down.

Alan walked into the café to say goodbye to Mary and Eldon. I filled up the plane, five gallons at a time. Mary had sandwiches ready as I stepped into the café. Alan was just finishing counting out $32,220. The cash lay in a big pile. It was a lot of money, and Eldon smiled from ear to ear. He'd probably wondered if Alan would be able to pay him. Alan proved true to his word and paid him every penny.

I made a phone call home. Ryan answered the phone. "Hi Son, I'm on my way home."

He yelled, "Alrighta!"

I asked Noreen if Tim had made it home and she replied, "Your pickup is dented everywhere. When Tim dropped it off he said that a bunch of guys had beat him up."

I replied, "We'll talk about it when I get home."

"Fly carefully, I'll see you tomorrow," she said.

As we walked out to the plane I asked, "You know who has the gold mine, don't you?" Before he could answer I said, "Mary and Eldon."

"Boy, you got that right!" Alan replied.

As we lifted off the snow was starting to come down. I turned north along the highway. A wall of snow cut the visibility to a quarter of a mile and seemed to be getting worse as we flew toward Glennallen. I decided to leave the highway. Off to the south was the Nelchina River, and maybe the lower elevation of the river would help. With a half-mile of visibility we finally found Tazlina Lake. The river out of the lake would eventually get us to the Copper River and Glennallen.

For a few minutes I thought we might have to turn back to Brandt's. "Watch out that side of the plane," I told Alan. I stared straight down at the ground as we eased forward, hunting for something we recognized. Alan slid forward in the seat to get a better view out the window, trying to point out anything that might be a hazard. I told Alan, "This might be the worst weather I've flown in all summer."

It was a great relief to see the snow let up and visibility go to ten miles. Alaska wasn't going to let us get away that easily. We were going to earn our right of passage out of the state. There are no free rides in this rugged land.

We landed at the little village of Northway, filled up with gas and filed a flight plan to Whitehorse. The flight guy asked, "Can you make Whitehorse before dark? It's against the law to fly VFR at night in Canada."

"No problem," I replied. There was no way we were going to get there before dark.

The plane struggled to lift the heavy load as we climbed out of Northway and headed for Whitehorse.

We bumped and jumped with the gusty wind conditions. As we turned the corner at Haines Junction a gust of wind grabbed the plane and rocketed us downward. Everything in the plane hit the ceiling, including us.

After seconds of dropping, the plane slammed to a stop. Everything fell back to the floor. The pain in my lower back was excruciating. The plane moved forward like nothing had happened. Both of our backs told us otherwise!

As we neared Whitehorse, darkness set in. I was having trouble seeing out the window. Close examination revealed oil coming out of the engine compartment and flowing up the window. "Whitehorse Tower, Cessna 61101 is ten north, inbound to land."

The tower cleared us to land. We made a slow approach and touched down on the numbers. The radio came to life. "Cessna 61101 clear to taxi to customs, it's the blue painted box next to the tower."

I repeated the clearance. Suddenly I remembered that pistols weren't legal in Canada. I yelled at Alan, "Hide my pistol in the back of my seat back." He grabbed it, pulled the Velcro that held the material in place, then placed the pistol in the hiding spot and replaced the Velcro covering.

"Did you get it in there?" I asked as I pulled into the blue square box. A customs agent stood glaring at us. After the engine was shut down he walked around the plane, shaking his head and talking into a hand-held radio. Then he walked up to my door and asked where we were coming from and where we were going.

"You guys stand over there in that white box," pointing at a little white square painted on the ramp. Two more agents showed up. They slowly examined every item as they removed it from the plane. My lower back ached so I lay down on the ramp.

One of the agents crawled out of the plane with my shotgun in his hand. "Whose rifle and shotgun is this?" he asked.

"They're mine," I replied.

He continued, "Are they loaded?"

"I don't see any reason to have them if they're not," I answered, *the wrong thing to say*. Two agents moved in toward us, their hands on their pistols.

I said, "Come on guys, give us a break. We just spent five months in a gold mine, all we want to do is go home."

Both guys glared at us while the other one finished emptying the plane. One of the agents walked up and handed me a blue slip. Then he said, "You have three days to get through Canada, I recommend you get it done." Then all three walked away.

They had looked in every spot, except the one that held the pistol.

We spent the next hour reloading the plane and then found a motel for a well-deserved hot bath and night's sleep.

At daylight we were in the plane, anxious to get home. A close check of the plane revealed the crankshaft seal protruding out of the engine case. There weren't any mechanics on the field so we departed for Watson Lake. We would need to stop every three hours for fuel; I could clean the oil off the windscreen then. In the meantime I could look out the side window to see where we were going.

I filled the plane with fuel at Watson, and Alan cleaned off the oil. I told him, "We only have two more stops, we can make it home the way it is."

Next came Fort Nelson and then Fort Saint John. The people on the ramp stared as we stepped out of the oil-covered plane, and to make it worse, neither of us had shaved or had a haircut for weeks. For the first time since we left the mine, I stood back and looked at the plane, and then said, "No wonder customs treated us so bad, we look like convicts!"

If everything went right we could make Kalispell nonstop. We loaded back into the plane and turned the key. Nothing happened. "Shit, the regulator is out again," I told Alan.

It had gone out a couple of times during the summer. Its job was to regulate the amount of electrical power to the starter and radios, but once the engine was running it didn't need the regulator to keep running.

I stepped out of the plane and told Alan, "Slide over into the pilot's seat."

"What are you going to do?"

"I'll hand prop the engine. Once it's running we'll be fine," I replied. "Do what I say, brakes on, mags on, mixture rich, crack the throttle. Here we go." I slowly pulled the prop through until the engine was on its power stroke. The propeller sat horizontal.

The 300-horse engine wouldn't be easy to pull through. If there were any chance of starting, I would need to pull the prop hard enough to get two cylinders to fire. If the engine came to life, the prop would spin up like a meat clever.

I swung my leg in and then back as I pulled down, the momentum of the leg moving back caused my fingers and body to move away from the dangerous propeller. The engine coughed and then came to life. We were in business.

I still had enough power in the battery to run the radio. The tower gave me a clearance to depart. I replied, "Saint John's Tower, would you open my flight plan to Kalispell?"

They acknowledged my request.

It had been a long summer, we were almost home and the airplane was doing its best to get us to our destination.

But we still had a couple of nagging problems that I hoped wouldn't get any worse. Oil splattered on the windshield continuously; it was just about more than I could take. After an hour the front window was covered in oil, forcing me to either stare out past Alan or look out my left side window.

The other problem bothered me more than the first, we had no electrical power at all. The engine was running fine, but I had no flaps or radios. All navigation instruments were dead and for the first time in months I had a map out to follow our progress down the east front of the Rockies. We were far enough out in the prairie that we could barely see the mountains, with the swamps and flat land below making it hard to hold my heading. I told Alan, "I'd rather be in the mountains than out here on the prairie. There are no landmarks to navigate by out here."

We passed Calgary to the west, and headed for Pincher Creek. The sun was starting to set low in the west. I was hoping that we could slip past Browning, Montana and through Marias Pass before dark. Now I could see that it would be dark before we made the U.S. border.

The oil problem seemed to be getting worse. Forward visibility was completely lost, giving me a big decision to make. Did we want to cross the 10,000-foot mountains of Glacier National Park with marginal visibility or land in Lethbridge and spend the night?

"What do you think, Al?" I asked as I looked at him.

He replied, "Do you think I would make any decision after all the dangerous flights you've made with this plane? You never hurt anyone and always made the right call. So now is not the time to ask me what to do. I'll agree with whatever you want to do."

He knew what I was going to do, I always pressed on. I said, "Dig out the flashlight, we're going to Kalispell." The outline of the tall peaks emerged high in front of us. The tired machine was giving one last effort to get us over the jagged peaks of the Rocky Mountains. The downwind bucked the plane from side to side, fighting us for every inch of altitude. "The old girl is working hard, but I'm not sure she's going to get us over the top with these downdrafts," I said.

The outline of a sharp flat-sided peak came into view on our right side, so I turned the plane toward the peak. Alan looked at me with a frown that said, what are you doing?

"If we can just get to the west of that mountain, with any luck we should find an updraft."

But as we flew toward it, the wind kept pushing us down and got stronger, creating an almost out-of-control descent that forced me to apply constant control input. The plane staggered as the high winds hit us from different directions. A big gust of wind slammed the plane to a near stop. Instinctively I shoved the yoke forward as the machine shuttered in a stall.

The mountain shot upward as we dropped. I yelled, "If we don't hit that updraft in the next few seconds, we'll have to dive out of this turbulence before it's too late!"

"God, it should be right here," I whispered to myself.

Alan's face showed the fear I felt. Right when I said "here" the plane soared upward. The vertical speed indicator showed a 2000-foot per minute climb and we sat back to enjoy the elevator ride. The altimeter passed 11,000 feet, then twelve, and the lights of the Flathead Valley were shining in the distance.

We were home free! Tears ran down my face, this was the home of our youth but would never look the same after being in Alaska.

Alan slapped me on the back and said, "You did it, you got us home!"

As we gazed at the lights, sadness and joy confused me. I had survived the harshness of Alaska; it had been a dream to go there and be a bush pilot. I could still feel the fondness and yearning for Alaska that I'd had for years. It's a grand place, but the harsh environment and a few shady people made it into a place of great danger. Many people and companies had lost everything there. But we'd survived, and with the grace of God just maybe we would go back.

Why had I survived the harsh flying conditions? I could only come up with one answer. Some unknown force had protected all of us. Call it luck, call it divine guidance. Whatever it was, I had survived some terrible flight conditions.

Maybe Alan could figure out a way to get back to the mine. Down the creek 20 miles more placer claims were available.

As we each parted for our own way home Alan said, "Let's take a few days to unwind, then get together to discuss the future."

For most of the last six months Alan and I had called the bunkhouse in Alfred Creek home, now it felt strange to go home alone.

Would we be going back to Alaska? I had my doubts. But for the time being, I was happy to be home.

XXIII
A FAMILY'S DREAM

The next three days were spent telling Ryan stories. "Did you shoot any more caribou? How many sheep did you see?" The questions and answers went on for hours and hours. It was absolutely great to be home. The endless shake in my hands slowly subsided.

But something was definitely wrong. An empty, hollow feeling remained deep in my chest. After six months of nerve-wracking flights, constant movement, and continuous anxiety, ironically it was now that I couldn't relax. The events of the mining season played over and over in my mind. If I did fall asleep, a nightmarish dream would wake me in a cold sweat. Slamming the plane into the rock wall at the end of the runway or a grizzly in the cookshack haunted my dreams.

I should have felt great. I hadn't killed myself or hurt anyone and was home with my family. Yet something was wrong and I couldn't figure it out.

After three days of calling I finally got ahold of Tim. "Hi, how are you doing? What the hell happened to my pickup?"

Tim replied, "You got a few minutes, it's a long story." He continued, "You can't believe how excited I was to be headed for Montana. It took forever to get to the Canadian border. My excitement was short-lived, they wouldn't let me cross the border. Since the pickup didn't belong to me, I needed a letter from you to take the pickup into Canada. The only option I had was to drive back to Tok. I left a message at Brandt's. When you didn't call back I called Delores and had her fax a letter for you."

Tim continued, "I held my breath as the custom agents scrutinized the letter. After an hour of sweating, I was on the road and headed home. Everything went well until I stopped at a bar for some food."

I replied, "That still doesn't tell me what happened to my pickup."

"Just let me continue," Tim said. "As I walked out of the bar three guys jumped me. They robbed and beat the shit out of me. I guess I should have cut my hair and shaved as you suggested. Anyway, thank God you had that hundred-dollar bill in the glove box. From there I drove straight through. Somewhere around Muncho Lake I fell asleep and ran the pickup into the ditch. I didn't roll it, but it was in both ditches before I got it stopped. Do you want me to get it fixed?"

The guy had already been through enough. I said, "No, I'll trade it in on something better." I thought to myself, *what hundred dollars?*

We spent an hour discussing the summer's operation. Tim had already found a job as a diesel mechanic, so he was going to be all right. He went on to say, "You know, Dave, I didn't make much money, but I had the trip of a lifetime. We did things that we can talk about into our old age. I wouldn't trade this experience for anything. The flying you and I did will be etched in my mind forever."

That evening I got a phone call from Leo. He said, "I just got to Brandt's with the D8 and D3. I towed the old swamp buggy out loaded down with most of the gear you guys left in the bunkhouse." He continued, "I brought the gold carpet out with me. I'll clean it and send Alan half the gold. David, I can't talk right now, but I'm hearing some rumors that you need to pass on to Dad, Mom and Alan. I'll call you tomorrow evening at seven. By the way, the wind is blowing 40 miles an hour and it is ten below zero. You guys got out just in time."

I hung up wondering what kind of rumor he'd heard.

The next evening the phone rang right on time. "What the hell do you want?"

Leo laughed and said, "You knew it was me."

I continued, "Evidently you got back into town all right. What was so important you couldn't tell me on the phone last night?"

Leo answered, "While I was sitting at Brandt's a miner walked up to me and asked me if I was one of the Montana miners. He went on to say that he bet we weren't coming back for another mining season. I asked him how he knew that and he said he used to work for Shorty. He has screwed a lot of miners. His scam is to get people from the outside to work his claims. He'll say anything to get people here. Then he promises to furnish a sluice box. When it doesn't materialize he tells the new miners that they have to hire someone like him to design and work the newly-built sluice box.

"Listen to this, you won't believe it," Leo continued. "The sluice box design will only catch the bigger pieces of gold. All the fine gold gets washed through the sluice box and then is conveniently piled alongside the creek by the miners."

"Let me guess," I replied, "Then Shorty and Melvin come back to the mine and run the neatly stacked and cleaned piles of gravel through a small sluice that just happens to catch the fine gold. What a scam!"

Leo continued, "That was the reason we never caught fine gold in the sluice. Remember Melvin never had an answer to why we weren't catching the smaller gold. Now we know why.

"The last thing the miner said to me was, 'It's sure funny someone hasn't shot the little thief.' I knew something was wrong from the start. No one would listen to me."

So all the rumors and suspicions turned out to be true. One thing for sure, we weren't going back to Shorty's claims.

"I thought you had leased an old Caterpillar from Shorty?" I asked.

"I did," Leo replied.

"You'd better be careful. You never know what that little shit is planning next," I replied.

Leo continued, "I have a plan to get some money from Shorty, I'll let you know what happens." We talked for a few more minutes. I told him to keep in touch and said goodbye.

Two nights later the phone rang. It was the Boss. He asked, "When did BC and Jim leave Alaska?"

I replied, "They left a day after I talked to you on the phone."

He continued, "They haven't shown up yet."

I didn't know what to say, then blurted out, "A grizzly tried to get in the cabin a few days before they left. It scared the hell out of them. You don't think they stole your gold, do you?"

He replied, "I don't know, but I'll find them."

We talked for awhile about all our deals with Shorty. I could tell that he'd had similar problems. Then he said, "Shorty has dealings with some of my friends in other cities. I'll pass on your story to them. I appreciate your help."

We said our goodbyes. The boss and his camp had been honorable and trustworthy during the time we had known them.

As it turned out, Leo passed along some information about BC to

Tony and Delores. From the very first time we'd seen BC, everyone had the feeling that they recognized him. Leo solved the problem when he saw BC's picture on the 'Wanted' board at the Post Office.

The next night I drove up to Tony and Delores's house. Alan was already there. It was like one big happy reunion. We spent the next two hours talking about the summer, laughing uncontrollably as story after story replayed. Reliving Tony's diarrhea problem brought the house down. Delores shook her head as I mimicked the look on her face when I ran into the cookshack after Tony had sprayed her and the bed.

Tony's foot was as bad as ever. The doctors were thinking about removing the foot right below the knee. Even that didn't shake him. He was still his old self, with joke after joke, story after story.

I relayed the information Leo told me about Shorty. Alan's hard-lined face told me he wanted to go to Alaska to permanently take care of the con-man. But without proof it was pointless.

Alan said, " Leo was right after all. From the very beginning he thought Melvin was stealing gold. I wouldn't listen to him. Remember how Melvin insisted we go back and work the sluice while he cleaned the gold? Then in the same area and same amount of time we gained 20 more ounces when Leo demanded we clean the gold with Melvin. I'll bet he got away with 30 ounces in just the first couple of weeks." He continued, "He sure was the laziest guy I'd ever been around. I just didn't want to believe anyone would steal from us.

"David, there is no way we can go back. I have talked the bank into taking only the land, not the farmhouse or the land it sits on. Tok Equipment is going pick up the machines and sell them for us. I found someone to buy the plane. All of us gave a 100 percent effort. It just wasn't meant to be." Alan lowered his head.

Tony spoke up, "I don't care how the gold mining ended, my life-long dream came true. Delores and I went to Alaska to live a dream, not to make money. You guys hold your heads high. Just think about what we accomplished. We found gold and got to fly all over Alaska. How many people can say they have done that?"

I said, "I've been thinking about this since we got home. Shorty's family doesn't even know what a crook he is, he lies even to them. I'm going to send a letter to Jimmy, Shorty's son, and tell him about his dad's dishonesty. Maybe it will keep someone else from being scammed like us."

Everyone thought it was a good idea. I left knowing we'd had a great experience, but now it was over.

I went back to work in the woods a few days later. Flying the airplane all summer made me soft. I suffered for a few days, but was back in shape in short order. I wrote the letter, but contemplated sending it for the next few months. Shorty was a bad guy, but I wasn't sure it was right to let his family know what he was really like. So the letter sat on a shelf, forgotten.

In February I received a call from Leo. "David, I'm in big trouble."

"What's the matter?"

"Shorty talked me into borrowing money from him and then gave me a connection to buy cocaine. I was supposed to give him his money back plus $20,000 when I sold the drugs. I got caught at the Chicago Airport with the drugs on me. You're my one call."

"You've got to be kidding! What's going to happen?"

"They're going to give me 30 years unless I turn state's evidence. What should I do?"

"Leo, listen to me. Tell them everything they want to know. In 30 years you'd be an old man."

He replied, "That's what I'll do, thanks."

I started to say, "Let me know," but the phone went dead. He was in big trouble.

I added Leo's part onto the letter and put it in the mail. I mentioned his shady mining practices, and how he lied to Alan and misled other miners. I told about the Idaho boys and now Leo's borrowing money and getting directions on how to buy and sell cocaine. *Your dad has caused a lot of people great sorrow and pain. He may think that he has gotten away with all his scams and bad deeds, but there is a time when everyone pays for their actions. Your dad will have to stand up and be judged. On that day he will pay. Everyone ended up losing except your dad*, the final sentence read.

Not a day went by that I didn't regret sending the letter. Even though Shorty had proven to be a cheat and a liar, his family were nice people.

A few days later I received a phone call, and the person on the other end wanted to know if I was interested in flying a Cessna 185 from Anchorage to Montana. He'd pay all the bills and wages. I jumped at the offer. A week later I departed Merrill Field in the strange plane and headed for Northway. This would be a great opportunity to get a look at our old camp.

At the Matanuska Glacier I turned left up Caribou Creek; it felt like home, sweet home. The whole area was covered with three feet of snow. The pure white mountains and valleys turned the area into a winter wonderland. The melting of the snow would bathe away any evidence of the previous year's assault on the land. Any evidence of machinery working the creeks would be wiped out by high water. The only objects left to indicate a mining operation had been there were the tailing piles full of the gold we left behind, cabins and gas barrels.

My heart pounded as I flew over our campsite. The snow was a lot deeper than I expected. Alan and I had blocked up the bunkhouse with six-inch tree stumps hoping to keep the building from caving in. As I floated over the cabin, I couldn't find it. On the second pass I lowered my elevation so I just cleared the steep canyon walls to get a better look.

The buildings were gone, completely gone! There was no sign of anything except the fuel barrels and big sluice box. All of Alan's mining gear was gone, or stolen. How could anyone remove everything during the winter? Tracks in the snow led around the end of Syncline Mountain and then to the highway at Gunsight Mountain Lodge. I could only guess who had stolen all the gear. Judging from the tracks, they must have used a big machine. I knew that Alan had sent a letter to Shorty telling him that he would remove all his equipment the next summer. But whoever stole the gear and buildings made sure we weren't coming back.

The rest of the flight back to Montana was spent thinking about Alaska. It was a great place and I'd gained a lot of experience. My love affair for the great land was stronger than ever.

The minute I got home I called Alan to let him know what I'd seen at the mine.

He said, "I thought that might happen. Thank God we brought all the expensive gold equipment with us. Leo hauled out anything else of value. So, whoever stole the buildings didn't get much more than wood."

"I hope they got frostbite." We both laughed.

Even though I was back sawing timber, my mind was continuously on Alaska and flying. Now I knew that I could fly with the best of them. The big question that remained was how to find or create a job where I was flying for a living.

XXIV
ANIMAL CHASER

The wolves circled the mother grizzly and her seven-month old cub. She would fight to the death to defend her offspring. As I circled overhead and watched the story unfold, I thought maybe the pack was just harassing the bears, not really out to injure them. Over the last 15 years this same scene had played out many times. But this time was different. The 18 wolves had blood in their eyes.

The big bear reared up on her hind legs and pushed back against a four-foot high fallen yellow pine tree. Her mother dwarfed the young cub. The little bear moved around her mother's legs, trying not to get stepped on or snatched by a wolf.

If one of the wolves grabbed the infant, it was all over. Ivory colored four-inch daggers extended from the paws of the bloodthirsty bear, ready to rip apart any trespasser that came within reach. From the savageness of the attack I could tell that this was a fight to the death. The odds were against the great bear.

My Cessna 185 circled lower, the highly modified wings kept me flying at 40 miles per hour. The airplane, an old friend, performed remarkably. I was almost at a hover as I circled to see the action.

Since my return from Alaska I had accumulated over 20,000 hours of flight time. Days were spent tracking animals; grizzlies, wolves, elk, moose, wolverines and even occasional fish were followed daily. The best thing about it was I got paid to do it.

As I flew, I often dreamed about how I got started in this career. The year in Alaska had been priceless, I had gained more than just five months of work. It gave me the experience and casual, calm presence that keeps me alive every day.

Glacier National Park and the Bob Marshall Wilderness are now my home. The worries that a swindler like Shorty would take what I had are gone.

Shorty paid for his indiscretions. A year after I mailed his son the letter, my brother, Larry, his son Cory, and Ryan and I went to Alaska to go fishing.

The shame and guilt of sending the revealing letter wore on me daily. I often thought, *What right did I have to expose a father?*

With great apprehension I stepped into Shorty's son Jimmy's office. As our eyes met, the stern look on his face cut through me. He pointed his finger at me and said, "I need to talk to you."

He disappeared into a back room. I followed hesitantly. I would stand and take the verbal abuse, I'd earned it.

He turned around and said, "You know that letter you sent me?"

I nodded and thought to myself, *Here we go.*

He continued, "When I read your letter I thought you were absolutely demented. But you know what, every statement you made has proven correct."

Shocked, I stuttered, "What are you talking about?"

"Since Dad died, we have been inundated with calls from people saying he had swindled them. He was even involved with the Mafia and now they want Mom to pay back everything Dad owed. They have threatened us with our lives. We've sold almost everything we own. But that's not near enough to get them off our backs."

As he talked his face got red and his voice got louder. "We found out that Dad had been scamming and swindling people for years. But you know what? That old son of a bitch got what he had coming."

"What do you mean?"

"He got so greedy he wouldn't let anyone else close to the mine. All your old tailing piles were producing a lot of gold for him. We offered to help, but he wouldn't even let me come to the mine. He had gold fever bad. It killed him."

"Your dad's dead?"

Jimmy continued, "Dad left town headed for the mine. The day he said he would be back came and went. A week later he still wasn't back, so I walked the 30 miles to Dad's cabin. The old swamp buggy was parked outside. Before I opened the door, I could smell rotting flesh.

"When I broke the door open, flies swarmed out in a black cloud. The stench almost knocked me back out the door. I had to hold my breath as I moved to the bed. His money and nuggets were spread all around him. His whole body was covered with maggots. He had been dead for quite awhile. We think he had a heart attack."

The shock of hearing the story gave me an empty feeling in my stomach. I didn't like Shorty, but even after everything he'd done to other people, no one deserved to die like that.

Jim said, "David, you were right when you said one day Dad would have to stand up and be judged."

As I walked out of the shop I remember thinking, *Even with all that gold and money he couldn't scam death.*

The wolves dove into the side of the grizzly. She turned toward the pain of the bites. Her reactions were quick, but not as quick as the wolves. Her giant arm swung at the attackers, only to miss the target. Immediately the canines would attack from the other side, only to have the same process replayed. Pieces of hide flew as three-inch canine teeth tore away flesh. The old bear wasn't going to survive long.

Sooner or later she would have to make a run for a more concealed spot. Maybe a rock cliff or being out in the middle of a nearby river would save her. But, if she moved, the cub would be left unprotected. Eventually, though, she would have to save herself.

As I watched the two bears fight for survival, I thought about Leo. He'd served his time in prison. He must have felt a lot like the little bear, trying to survive in a bizarre world. Seven years of his life were squandered. He'd made mistakes and paid for them. At least he survived and worked his way back into society.

We still communicate occasionally. He now owns a rain gutter business and is doing well.

As for Tim, I think about him often. He had been a valuable part of the gold mine. When he walked into my office ten years later, his unkempt appearance had improved to a slim, well-kept demeanor. He had a beautiful young wife and two preschool boys. The boys had been hearing about the pilot who had kept his dad safe. As we relived a few of our Alaska stories, the boys stared at me with wide eyes. When Tim drove away to his California home, I knew I had a friend for life, even if I never saw him again.

The attack on the mother bear was taking a big toll on her strength. Survival instinct kicked in and as she ran she would oscillate around at the wolves as they assaulted from behind. They pursued like a swarm of bees, easily keeping pace with the sprinting bear.

But the grizzly was cunning, leading her chasers into thick underbrush, which gave her the advantage. The wolves couldn't get away fast enough. A big black wolf moved in for a bite. His reactions were quick, but the huckleberry bushes stopped his escape. The big bear stood up, giving me a better view. She had the wolf in her mouth! The wolf lay limp as the fight moved away.

The attackers were slowly becoming the attacked.

The wolves stood back, not wanting to be the next victim. I circled back to see where the cub was. I figured a couple of the wolves would have it ripped to shreds, and strained to see any sign of the small bear.

"There it is," I said to myself. High in a Douglas fir tree sat the infant. I smiled as I thought how the mother bear had outsmarted the wolf pack. She had used cunning and wit to make survival possible for her and her offspring.

As I flew back toward town I thought about how we had survived that year in Alaska, or had we survived? Well, physically we all made it back to Montana. As for our mental condition, the jury was still out.

Alan had moved to California, starting a very successful hardwood floor business and recently moved back to the Flathead. At 49 he is semi-retired and has a new wife and son. We visit often and reminisce about Alaska. The years have diminished the anger and pain. I often remind him of what he did for his mom and dad.

As for me, I have a successful flying business, Red Eagle Aviation, in Kalispell. What started out as a one-plane, one-man operation has turned into five planes and a helicopter. I've also remarried, and live with my wife, Linda, on Flathead Lake.

Ryan is following in my footsteps, flying wildlife surveys and wilderness charter flights.

Over the years I've had a lot of exciting flights and great memories while keeping track of two endangered species, grizzlies and wolves. On one of these flights my job was to fly a wolf pack that had been killing sheep in Pleasant Valley for a couple of months. My job was to locate the pack, then report their location to the wildlife biologists. The seven wolves were lying in the airplane, one beside me and the rest behind. I had a 30-minute flight to get them to the wilderness airstrip. The drugs that kept them asleep were good for only 40 minutes. I didn't even want to think of what would happen if they woke up prematurely.

The biologist waited at the airstrip as I pumped down the skis for a snow landing. As I turned final on the wilderness airstrip, the alpha female sleepily raised her head and pierced me with her big yellow eyes. Her six pups were lined up like cordwood between us. I looked at her and said, "You just lay your head back down, old girl. I'll have you and your family on the ground in a few minutes."

I figured there was no reason to get to excited now, Alaska had provided more frightening situations than this. A few minutes later the wolves were on the ground exploring their new home.

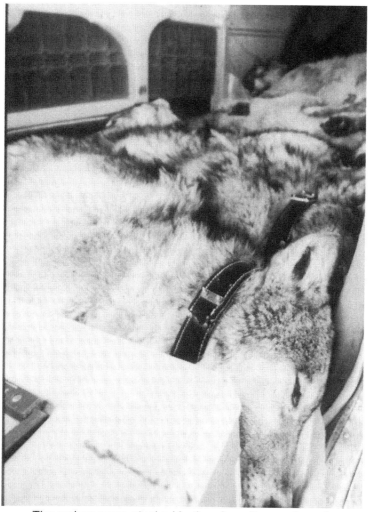

The wolves were stacked in the plane like cordwood.
I was sure glad the Alpha female was in the back.

Another exciting flight etched forever in my memory ensued while moving a grizzly, asleep on the floor of the plane beside me. The young bear had been getting into an outfitter's camp and would get one more chance, so a biologist and I would move the bear to a deserted wilderness airstrip. The problem with grizzlies is that each one reacts differently to the drugs. This bear should sleep for an hour. As I started to add power for takeoff, the bear let out a low growl. The drugs paralyzed muscle use, but now the bear had enough control to growl. This wasn't good. The grizzly was waking up.

I slammed on the brakes and slid to a stop. The biologist and I were out of the plane in a flash and opened the door. We grabbed the grizzly, pulling the bear out and to the ground.

It was time for us to seek the safely of the plane. The drug wore off and the bear slowly walked into the trees. He gave us a disdainful last look and was gone. It had been a good day. The adrenalin rush brought back memories of Alaska.

After thousands of grizzly and wolf sightings, I have learned to trust the old sixth sense. My subconscious tells me where to go, and nine out of ten times the animal is where I thought.

I felt this unusual feeling for the first time while flying gold in Alaska. Whenever danger threatened, my hands would tremble; the hair on my arms and neck would stand up. This feeling has kept me alive for the last 20 years. I thank God for that gift.

The short and rough Alaskan airstrips had pushed me beyond my abilities. Should I go or should I shut the plane down and refuse to go? That was always the choice I had to make. Nine out of ten times I'd push the envelope and fly.

I'd been lucky, sure. But I also realize that we make our own luck. If good decisions are made, then good luck will follow. I had made a commitment to my cousin. Flying is what he hired me to do, and it took a lot of bad weather to keep me on the ground.

Not many days go by without reflecting back to Alaska; the yearning to be there haunts me still. The towering Alaskan mountains, snow-capped peaks and yellow-orange lower slopes call me back to the gold mining summer. My mind's eye lets me see silver-maned bull caribou swinging their magnificent antlers. Alaska is a place where dreams are made.

The gizzly looked liked a teddy bear, until he woke up.

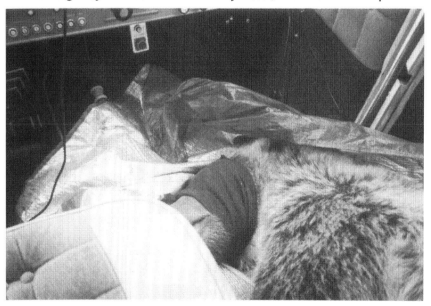

The bear let out a low growl, he was waking up in the plane.

Sometimes I imagine Uncle Tony sitting in the right seat, trying to spot an animal before I did. Or Aunt Delores staring at me saying, "Don't you kill me," as we descended through the clouds with the broken engine. Once we were safe on the ground she said, "I knew you could do it."

I don't believe any of the flying I do now would have happened if I hadn't wandered to Alaska and acquired the experience of a lifetime. Tony, Delores, Leo and Alan made it possible. I will eternally be in their debt.

For a long time we all thought that the summer gold mining was a complete loss. We had struggled, and the effort to survive had tried our souls. But through all the struggle and effort we grew, became better people, and a closer-knit family.

Alaska is a magnificent place, but its beauty and enchantment can be misleading. It is a place of extreme peril. The high winds and poor weather conditions have claimed many lives. It will devour the unprepared or misguided. I still wonder why I survived and so many before and after me never came home.

There are days when I crave to go back north. I miss handling real gold nuggets, seeing huge glaciers, landing on short mining airstrips and even landing at Merrill Field.

As I scanned the help-wanted ads this last year I noticed one that said, "Enstrom helicopter pilot wanted in Alaska to fly fishermen." Maybe I would be going north again!

My aim was on the middle of her chest. Then the griz turned and headed back up the hill. About halfway up she met the cubs coming down and stopped and looked at us while the cubs turned and followed.

I still had the site on the bear. Mark said, "Put another one in, put another one in!"

I had been concentrating so hard I didn't understand what he wanted me to do. He surely didn't want me to shoot the retreating bear.

"What do you want me to do?" I asked.

Mark replied, "Put another bullet in that empty chamber." He was right; I was down to four rounds. If the bear decided to come back, I would need all five.

The bear stopped at the top of the hill and shook her head, then disappeared out of sight.

All four of us stood and looked at each other. I said, "Look at this!" I still had the hook in my hand.

Then Naomi said, "What would we have done if David hadn't had the pistol?"

Mark stood with a ten-pound fish in his hand. "I would have thrown her a fish." We all laughed and decided we had enough fish and left for the lodge.

For some reason Mark didn't call me Cowboy again.

The next day I was leaving the lodge for Montana. I had a great time. Even though I was leaving again, I knew someday I would be back. Maybe I would move part of my flight operation to Alaska. My love of the great land is as strong as ever. My thoughts turned to some words Uncle Tony said to Alan and me 21 years ago.

"My lifelong dream came true. You guys hold your heads high. Just think what we accomplished. We found gold and flew all over Alaska. How many people can say they did that?"

The next morning I departed Anchorage International Airport headed for Montana. There wasn't a cloud in the sky. The jet circled north and climbed. The flight path would take us over the Matanuska Glacier. I sat with anticipation of seeing Caribou Creek, then Alfred Creek and the spot where we mined gold.

The sight of the mine stuck in my mind as the plane flew south. My head leaned against the side window. My thoughts went back 20 years to Uncle Tony and Aunt Delores.

They had arrived home in a couple of days from Alaska. The infection had spread up the leg. A few months later the foot was removed below the knee. For the next year Tony grappled with the healing. I stopped to see him many times. He was still his old self, making jokes and hiding around corners, only to scare the next victim. He would laugh until he would almost fall down.

The infection wouldn't respond to the medication. The amputation of the rest of the leg was to be performed in Spokane. While on the operating table he had a massive heart attack, which resulted in open-heart surgery.

Tony survived the surgery long enough to play one more trick. Alan relayed the story: "After the surgery Dad was wheeled into a special recovery room. We peered in the window for any sign of life. The light flashed on his heart monitor. I stepped into the room and walked to the bed. As I reached down to hold his hand, Dad raised both arms and hollered, then laughed for the next ten minutes. He had been waiting, God knows how long, to scare just one more person."

That evening I got a call from Delores wanting to know if I would fly to Spokane to bring Tony home. He had died during the night.

The next morning I met the hearse at Felts Field Aviation and loaded Uncle Tony into the plane beside me. The blanket slid off his face. I talked to him about Alaska and gold mining all the way home. An empty feeling and the great loss of a friend pained my soul. Tears flowed as we addressed the gold mine and the future. I could still hear him say, "I hate flying, but I'll fly anywhere with David. He needs my help."

The last thing I said to him was, "My best friend Tony, I'll see you in the future. When that day comes, we'll fly together again."

Made in the USA
Lexington, KY
31 July 2010